Front Line

by the same author

THE THREE WEEKS' WAR IN POLAND
THERE'S A GERMAN JUST BEHIND ME
MAO AND THE MEN AGAINST HIM

Front Line

CLARE HOLLINGWORTH

JONATHAN CAPE
LONDON

First published 1990
© Clare Hollingworth 1990
Jonathan Cape Ltd, 20 Vauxhall Bridge Road, London SW1V 2SA

A CIP catalogue record for this book
is available from the British Library

ISBN 0-224-02827-8

Phototypeset by Falcon Graphic Art Ltd
Wallington, Surrey
Printed in Great Britain by
Mackays of Chatham PLC, Chatham, Kent

Contents

Illustrations

The author acknowledges with thanks the following sources: 7,
Middle East News Agency; 9, Camera Press Ltd; 10, Joint Public
Relations Staff, HQ Middle East Command; 14, *Daily Telegraph*.

Acknowledgments

Graham C. Greene persuaded me to write this book, but I must stress from the beginning that it is the events I was fortunate enough to watch and the powerful people I met that I hope make the book interesting and exciting – not myself.

Sometimes there was a combination of luck and a feeling for news. This was the case when I stayed in Persia to meet the 'young' Shah who had just mounted the Peacock throne after his pro-German father had been forced to abdicate by the Allies. It was entirely luck that my husband (Geoffrey Hoare) and I had just returned from Haifa when Jewish terrorists, from Irgun, blew up the King David Hotel, where we were staying, only a few minutes before we reached it. It was luck that I had alert foreign editors who sent me to the right place at the right time. And, on a different level, it was pure luck that when chatting with Donald Wise in Vietnam, a sniper's bullet whistled by between our two heads.

I am grateful to John Dudman, former deputy foreign editor of the *Daily Telegraph*, who has helped me with the research and writing of this book. The *Daily* and *Sunday Telegraph* have provided me with many facilities and assistance. I must also express heartfelt thanks to the excellent staff of the Centre of Asian Studies, University of Hong Kong, from the director, Professor Edward Chen, through the remarkable and efficient administrative officer, Ms Kripalani-Thadani, down to the splendid girls who use the word processors.

I am fortunate in having some excellent friends who have encouraged me to work and, indeed, helped enormously with their advice and criticism. I should like particularly to thank the Dowager Lady Egremont, Sir Denis and Lady Wright, Mrs E. Robson-Scott and Elizabeth Wright for their wise counsel and constructive suggestions. Both Mrs Robson-Scott and Miss

Wright read chapters, made suggestions and corrected proofs.

Lastly I must mention, indeed, pay tribute to the two editors who have faced the hard work of dealing with the manuscript. First, Anne Chisholm, and then, Jenny Cottom, who with noted efficiency and kindness accomplished the last and most difficult lap.

1 Childhood Battlefields ... League of Nations Union ... Marriage ...

People have often asked how I, a woman, became fascinated by war. It began when I was taken by my father, who instilled in me an early interest in history, literature and, to a lesser degree, geography, to the old battlefields of Naseby and Bosworth during school holidays. Later, we went to France and visited Crécy, Poitiers and Agincourt. He would always explain most succinctly the battle line-up, who attacked where and why, the mistakes that were made that resulted in defeat, the reasons for the battles – that war, in fact, was and has always been an extension of politics and the ultimate result of the failure of statesmen to keep the peace. So battlefields of old have always possessed a magnetism for me.

Bosworth Field, however, was the favourite battle site of my childhood as I lived near Leicester and I knew almost every thorn tree in the marshlands and fields where Richard III deployed his men just off Watling Street. The king's tombstone also intrigued me because it was built into the stable of a large mansion, constructed during the industrial revolution, that stood beside the Midland Canal near the city centre, and the legend was that he was carried there on horseback with his head hanging lower than his feet – a dreadful fate for a king.

From Granada in southern Spain through France to Italy, some of the most interesting trips I can recall have been to battlefields. I liked Crécy, perhaps because it is free of the huge cemeteries that make twentieth-century battlegrounds so depressing. It is within easy reach of Abbeville and provides an excellent excuse for a break in that rather dreary journey from the Channel ports to Paris. It is still possible to see the potholes that were dug to hinder French cavalry and thereby protect the English archers who, during the battlefield established in Europe 'the supremacy of the long-bow with its effective range of 200-500 yards'. This alone gave England the standing of a great military power. My childhood notes recall that the French force, including the Genoese crossbowmen, failed to regroup before they attacked and that they were hampered by wet bowstrings caused by a thunderstorm.

My earliest personal memories concern growing up and independence. I was born at Knighton, a village south of Leicester. There were fields on all sides. During the First World War the family moved to Bodkin Farm in Charnwood Forest, an enchanting spot a few miles from the village of Shepshead. We went there because father's war work was to manage a boot and shoe factory, which my grandfather had established at Shepshead some years before, in order to pay wages lower than those demanded in an industrial city such as Leicester. Father, who had no training for the job, ran the factory during the war and my grandfather, James Riley, drove over with the wages every Friday in a green Arrol Johnson car to review progress.

We children had a wonderful life, playing in the brook, exploring the farm together, watching the cows being milked and the pigs born. We knew the names of the birds as they built their nests every year and, after life on a farm, we took sex for granted and had but little curiosity about it. We were rightly not allowed to collect birds' eggs but we were allowed to pick flowers and press them into books as we absorbed their names.

In the neighbouring farm there were two small hills – outcrops of rocks. We were always climbing them and at weekends we walked to the top of St Ive's head, the second highest hill in Leicestershire or strolled in Longcliff woods – part of Charnwood Forest. We joined in the haymaking and harvesting, sadly watching the rabbits shot as the corn was cut down. I loved the many picnics in summer and the shooting parties in winter. We had splendid farm food. I noticed that the farmer, Mr Lee, and his so-called labourers, who fed together in the large kitchen, had their 'sweet' – usually a suet pudding – before the meat course.

Mrs Lee explained that this took the edge off their appetite before they came to the more expensive roast.

Mother's contribution to the work of the farm was to churn the milk on Wednesdays. We took the butter to Loughborough market on Thursdays in a small trap pulled by a pony called Polly. On other days we rode Polly around the fields, mostly bareback.

On one night during the First World War, mother and father went into the garden to watch German zeppelins flying over. We children were awakened by the excitement and were taken into the garden to see those great silver flying machines slowly crossing the sky. Loughborough was bombed that night but when we visited the town the next day the only damage appeared to be a few really small bomb craters in the road. Local lore claimed that the Germans thought that they were bombing Leicester, which was never touched during the First World War.

At an early age there were lessons in the mornings with mother or a governess. I learnt the alphabet from them and I could read a few words and count when we returned to Leicester and I was sent to the Collegiate School.

There I found out about the bourgeoisie and the acute snobbism of a provincial town where lawyers did not enjoy mingling socially with the industrialists, who were, by that time, making large fortunes out of boots and shoes as well as hosiery. Mercifully, we still spent a good deal of time in the country and at unfashionable seaside resorts where we learned to swim.

I recall that the Collegiate School had joint headmistresses, Miss Jackson and Miss Thomas, who were certainly dedicated to producing girls able to stand on their own feet in a masculine world without losing any femininity. The latter took the boarding section of the establishment to Eastbourne when space became scarce as a result of more and more industrialists wanting their daughters to have a secondary school education. Many 'day' girls liked the idea of being a boarder in Eastbourne and, at the age of twelve, I was able to persuade my parents to allow me to join some friends at South Lynn, as the school was called. In many ways the move was a mistake on my part because it 'wasn't done' to do any work in the class there and I was afraid I should be called a 'swot' if I studied openly. The girls were only interested in sport, and I was not. We had to change every evening for dinner and, after the meal, we danced in the gymnasium to the latest jazz tunes. Lesbianism was not unknown.

Despite the beauty of the school grounds and frequent visits to London, which I immediately decided was a far more interesting place than Leicester, I was not sorry when I was moved to the grammar school at Ashby-de-la-Zouch to join my sister, who was not strong and had to be at a boarding-school near home. Here I was encouraged to work hard by the headmistress, Miss C.M. Hopkirk, who had been my mother's mathematics teacher twenty years before at the Wygiston Grammar School in Leicester.

My sister Edith – known then as Peg but later in life as Holly – and I regarded our father at the time as 'rather odd' in his attitude to women. In many ways he was an egalitarian but he made us both attend the domestic science college in Leicester. This provided me with the time to read. Although it is useful to be able to make an omelette, my domestic science training caused me to hate having anything to do with housework. Mother was in many respects ahead of her time and I recall her standing up for male and female homosexuals, declaring that 'after all they never caused any unwanted babies'. However, Peg who never had a job and entered into an extremely happy marriage at an early age complained that mother was too dominating.

In Leicester I lived a reasonable social life and became engaged to a suitable young man in the county who was also active in the Territorials. I made friends with people in all three political parties and gradually veered towards Labour. At that time, many young people I met of my own age were inclined to the Left politically but not so my fiancé. Even though I was engaged, I was keen to get into journalism and I recall the first piece I ever wrote for publication was an appreciation of Miss Hopkirk, my old headmistress, the day after her death.

My family gave me a small dress allowance so that if I lived at home I could make out and even spend the allowance on travel. Although I did not realise it at the time, my life became divided between the hunt-ball existence which I shared with my fiancé, family and some friends, and the scholarly and politically interesting side. I recall I wrote a series of essays on the various plans for the division of the Austro-Hungarian Empire after the First World War. My friends on this side of my life were generally interested in both party politics and the League of Nations, indeed, some were actually working for the League of Nations Union (LNU).

I took what would now be dubbed a mini-secretarial course and obtained a job as Secretary – later to become Assistant – to the League of Nations Union organiser for Worcestershire.

A friend, the Principal of Leicester University, Mr Attenborough was increasingly anxious for me to take an academic turn. Thus under his guidance I worked towards securing a scholarship to the School of Slavonic Studies at London University where, later, I worked under the brilliant direction of Professor Seton Watson.

I decided to take a course at Zagreb University. Initially I went there in an effort to learn a Slav language. Someone reliable produced the name of Mrs Esti Poliak who was anxious to have an English 'lodger' who would pay for at least part of their keep by speaking English; she had a flat at Savska Cesta 7. We got along well together but I learnt little Croation, partly because I am a bad linguist but also because most of the people at the University and all Esti's friends were Jewish and wanted to speak English. Later I remember I was unable to stay with Esti because she had what was then called a 'black' man living in the guest-room who had escaped from Nazi Germany and had no papers nor right to be in Yugoslavia. But Esti got him out eventually – with her entire family – and they all settled in America. I returned to Zagreb for lengthy periods on two or three successive summers and enjoyed the life there with its excellent inexpensive restaurants and outdoor cafés where one drank the local wine as violinists moved around amongst the tables. Swimming in certain parts of the Sava was good and I used Zagreb then and later as a base for touring Yugoslavia, Hungary, Bulgaria and even Albania – all on a shoe-string.

Working for the LNU certainly had many advantages. Because there was no work in the Worcester office during the summer, I was encouraged to take months of 'sabbatical' leave for study and travel on condition I included a visit to Geneva to collect material for articles for *Headway*, the LNU magazine, as well as for speeches. During the Annual Meeting of the League Nations in Geneva I met Trilby Ewer and Vernon Bartlett. Although working for the Labour orientated *Daily Herald* and the Liberal *News Chronicle* respectively, Trilby and Vernon were the best known diplomatic correspondents at the time and on excellent terms with Anthony Eden. Standards of journalism were then far higher than now. Eden could give Ewer and Bartlett a great deal of background to enable them to understand government policy with no fear that they would ever quote him. The manners of the correspondents, too, were far better than they are today when I have seen important men, such as the Governor of Hong Kong, bullied by the local press.

Trilby had an interesting background. During the First World War he had been a Communist and, at the time of the Russian Revolution, had smuggled some of the Tsar's jewels out of Russia covered with milk chocolate in a large blue Cadbury's box. When offered a generous fee by the consortium of jewellers that was set up to deal with this major consignment, Trilby said 'Please add my commission to the price you pay the Russians.' But like so many people of that epoch, Trilby gradually veered to the Right and, although he went on working for the *Daily Herald* until he was eighty, he called himself a Socialist while expressing views that hardly differed from my Conservative family.

A second advantage of working for the LNU was that I had to make frequent visits to the London headquarters where I met people like the Chairman, Viscount Cecil, Professor Gilbert Murray, Victor Cazalet MP, Vyvyan Adams MP, Noel Baker MP and, from time to time, I was allowed to attend the meetings of the Executive Committee on which, in the early days, Austin Chamberlain and a mass of other VIPs were serving.

In both London and Worcester I learnt something about writing for the press – announcements, reports of meetings, speeches and an occasional article for the oldest newspaper in England – *Berrows Worcester Journal*. I lived in Malvern and bought a car for around £20 that took me to the Worcester office. Although I still went to the odd race-meeting or hunt-ball I decided provincial life was not for me and, without drama, I broke off my engagement. Shortly after this I met Vandeleur Robinson who was then Regional Organiser for the LNU in the south-east and lived in Guildford. It was odd that there was no romantic encounter but on trips to London we soon discovered we had much in common, especially an interest in the politics of central and south-eastern Europe. Vandeleur, who had passed high on the list in and out of Woolwich, had decided he did not like Army life and, after taking a degree at Cambridge, had taught for a time at Prague University.

We decided to marry and went for our honeymoon to Yugoslavia and Albania. For family reasons we were married in a church in Leicester after the legal ceremony at a registrar's office in London. My family approved of Van – as he was known – and his family of me, although his mother was one of the world's greatest snobs. She suffered from having married a regular soldier, a gunner, whose name was Robinson. In retirement they lived in Leamington Spa where she spent much of her time working for the Conservative Party whose member of parliament was then Anthony Eden. She was related to the Bowes-Lyons and signed all her cheques, Ianthe Bowes-Lyon Vandeleur Robinson. Van and I made our base first in a modest flat in Ebury Street and then in a delightful 'maisonette' in Marsham Street.

I returned to Leicester early in 1937 to organise the Peace Ballot there. Considering the Conservative member of parliament for South Leicester was deeply opposed to the Ballot, my family were extremely loyal and supportive. I used their car and telephone when at home although we had an office in the town. Van came down to spend the weekend with me when I was too busy to get to London.

During the holidays we generally managed to travel together. Shortly after marrying we were fortunate in meeting Terence Donovan, KC, then a barrister specialising in income tax. Van, who by that time had joined the Labour Party with me, met him at a meeting of the Westminster Branch. Shortly after that I recall Van trying to guess which public school he had attended! Terence was amused as he told me he had often been cold and hungry as a child. The First World War gave him his chance and, after it, he joined the civil service and read for the Bar.

Terence was on hand with advice and when I was moaning that I should have to take out a passport in the name of Robinson, he said there was no need for this as I was known as Clare Hollingworth and wrote for various publications, albeit small ones, under that name. In England he stressed your name is the name you are known by. He wrote a letter for me to take to the passport office and sure enough a passport was issued in the name of Hollingworth. On one of the inside pages was added 'Clare Hollingworth, a British subject by birth, is the wife of

V.D. Vandeleur Robinson a British subject by birth.' I gather I was about the eighth woman in England to have a passport in her own name.

By the late 1930s, both alone and with Van, I had seen much of central Europe, including Hungary and Czechoslovakia, Austria, Yugoslavia and Bulgaria from the grass roots. I wrote occasional pieces for Kingsley Martin, who was then editor of the *New Statesman* and, when working in London I talked with Trilby Ewer, who influenced me to move away from politics towards journalism as a career. The war clouds grew blacker as Hitler took over Austria, then occupied the Sudetenland.

As a result of a chain of administrative accidents, I was appointed as the senior official in Warsaw in charge of the News Chronicle Fund for Refugees from the Sudetenland, which was later amalgamated with the Lord Mayor's Fund for Refugees from Czechoslovakia with its Polish headquarters, for which I was responsible, in the same building of the British Consulate General in Katowice.

The refugees were, roughly speaking, divided into political and religious groups whose leaders generally, though not always, arranged for them to cross the border illegally into Poland. There were Jews, Catholics, Communists, Socialists and I held a conference with the leaders every day in Katowice when I was there.

I sent through the diplomatic bag, or by safe hand to London, the names of the hundreds of men and women as they arrived and for whom I was responsible. London then advised me of the visa situation and travel plans made for these fugitives. Generally, we arranged for a large group of one hundred or more to travel together. Few had passports and they travelled on identity cards with photographs with an appropriate caption verifying their background. I signed all the cards. I learnt subsequently that Sir Stafford Cripps was interested as well as surprised that sovereign states stamped their visas or transit visas on these documents.

My small office was staffed by two German-speaking British secretaries and a few volunteers. We were greatly helped, it seems odd to report, by the Polish authorities and the police. Not only were there hundreds of refugees in Katowice but also in Krakow where my assistant, Mr Herman Field, later became known for his Communist activities. He was sent out as an assistant for me from London by Dorothy Layton, daughter of Sir Walter Layton who was then Chairman of the *News Chronicle*. They had no idea that he was a secret member of the Communist Party.

The refugee organisation was fortunate in that so little money had to be spent on board and lodging as Jewish, Catholic and political organisations tended to look after their own, although there were scores who, for one reason or another, had to be fed and given accommodation. I had to go frequently to Warsaw where the British Embassy in the person of 'Robin' Hankey (now Lord Hankey) helped me to deal with the Polish authorities. Such an organisation is unthinkable today. I changed almost all the funds on the black market, which was not difficult as so many Poles were trying to get their money out of the country. I also visited Gdynia frequently where the Honorary British Consul helped to obtain cheap transport by sea for the refugees who, obviously, could not cross Nazi Germany.

There was little or no time for social life but when I was in Warsaw I did meet the brilliant and unusual wife of Clifford Norton who was Counsellor (number two man) in the British Embassy there. Her real name was Noel, but she was always known as 'Peter' and she had opened the first modern art gallery in London some years previously. Indeed, she had to sell it soon after she married Clifford because it was rather frowned upon by senior people in the Foreign Office. However, even in Poland in those immediate pre-war days her interest in pictures was undiminished. Not only did she become a great friend but she had considerable influence on my life, especially later when I was living in Paris. She had revolted against a conventional upper-class life and gone out to earn her own living. I recall she told me she had taken a job as a cook and, more than once, had spent the night on a bench in Hyde Park. Peter was tough both physically and mentally. We were to see much more of each other.

I remember that as war approached, Hans Henry (Count Hochberg) son of the famous beauty, Daisy, Princess of Pless, came to the Consulate to try to obtain a British visa. The Consul-General, John Anthony Thwaites, told him that visas to Poles could be issued only on special orders from the Foreign Office in London. Hans moaned a little and then said: 'What a pity as I was born in Berkeley Square and the King and Queen were my godfather and godmother.' 'Well,' said Thwaites, 'I can't give you a visa but if you give me a copy of your birth certificate I can give you a British passport.' I arranged for the birth certificate to be sent to Katowice and he received his passport. After Poland was overrun by Germany, Hans Henry lived in Paris in what are called 'straitened circumstances' but he managed to reach London before the Germans moved into France, and joined the Polish army in Scotland.

While working for the refugees, I made up my mind that when that particular job ended, I would pursue a career in journalism. Obviously a war was upon us and it was impossible – or so I thought at the time – to obtain a job in Fleet Street while I was working in Poland.

My husband was all for my pressing ahead in journalism but my parents were horrified and told me so in very direct terms. They had 'taken' the shock of my joining the Labour Party and even becoming a parliamentary candidate without much fuss or trouble. But they abhorred the press, apart from *The Times* and to work for any newspaper other than that august journal was, to their way of thinking, out of the question.

The London office of the Lord Mayor's Fund recalled me for consultations in July 1939 and explained the work could not continue in Katowice or, indeed, in Poland because of the threat of war. A pleasant woman was appointed to take over from me whose job was to run down the organisation while doing everything possible for the refugees already there. I returned to Katowice for a brief spell to hand over to her. Then back to London to look for a job with the help of my good friends Trilby Ewer and Terence Donovan.

2 First job for the *Daily Telegraph* ... The Germans invade Poland ...

Arthur Watson, editor of the *Daily Telegraph*, regarded me from his chair on the other side of a large, oblong desk. His office was spacious and the atmosphere contemplative, reflecting the mood of the portraits of his predecessors that decorated the oak-panelled walls. I had received a telephone call from his secretary, who asked me if I would be prepared to see him. He had heard from friends of my work among refugees in Poland and he had read my articles in the *News Chronicle* on the approaching war in Europe.

I arrived for the interview on 25 August 1939, intrigued and curious. I was twenty-seven. I explained to Mr Watson that I knew Poland extremely well after months of helping Czechoslovakian refugees to escape into Poland following Hitler's seizure of Prague in 1938.

He said, 'We would like to take you on if you will go back to Poland.'

'Delighted,' I replied.

'Get back there quickly. I would like you to go as soon as possible. Tomorrow. Report to our man in Warsaw. Hugh Carleton Greene. He is staying at the Europejski Hotel. But first talk to Bob Skelton, our news editor, who will brief you on our requirements, filing times and so on.'

I do not remember whether we discussed money but it had never been of any particular importance to me. I was thrilled at the thought of the assignment and could not wait to get moving.

After talking to Skelton, I hurried off to dine with friends and break the big news. I learnt that the next direct flight to Berlin left early from Hendon the next morning. I broke off from the dinner party, rushed back to my flat in Buckingham Palace Road to pack – and then a stream of telephone calls delayed my preparations. It was after midnight when I began packing only to realise that my suitcases were too big for the aircraft. This was far from being an insoluble problem. I telephoned Harrods where the night staff reeled off the measurements and prices of their available luggage. I quickly made my choices – and the suitcases were delivered within an hour. (It seems rather odd to me today that such a night service no longer exists when there must surely be many ingenious and enterprising victims of unemployment able to exploit demands for new service industries.)

At the airport early next morning I met William Forrest of the *News Chronicle*, who was far from popular in Germany as a result of his reports from the Republican lines in the Spanish Civil War. We were kept waiting for hours 'owing to problems concerned with landing in Berlin'.

Finally, we took off. It was an uneventful trip until we approached the capital. As our pilot banked, I looked across the dipping wingtip as Tempelhof Airport appeared. The concrete runways were full of 'Lufthansa' aircraft, which had been taken out of service a few days before. And every corner of the airfield was packed with German fighters, ranked nose to tail, like black insects from H.G. Wells's *The Food of the Gods*.

Soon after landing, Forrest and I were separated from the other passengers and marched off to a wire mesh pen. Officials told us that Hitler would be making a speech in Tannenberg later in the day that would be a declaration of war and, as journalists, we would be 'held' at least until the Nazi leader had made his broadcast. I suppose I was too young and inexperienced to be frightened by the situation, which resolved itself after a couple of hours when loudspeakers announced that the speech had been postponed. We were released and told we could go to Warsaw.

We took off again and the plane followed a carefully prepared route at around 1,500 feet. We saw nothing of significance on the ground, which was the point of this particular piece of navigation for the last British airliner to cross Germany before the outbreak of war. It was dark when we landed in Warsaw. There was no sign of tension as I drove into town through well-lit streets, occasionally hearing music from pavement cafés. At the Europejski Hotel I reported to Hugh Carleton Greene, a tall, friendly character. I realise now that few foreign staff correspondents would have so cheerfully welcomed an unknown female as an assistant but he could not have been more cordial.

In his room we discussed plans over drinks. 'One of us', he said, 'must go to the German border.'

'Let it be me,' I said. 'I know the area on both sides of the frontier around Katowice and Krakow extremely well. My German may not be very good but I do have influential friends in Silesia.' He agreed that I should go.

The air service between Warsaw and Katowice had been suspended because of the worsening crisis with Germany. So I took the night train southwards. We stopped at stations on the way and I saw policemen and other officials posting up notices proclaiming the mobilisation of the Polish Army.

In Katowice I notified the British Consul General, still John Anthony Thwaites, that I had arrived to report developments for the *Daily Telegraph*. As Polish officers had taken all the hotel rooms, Thwaites offered to put me up in his flat: his wife and family had been evacuated to Britain. I accepted his kind offer and the next day I set off on my first major story for the *Daily Telegraph*.

I found officials genuinely cheerful and confident that in the approaching war, which most of them expected to break out in a few weeks or months at most, the Poles would give the hated Germans a good hiding. Indeed, optimism was everywhere. Even so, the wives of wealthy citizens had left for Warsaw or towns in the interior.

The border with Germany, of course, was closed except for flagged cars that enabled German consular officials or staff officers in civilian clothes to travel across the frontier as they pleased. This gave me an idea and I asked Thwaites if I might borrow his car.

'Where do you want to go?' he asked.

'Into Germany,' I replied.

He roared with laughter and disbelief. However, he did allow me to take his car and so off I went into Germany with the Union

Jack fluttering from the bonnet. Nazi officers seemed somewhat
surprised when they realised that they had been saluting the British
flag but, in fact, no one tried to stop me and I crossed the frontier
at Beuthen without trouble. It was almost deserted now that all
civilians had been evacuated apart from a few traders. Soap was
strictly rationed, there was aspirin – that excellent German product – and oil and fats were obtainable only with special permits.
Tea, coffee made from burnt maize, and meat were also rationed.
Yet amid all this shortage, a waiter I had tipped well in the past
produced from a restaurant kitchen – a partridge!

I thoroughly enjoyed that meal and then went off to buy all
the films I could find along with bottles of wine, electric torches
and other oddments in short supply in Poland.

I drove along the fortified frontier road through Mindenburg
to Gleiwitz, which had been transformed into a military base. Just
as I was leaving the town sixty-five motor-cycle despatch riders,
bunched together and riding hard, overtook me. By the roadside
there were large numbers of troops, literally hundreds of tanks,
armoured cars and field guns. Screens of hessian beside the road,
constructed to hide the military vehicles, blew in the wind, thus I
saw the battle deployment. I guessed that the German Command
was preparing to strike to the north of Katowice and its fortified
lines and this, in fact, was exactly how they launched their invasion in the south.

Back in Katowice, I described what I had seen to Thwaites, who
listened with obvious disbelief; he did not consider it possible even
to cross the border into Germany. 'Then see for yourself,' I said,
and opened 'his' car door to reveal my purchases – things that
were just not available in Poland. Finally convinced, Thwaites
locked himself in his office and enciphered a top secret message
to the Foreign Office via the British Embassy in Warsaw.

I telephoned Greene in the Polish capital and dictated my
story. He relayed it within minutes to the *Daily Telegraph*.
In those days there were no bylines in quality newspapers in
Britain, which was a good thing because my family would have
been worried.

The following day I drove to nearby towns in Silesia to
try to contact British subjects working there and warn them
on behalf of the Consul General to leave. More and more Polish
soldiers appeared in the streets to be cheered by schoolchildren

and townsfolk. In Katowice itself anyone owning a car packed their belongings and headed out of town. Everyone was tuned in to the BBC as well as German and Polish radio stations. The count-down to war was nearing zero hour.

As the first light of dawn pierced the sky over Katowice on 1 September, I was awakened by explosions. Distant gunfire created a noise like banging doors. Aircraft roared over the city. More heavy explosions. From my window – it was not even 5 a.m. – I saw the bombers riding high in the sky, and looking towards the German border less than twenty miles away I saw the flash of artillery fire. There was a lightning burst in the park, then another . . . then another. So the invasion was on and Britain and France were on the brink of war through their promise to defend Poland if Hitler attacked.

I woke up Thwaites and then dashed off to telephone Robin Hankey, second secretary at the British Embassy in Warsaw. 'Robin!' I shouted. 'The war has begun!'

'Are you sure, old girl?' he asked.

'Listen!' I held the telephone out of my bedroom window. The growing roar of tanks encircling Katowice was clearly audible. 'Can't you hear it?' I cried.

He seemed convinced and wisely advised that I got out of Katowice as soon as possible. I rang off, then telephoned Greene and broke the news to him. It was 5.30 a.m. Greene contacted the Foreign Ministry in Warsaw. 'I hear from our correspondent in Katowice that the Germans have crossed the border and are advancing,' said Greene.

'Absolute nonsense,' came the reply. 'We are still negotiating.'

But as they talked the air-raid sirens wailed in Warsaw. For the first time Nazi bombers flew over the capital and the bombs fell.

Greene telephoned my story to London and suggested that I remain as near as possible to the action. In Katowice, Thwaites stowed his valuable pictures in the cellar of his home while we waited for his car and driver to take us to the consulate. There the senior and most trusted member of his local staff, a German-Silesian, was in floods of tears. 'This will be the end of poor Germany,' she kept moaning. While she wept, I emptied file after file into the heating furnaces until ashes danced around my feet. Thwaites burnt all his ciphers and telephoned the British subjects who were still in the town.

The telephone rang repeatedly. The city police chief advised that it seemed that the Germans were slowing down after they crossed the border; he thought there was no immediate threat to Katowice. A Polish army contact predicted that the invaders would mount a pincer movement without inflicting any damage.

From the street outside the consulate came a shrill voice urging children to go to school and adults to their offices. The loudspeaker insisted that the report of a German invasion was rubbish. This was one of the first examples of German psychological warfare and their agents were doing their job well. For a moment I thought that I had started a phoney war. But the guns were still firing and they grew louder . . .

For the consulate official in charge of Czech refugees – the job I had been doing until a month earlier – there was a formidable problem. Miss M.L. Dougan knew too well that more than 1,000 refugees remained of those who had escaped from the Gestapo in Vienna, Germany, Bohemia, Moravia and the Sudetenland. Through lack of interest in a visa to the United Kingdom, they had waited in Poland for months in the hope of getting a visa to the United States. Now the Nazis were coming to claim them.

All that long day, Miss Dougan struggled with a transport system that had jammed. Groups of refugees started walking to the east, a train packed with women and children left for the south. Many were overtaken by the German offensive.

By 10 a.m. the gunfire had subsided. I decided to visit the frontier. I drove past Polish troops on their way to the front. In the suburbs and villages around Katowice there was no obvious alarm. People stood outside their houses, looking slightly stunned and gazing at the sky. There was no rush to leave.

I stopped when I saw a Polish captain whom I knew well. His men were covering and oiling heavy artillery. 'It's a great pity', he said, 'but the concrete of our gun emplacement hasn't yet properly set.'

I drove on to Przysyowice and looked down on the German fortifications on the Gleiwitz front. I found empty factories: dwellings near them had been evacuated, too. Along the frontier to Rybnik through unperturbed countryside and then back to Katowice, I was not challenged even once during my foray to find the fighting on that first day of war. Indeed, in some villages it was business as usual in the markets. I visited several churches expecting to find them full. They were all empty.

In the ugly industrial town of Chorzow, I saw children in brightly coloured clothes climbing into coaches to be evacuated from the frontier zone. There was a holiday mood about it all; one might have thought that the people were waiting for a carnival procession.

Back in Katowice, the mood was very different. Air-raid wardens with yellow arm-bands were on the streets and ambulances were parked in the side streets. All trains and buses had been stopped; the telephone system was cracking up. Most of Katowice's rich fraternity had left but there were a few cars, laden with blankets and suitcases, still heading out of town.

I reached the consulate to find everyone suddenly running to the windows. Thirty or forty young men – the eldest could not have been more than twenty – were being marched along under double guard. They all wore swastika arm-bands. When they had heard the sound of gun-fire, they had rushed on to the streets, yelling 'Heil Hitler!' Instead of leading an uprising they had run into a group of Polish soldiers who quickly disarmed them.

A few minutes later, two lorries rattled past the consulate. They were full of workmen, their clothes ripped, blood and dirt smearing their faces. They were crouching, surrounded by Polish troops. Every time a head was raised, a rifle butt drove it down. They had all been involved in another pro-Nazi revolt that went wrong. When I left the consulate for a lunch-break, I discovered what kind of immediate justice the Poles were inflicting on their captives. I glimpsed a line of figures with raised rifles and I heard the volley as I sped on in my car.

Throughout that afternoon, rumour and counter-rumour reached the consulate but by evening it was established that the Nazis were through at the two points I expected: from the north of Gleiwitz towards Czestochowa and through the Moravian Gate, the gap in the mountains which historically had been the invasion avenue from Czechoslovakia into Poland. Sensing the real possibility of a night attack on Katowice, I decided to sleep in Krakow, seventy kilometres away, and return to the consulate the next morning.

I left at nightfall. For miles the road was a jostle of peas-ant waggons. My headlights, that I used but rarely, picked up humped figures, carts over-piled with household belongings and everywhere the white discs of children's faces.

In the villages there were big crowds which suddenly vanished at the sound of an air-raid siren. Occasionally, I entered a village without knowing that the warning had sounded and wardens and townsfolk ran from houses to try to stop me. They explained that they had been told that all cars should remain stationary during a raid. I ignored their advice and continued my journey. I stayed the night in Krakow, which was quite barren of news, and headed back for Katowice. By now there were control points in every town and village and even with my pass from the commander of the southern army it took some time to get through. The Polish army was on the move with troop trains heading for the front, bivouacs in the fields, trenches appearing as a new defence line emerged.

In Katowice the consulate staff were trying frantically to contact an Englishwoman who was known to work at the Zaklady Electro factory, the biggest electrical and carbide enterprise in western Poland. Each time they telephoned and got through the receiver was banged down. Finally a voice at the factory said: 'For God's sake, let us be, we are on fire!'

A few minutes later from a different telephone came the voice of the missing woman saying 'I'm sorry. I can't leave. The Germans have already passed through here and I doubt if our special train for the factory personnel will run.'

'The Germans are there!'

'Yes, they didn't disturb us and they told us to carry on with our jobs. Then they went on.'

'But aren't you phoning from behind German lines?'

'There aren't any lines. They went away.'

It was incredible but true. The big breakthrough came soon after 11 a.m. on the second day of the war but it was not known to the Silesian civilian authorities until mid-afternoon. The tension in Katowice was reaching snapping point. The radio station had been hit and, just before lunch, a train-load of ammunition was bombed and blew up with an explosion that shook the city. Reports flooded in from nearby towns. At Semianowice, the Nazis had started a riot and set most of the town ablaze with incendiaries. About fifteen miles from Katowice, a cordite factory flamed above the skyline. Above us, the bombers circled constantly.

Later in the afternoon, Polish officials asked the British and French consuls to leave with the last of their nationals. I put my typewriter and a few possessions into Thwaites's car. The British refugee workers joined us. We called on the French consulate, where the consul, a charming man, insisted on my taking a case of champagne for which he had no room in his car: it was to provide me with much needed refreshment later on.

As we set out, a Polish machine-gun opened up against Nazi planes swooping down to rake the streets with bullets and bombs. We all dashed from the car for cover and immediately the raid was over, back we clambered into our seats and raced out of Katowice. We found dozens of other British and French cars heading for Krakow and, at some points, the Polish army had closed the road. So for most of the way we were forced to drive across country, over fields made hard and bumpy by the hot summer.

We reached Krakow to endure a night of air-raid warnings but little else. Soon after dawn there was distant artillery fire and it was clear Krakow would not be secure for long. To the south, the Polish cavalry launched a gallant attack against the invader without any hope of being able to stop the advance. I wanted to get to the front and, again, Thwaites allowed me to take his car. I did not get far. The road was blocked with retreating troops and German shells were not far off. There were scores of dead and wounded troops and dead and wounded horses everywhere.

The Poles had concentrated around a cluster of farms in a hamlet and they were still digging support-trenches in the iron-hard soil. Field telephones were being laid. But away to the north-east, horse-drawn field kitchens, fodder and supply waggons and transport of every kind were on the retreat. Above us, German bombers watched the scene of war where buses, converted into ambulances with their windows blacked out to conceal the wounded, drove back to Krakow.

Yet there was still some optimism to be found at the Polish military headquarters. 'You will understand, mademoiselle, that we must yield ground to strengthen our line. Our real defence must lie along the rivers, San and Vistula,' an officer explained.

'You will sacrifice all this region then? And the Silesian heavy industry as well?'

'We are prepared for that. It's for ultimate victory. Poland will lose territory during the war, but she will gain more – much more – afterwards.'

Like other officers, he failed to appreciate that from the opening of the invasion, the Polish army was being beaten to the punch all the time and that they were in danger of being split into fragments by the German blitzkrieg. Instead of acting upon the advice of the British and French experts in the months leading up to the war to plan delaying actions and establish a trip wire to delay the invader and enable them to fall back to a strategic line, the Polish Command had foolishly deployed large concentrations of men and guns on the border. The German armoured and motorised columns drove through them 'like spears', according to a Polish general I talked with weeks later.

At my hotel in Krakow, Thwaites told me that the Polish authorities, who had been anxious to establish a British consulate in the city the previous day, were now pressing him to leave without delay. 'We must go to Lublin,' said Thwaites.

As we walked down the stairs, a radio in the crowded foyer was announcing that 'a state of war now existed between Great Britain and Germany'. Then came 'God Save the King'. It was 3 September 1939. A porter approached me and kissed my hand as the radio switched to the 'Marseillaise'. It was the worst moment of the war for me and I felt slightly sick. I steadied myself against the wall and thought of my years on the staff of the League of Nations Union and the organising of the Peace Ballot. All that we had worked for seemed lost. London would be bombed and friends and buildings I loved destroyed. And now neither Britain nor France could prevent all these people around me from falling into German hands.

Then we prepared to leave once again in Thwaites's car. As we were about to depart one member of the party, a middle-aged Englishwoman, was missing. She had gone off to buy toiletries. She returned festooned like a Christmas tree with a collection of little bags. Then she summoned up holdalls, carpet bags, suitcases, handbags and a typewriter and insisted on bringing them all with her.

Thwaites had abandoned his luggage by now and I put a few oddments into a pillow case and sat on it. His four-seater car had to hold six and his chauffeur was not happy. He knew what the roads to Lublin were like.

Leaving Krakow was like leaving Katowice. It was on fire in three places and so much smoke drifted across the rooftops and through the streets that some people thought a gas attack had begun. There was sudden firing and machine-guns perched high above us opened up at attacking planes. We drove on, ignoring the shouts of air-raid wardens and soon found ourselves moving along on empty roads.

We were stopped repeatedly in villages by police and militia who were suspicious of Thwaites's diplomatic number plates and personal pass. But with our chauffeur muttering about the stupid 'peasants' we were able to continue until we came to a level crossing just as the barrier fell. The railwaymen were shaking with fright.

'There's an alarm. We've been ordered to close the gates.'

'But we want to get on. This is an official car.'

'We have orders to close the gates at an alarm.'

A long line of cars behind us waited as a single German bomber wheeled overhead.

'Please, we should like to move on,' I said.

'We have orders to close the gates at . . . '

'Konsulat Angielski!' roared Thwaites. These were the only two words of Polish he knew.

'We have orders to . . . '

'These peasants!' exploded the chauffeur.

Nearby was a handy ditch but we did not have to use it for cover. The German bomber flew off, the barrier was raised and on we drove.

It was a hair-raising journey made frantic by our inability to find a telephone to try to contact Warsaw. We stopped in villages, pleaded at restaurants and hotels. None could help.

So, cut off from Warsaw by telephone, we decided to go there via Sandomierz. We came under machine-gun attack from German fighters strafing the roads, we rocked in and out of great pot-holes, we were covered in dust and after dusk we found ourselves driving without lights along an invisible road in unknown country.

Suddenly a light beamed at us. A man holding a rifle and bayonet ran out with his hand raised. 'You can't take the left fork here,' he called. 'We've had word that the Germans are coming through fast in the west.'

So we took the right fork and, a few minutes later, two cars with luggage piled high on the roofs turned in from a side road on the left. 'They're from Kielce,' said the chauffeur. 'Refugees.'

'By Jove!' Thwaites turned to me. 'If we had gone by Kielce we'd have been ... we'd have been cut off.' He thought for a moment. 'I think we must be running parallel with the German advance now, but well ahead, I hope.' Just then a sentry stopped us at a bridge, a long tunnel of girders. Through the steel lattice we could just see the water. 'Please drive slowly,' he said. 'The bridge is dynamited.'

As we drove across the bridge and on to the road piercing the plain ahead, the wide country was illuminated briefly by the moon and I felt the loneliness and helplessness of a nation awaiting the relentless approach of the invader.

Hours later, we rumbled on to the cobbles of Sandomierz, which stood at the junction of the San and Vistula, the key point of the projected defence line.

I telephoned my story through to Greene, who sounded singularly placid. I did not tell him that I had had to obtain permission from six officers to file my copy. When I returned to my party, I found them in a highly uneasy state. They had left their hotel to find themselves stopped in the darkened streets by cloaked figures, who flashed shaded torches and asked for their credentials. They were forced to return to the hotel – a particularly smelly one – where they had been watched by a group of staring Poles as they ate eggs and bread and cheese. Every mouthful was regarded with such intensity that the two women with us dropped their food into their laps out of embarrassment and anxiety.

It was then that Thwaites decided to move on so we set off again to the Jewish town of Rozwadow. The Jews in Poland were generally a fastidious section of the population but one would never have accepted this description from the hotel where we stayed for the night. The three men slept in one room and the women were in cubicles where we slept in bug-marked sheets. The following day we arrived in Lublin, an important centre for the Polish High Command and one of the chief manufacturing cities of Poland. It was packed with buses, lorries and waggons bringing in workers from as far away as Poznan. According to the authorities, industry in Lublin was to be super-staffed, speeded up and geared for twenty-four-hour intensive war production. The population was also swelled by wealthy families from Warsaw and western Poland seeking safety.

But poor refugees found that there was no room for them as they trudged from house to house seeking lodgings. When they sought sanctuary in churches they were startled to find them stripped of all statues, pictures and ornate embellishments.

Meanwhile, the public authorities provided a flat for us all. It was lent by Madame Sophie Wyszynska, widow of a former Polish diplomat in Berlin, who left with her child by the last train out of Lublin. The apartment was quickly transformed into the British Consulate with the Union Jack hanging from the balcony.

Soon Thwaites was swamped with enquiries from Jews trying to reach Palestine and their relatives, Poles trying vainly to buy British passports and people who wanted anything from petrol to a commission in the British Army. The two women in our party also posed problems for Thwaites, who gave me the job of escorting them to Warsaw to obtain transport to the UK via Lithuania. I needed to return to the capital to renew contact with Greene and from there our companions would be able to continue their journey to Riga and then sail for England. That, any rate, was the plan.

The drive to Warsaw on Tuesday, 6 September, was straight-forward enough despite heavy traffic. Among the cars and lorries came a stately Rolls, taking President Moscicki to 'an unknown destination'. But the German radio had already disclosed his journey was to Lublin to set up a new capital.

We reached Warsaw in the early afternoon and the situation there quickly became bizarre and frightening. I left the two good ladies outside the consulate while I went on to see Greene at his flat. To my surprise I found that he had left his apartment in rather a hurry. I rang through to the Europejski Hotel, where other journalists had been staying, to be told that all remaining British subjects had been ordered to leave Warsaw and that they had departed earlier that day. I rushed back to the consulate to find the two women in tears because it was closed and the Consul-General had already left.

There was a train leaving that night for Riga but the two ladies refused to wait for it and insisted on returning with me to Lublin. But we had only five litres of petrol in the car and supplies without a military permit were unobtainable. A useless car, two half-hysterical passengers and a city already evacuated. I had really put my head in a trap this time. And I knew, too, that without his car, Thwaites and his staff would be stranded in Lublin.

I sought help at the British Embassy. The military mission was still there with lorries and cars ready to follow the diplomats and staffs who were all on the road by now. I obtained varying amounts of petrol from cans in the waiting vehicles; everyone was very kind and anxious to help although they had their own problems. We went on to the US Embassy where they were even more sympathetic. More litres of petrol and, eventually, I had enough for the journey back to Lublin.

I had been really scared and now I was exhausted and hungry as I had not eaten all day. Happily, I had 'collected' a bottle of champagne from Greene's flat. Since my companions were not interested in alcohol of any kind, I consumed most of it myself. At 2 a.m. we reached Lublin and I hardly noticed the air-raids as we sped through the murky suburbs.

After a few hours' sleep, I was awakened by a soldier demanding that the Union Jack be removed from the balcony as it might pinpoint us as a target for bombers. I wandered into the streets to find a city that had changed dramatically in twenty-four hours. Now there were air-raids every few hours. It was a frightened city with little food and a population that had given up listening to the Polish radio reports of the German offensive and had switched to the German broadcasts to find out exactly what was happening. Even the British Embassy, which had moved to Nalenczow, a nearby spa, was cut off from all sources of news. Not one of their cables reached its destination and it was taking up to twenty-four hours to contact London, Paris or Washington by telephone.

It became very clear that the Polish government's decision to quit Warsaw was disastrous.

Once out of the capital, the government was never able to get the administrative machine working smoothly again. The government had but few facilities for telephone, telegraph, railways or aviation and ministers were not allowed to remain long

in one place for security reasons. German espionage and bombing ensured that they had to keep constantly on the move. There
was also the depressing moral effect of the flight from Warsaw.
Many Poles felt the war was lost the moment their President left
the capital.

After two nights in Lublin, Thwaites received orders to move
on immediately. By that time he had inherited from the British
Embassy three more adults and a child for evacuation. This
meant nine adults and a child in his four-seater car! Thwaites
spent an entire night telephoning the military authorities before
he obtained another vehicle. Everyone including the two Englishwomen and all their luggage somehow squeezed themselves into
the cars and at 5 a.m. we set off for Lvov (pronounced L' - voof)
via Luck (pronounced Wootsk), the capital of the eastern border
province of Wolhynia, which is now part of the Soviet Union.

Across eastern Poland the roads pushed out white and whiter,
trails of packed dust. First we passed peasant carts and then the
inevitable cars. We waved to one and stopped. Out jumped
young Hankey, whom I had last seen, impeccably dressed and a
model of correctness, at the British Embassy. Unshaven, rumpled,
ankle-deep in dust, he still had the same pale, merry eye. 'Good
Lord, fancy seeing you here!'

'Where are you off to?' I asked.

'Why, an unknown destination, of course,' he chuckled. 'This
war gets me down.'

3   Eye-witness in Poland 1939 . . .

We reached Luck with its wooden shacks and open booths of craftsmen that formed a vast suburbia around the city centre where neither accommodation nor food was available. I traipsed from hotel to lodging place for hours and finally found a bed at a monastic college in a room which I shared with three men.

We were all thrown out the next morning to make way for the general staff. I wondered how many generals would sleep in my room.

Thwaites finally solved my problem by goading local officials into producing another address for me: a large house at Polonka, several miles from Luck, where a Polish countess lived. It was a long drive and we did not reach the home of Countess Chodkiewicz until after nightfall. We entered a long drive and drew up at darkened steps leading up to a barrack-like establishment. 'Ask if anyone speaks French,' I told the driver.

'Mais certainement,' came a beautiful deep voice. I introduced myself and explained my plight. 'But, of course, mademoiselle, we will find you a bed, and your chauffeur, too.'

The torch-light showed only that the Countess was tall and grey and her house a sanctuary of stone halls and echoing corridors. I sensed her kindness and was happy. She found a bed for me and I dropped into it and slept.

The morning sun revealed a most charming house, an eighteenth-century white bungalow, simple and pleasingly proportioned and surrounded by a lawn like a fresh meadow with a protective screen of trees. Semi-circular porches stood out in groups of pilasters at the front and back of the house: their connecting stone hall had lost its pictures but animal heads and horns were still strung along its walls. In the rooms on each side of the hall there was Russian-designed furniture: the oil lamps had been bought in Petrograd. For this was the summer residence of a Russian landowner – the Russia of another epoch – of which Countess Chodkiewicz was the fitting centre.

She seemed more than sixty and her hair was greying but her tawny skin was as supple as that of a woman thirty years younger. There was youth, too, in her eyes, which the cheekbones underlined, giving proportion to the length of her face. She had a simple way and a certain ruggedness, which made her seem, as fully as the peasants, a part of her own fields. She possessed stoic dignity. She realised, even then, that she might not live many days. Yet she said only: 'Mademoiselle, do you know how far it is to the Russian frontier? A hundred and fifty kilometres. It is not the Germans we think of here.'

She never showed any anxiety for herself but betrayed a shadow of concern for the tiny grandchild, asleep on the lawn while his father fought in the Danzig Corridor. The children of the Countess had none of their mother's vitality: her daughter was a heavy blonde with pale, opaque colouring and her youngest son was a shambling figure who lisped owing to a cleft palate. But she had taught them both repose.

The gardens of this lovely house were raised above the surrounding marsh and ringed by a great hedge, from which many of the trees grew. Through gaps I could see, from the terrace, the wooden church of Polonka looking like a white miniature.

As I walked along the causeway to the village, I noticed frogs and toads, which seemed larger than I had seen before, lizards and highly-coloured beetles. The marsh flowers made larger patches of colour and all around the peasants were cutting the tall grass for winter bedding, and even in mid-September sinking a little into the mud as they worked.

The village itself was a huge square, Russian-style, with wooden houses on three sides. In the centre ducks and geese swam in the communal dirty pond. A scattering of villagers stood outside their huts: a young woman in a red kerchief, an old moujik of a man and others. They all spoke Russian. Their houses varied in size and cleanliness but I could read poverty in the inertia of the people and the lifelessness of the hamlet.

There was no shop nor any place where one could buy food had there been any to buy. There was no movement, no animation, not a plot of private ground that I could see. Yet these people were farming one of the richest soils of Europe. I found no concern for the war. No one spoke to a small group of Polish airmen in the village and this was symptomatic of countryside fears of impending conscription. Many peasants in eastern Poland hid in the forests to avoid call-up.

Polonka's only offering of interest was the Orthodox Church, which I had seen from the house. I sat with my head against the church wall, hearing the chant through the thin planking and gazed across the marshes. The red earth burned through a thin covering of grass. The plain was patched and striped with yellow, russet, olive-green and purple between great clumps of black trees. The sun hung rayless from a burnished sky that made cloud and land blush and gave distinct form to haycocks and cattle. Cold smoke lingered on the horizon.

High above somewhere there was a tremor, a familiar sound. The men in the fields looked up and I, remembering the machine guns, sheltered close to a hayrick.

Three bombers slipped out of a cloud bank and the sound of those slamming doors drifted across the landscape. The shell puffs in the distance were wide of their targets. Then came the thump of bombs. A cylinder of smoke pushed up from Luck, toppling slowly in the wind as the sun set over eastern Poland.

My fellow guests at the house were poor game for a journalist. Among them were a surly provincial governor, an ex-minister who evidently thought I was a spy and a stodgy bourgeoise with giggling daughters. On the second evening some twenty airmen with faces black from exposure and petrol fumes arrived; their fighter planes were hidden in the woods across the valley. I stole back after supper and looked into the big room where they were crowded at table. Two or three candles gave all the light, catching features, the breast of a tunic, the shine of a button. Countess Chodkiewicz and her daughter were serving, grey and blonde heads stooping over officers, moving in and out of shadows . . .

The airmen were at the house the next day. Their lieutenant, a nice if somewhat stringy boy, apologised for his hoarseness. 'I had a bad throat before the war started and I've not been much on the ground since. Ah, mademoiselle, it's cold, you know, up there.' They would not speak of the war in the air but told me of the long caravans dragging desperately across central Poland and how as they went the German fighters would dive and machinegun men, women and children. Very few of the poor with their slow-moving waggons ever escaped from Poland.

By now, even at Polonka, we were aware of the rising intensity of the air-raids. With every dawn, the bombers were up, raiding Luck ten or a dozen times by noon. German spies had discovered within forty-eight hours the arrival of government and military headquarters in Luck and the bombers were pounding it with little resistance from the anti-aircraft batteries.

Meanwhile, our group of airmen looked at the skies as they waited for petrol supplies and listened to the BBC announcing yet another RAF excursion over Germany on a pamphlet dropping mission.

Indeed, it was hardly surprising that the pilots shared the popular anti-British views arising from the growing realisation that Britain would move neither man nor aircraft to defend Poland, that our concern was focused on the western front. The pilots even blamed Britain for their petrol shortage. 'Had the Anglo-Polish loan been adequate, we could have imported petrol and stored it throughout the country,' they argued, adding, 'We were prevented from doing so because you kept us short of foreign exchange.'

I knew that one reason for the shortage was the breakdown of their own transport, due partly to poor organisation but also to the raiding of convoys and reservoirs by the Luftwaffe. The Polish fliers also held Britain responsible for the failure of trade negotiations. But I was aware, too, that Poland had been obliged to sell us anti-aircraft guns, which she needed so badly, to finance her purchases of petroleum.

In Luck, I met great antagonism when I went to the Post Office to cable a story to the *Daily Telegraph*. The clerk insisted on seeing my military press pass and, when I produced it, he said that the British Consul should accompany me before the cable could be accepted. Thwaites obliged and finally I was able to hand over my story, which the clerk read and then he cursed me in German. I discovered subsequently that the story never reached England.

Just then the whistles blew. I was still in the Post Office and, in a moment, the reverberations of bombs began. The big building stirred uneasily. The doors were being locked but I broke free just as the nearest bomb exploded.

A warden tried to stop me. Like some old spinster, I shouted, 'English! English!' and waved my passport at him. He spat. Behind him a group of Poles sheltering in an archway jeered and cursed me. I felt it was time to be on the move again and dashed back to the house. The embassy had warned me that the long German pincers were closing in and that German tanks were in Lvov.

Only one person remained absolutely calm amid the local hostility and the approach of the Germans: Countess Chodkiewicz. I told her that it was necessary for me to escape from Poland by making for Rumania but I had run out of petrol.

'Now don't worry, mademoiselle,' she said. 'I believe the air force officers are expecting petrol. Let me speak to the colonel.'

I watched her talking with the grim little man, gracious yet deferential to his rank. His face was like a war-idol: her warm skin caught the light as she spoke, quietly, persuasively. Soon she returned, successful. When at last the petrol arrived and the little colonel had strutted away, dangling a bottle of whisky, I tried for the last time what I had attempted before. 'Madame la Comtesse, won't you let me arrange for you to leave for Rumania? There is still time and there is always danger.'

Unlike her government, Countess Chodkiewicz proved unwilling to leave Polish soil. 'Thank you, mademoiselle, thank you. I have no one in Rumania. We could not be beggars in a foreign country.'

As we drove away she watched from the steps, son and daughter behind her. The blue uniforms of her airmen guests moved about in the shadow of the porch behind her . . .

I had been advised by Thwaites to make for the latest government retreat in Krzemieniec, which was even closer to the Russian border. The first town on the journey was Dubno where the Ministry of the Interior had taken refuge. Bad roads forced me into a detour which led to a moated castle. It was a huge, curving curtain-wall built of dark red stone, without crenellation or any architectural feature. Over a ruined parapet I could see the roofs of dwellings in the inner bailey. Against ramshackle Dubno, it looked so incongruous that it seemed to be a relic of a tale from Grimm. I wished that the Poles had a Society for the Preservation of Ancient Monuments to take care of this one.

Suddenly, the scream and roar of an air-raid. I drove under the trees. German espionage again! They must have already traced the Ministry of the Interior to Dubno and the Luftwaffe was on its tail again. The targets were a barracks, a railway line, gasometers. After a few minutes, explosions close by. A horse came charging up a path, then another, their light droszkies harnessed to them still. They galloped with a hideous high action of the forequarters and below, blood and intestines came away.

I drove on to Krzemieniec unable to rid the picture of those agonised horses from my mind. Krzemieniec, where the British Embassy and the Polish Foreign Office had established themselves, looked like the set for a ballet. The little town was built on the side of a hill and it rose from the main road in tiers of brightly painted, fretwork houses. Across the valley, a sugar-loaf hill balanced a citadel rather like one so often floodlit in Budapest. I discovered that the British Embassy had made its headquarters in the modest Hotel Bono, a one-storeyed building in the main street. In one of the rooms leading off a long corridor I found Robin Hankey again. He and a young wireless operator wrestled with a huge transmitting set, nicknamed 'the iron lung', trying constantly to reach London. They succeeded only once. And London refused to reply because Whitehall officials feared that the transmitter was being operated by the enemy.

Only the Ambassador, Sir Howard Kennard, enjoyed the privilege of a room to himself. I was sitting on a soapbox with Mrs 'Peter' Norton, and indulging in a rare glass of sherry when Sir Howard came in and greeted me.

'Hmm, you're a peculiar woman, Miss Hollingworth,' he said. 'What are you doing running about in the middle of all this? Love of excitement, I suppose.'

'I'm a journalist, Sir Howard. This is how I earn my living.'

Tall, slim, handsome in a grizzled kind of way, Sir Howard enjoyed immense prestige with the Poles before Munich. In those days he could, as he said, talk to Foreign Minister Beck 'like a father'. Afterwards, he was cold-shouldered. He had put Peter in charge of the evacuation of the embassy from Warsaw and at all onward stopping points. When he told her she would be the first to leave Krzemieniec, she protested vigorously, stamping around, hitching her eye-shade and exclaiming, 'Why should I go first? I am here because I can do a man's job.'

Indeed, I have not often found a man to match Peter's strength and efficiency. She had engineered escapes for many Polish refugees and in the evacuation operation of the British Embassy she ensured that the diplomats reached safety without harm. Clifford was equally effective, belying an assumed manner of vagueness. Yet he, too, possessed a fiery nature. During the Munich crisis when he was dining with other diplomats, a German representative said, 'Ah, I fear there may be a war, but a short war, I think, don't you? With a negotiated peace.' Norton lost his temper, and smacking his hand on a mantelpiece, declared, 'No! If Germany destroys the peace of Europe twice in a generation, I cannot foresee either a short war or a negotiated peace. It will have to be stopped once and for all.'

The fourth member of the diplomatic team was Hankey, whose father was Cabinet secretary in the First World War. Robin Hankey was then a good operator in the high echelons of the world's chancelleries. Throughout the war, his white terrier, 'Small Size', tumbled at his heels.

That night, I was taken to dinner in a barn of a building which could have been a disused school or college. On trestle tables set out in a long, bare room, the Polish government was trying to feed the diplomatic corps and the staff of their own foreign office.

Ministers, secretaries of embassies, heads of departments, Chinese, Italians, Central and South Americans all sat jumbled together along the benches like schoolboys. There was not enough space for a quarter of them. Some, in fact, avoided the scrum. The US Ambassador, Francis Biddle, sat with his wife and daughter with Sir Howard in a café opposite. Suddenly there was a momentary frenzy. Sir Howard had left his door locked at the 'embassy' with the light switched on and beaming out into the blackout. Ambassador or not, wardens stormed at the British envoy and then invaded our strange dinner party to find the key to the locked door. It was, of course, produced and the offending light turned out.

Over dinner of one egg and a portion of rice, I proposed the bright idea of returning to Warsaw. I had been told that the road to the Polish capital was, strange to say, still open and as air-raids and retreats were ceasing to be news, why should I not go back for the latest story there before the Germans took the city? My suggestion was greeted with horrified expressions. Then, a guarded discussion. After all, there were two Englishwomen stranded in Warsaw, there was a Briton in hospital in Lublin, there could be others . . . Indeed, some English people in Warsaw were abandoned by the British Embassy, which was unable to trace them in the confusion of the outbreak of war.

Much to my surprise, the diplomatic corps offered to provide precious petrol for this mad escapade. A map was produced. French, American and Polish diplomats advised on the best route to take. Some 'hard rations' were handed over plus a bottle of whisky.

I was not being brave – I certainly did not feel courageous – ignorant, perhaps and naïve. My over-riding feeling was enthusiasm for a good story, the story on the fall of Warsaw to the Nazi divisions. Who could resist that? So off again, this time I went alone without a driver, through Luck and retraced my journey towards Lublin.

Police stopped me from entering several towns and villages so I drove off the main road on to the hard-baked fields and picked up the route further on. Traffic was almost non-existent but the roads were jammed with thousands of refugees, many of them dragging prams loaded with children, some falling so far behind that they were lost or abandoned.

Then, another strafing raid. No sirens out there in the country to sound a warning. Two fighters, lower than I had seen them before, hurtled towards us raking the road with bullets. There was a confusion of running figures, flying skirts, falling shapes, over-turning carts and prams. Flat in the fields, they covered their heads under coats or sacking with the ostrich-impulse of terror. A horse dropped and lay kicking. Ten minutes later, the peasants returned to the road, picked up their belongings and started walking again. Few ever reached the safety of Hungary or Rumania.

That scene was repeated many times on the road to Warsaw, a road pitted with craters. Lublin itself was unrecognisable. Half an hour was long enough to view the ruins of shattered houses and offices, the flies almost covering the bodies of men, horses and dogs on the pavements. The windows of a few surviving shops had been pushed in and the stores rifled. I suppose the handful of survivors had to find succour somewhere.

I continued my journey following the course of dried-up rivers, down bridle paths, over fields and along cart tracks. The countryside was deserted, fields brown with the stumps of maize, cottages empty. There was no one to be seen on the route I took. When it was too dark to drive I stopped, ate some biscuits, took a pull of whisky, and curled up for the night with my electric torch and revolver on the seat beside me. Sleeping in the car caused me to wake early.

It was a clear morning, already light, and I could smell that it would be hot later on. I drove on, slightly disturbed by the absence of human beings and intrigued by dust rising ahead. I could see men marching and wondered if they were part of a retreating army. But these soldiers strode with a precision that had nothing to do with defeat. I was sitting there looking at a detachment of the German army.

For a moment I was so scared that instead of turning the car, I actually shut off the engine and gazed at the green uniforms approaching. Then I shook myself, switched on the engine and drove madly across the fields. Running over firm meadows, bumping through maize-stubble, rolling into rutted tracks, springs creaking, I stopped being afraid and thought only of my driving. I was going in the right direction but certainly not on the carefully chosen route.

After two hours, I was stopped by a broad stream. I had to get across it and I drove along the bank searching, methodically, for a shallow spot and then, desperately, for a bridge. I had gone too far to the south.

Eventually, I came to an old wooden bridge. A group of peasants stood on the far bank. 'Can anyone tell me the way to Lublin?' I shouted. 'Will one of you show me the way?'

Mutterings. I called, 'Have the Germans passed this way?'

'No Germans. Only the machines.'

'Do you mean tanks? When did they come – and where from?'

'Ah, I don't know. They came last night and crossed the river. But where they came from, I don't know.'

'Well, from which direction?'

'It would be over by Radom or that way.'

'And where were they making for?'

'It was towards Policzna or maybe Gotah. But we've seen no Germans.'

I drove over the bridge realising that the Lublin–Warsaw road was cut and there was no hope of continuing to Warsaw. I made my way back to Lublin and, on the outskirts, I passed a big American car with a uniformed figure inside. We smiled and waved. It was the American military attaché. He knew – but I did not then know – that I had emerged from German-occupied territory.

The raids began again on the bomb-cratered road to Luck. It ran parallel at one point with the railway a quarter of a mile away. A train appeared and immediately there was the sound of planes. I wrote in my diary at the time: 'There was a detonation, the crack of a small bomb with the ground-thud following, then another and a third as the train slid to a stop. Its sides opened and I saw figures running, jumping and diving into the long grass.' I was a safe distance away but I could not look at the planes as they dived twice, one after the other, to machinegun the passengers lying in the grass. I was surprised so many survived although one woman was out of her mind: she ran forward and clung to the rails in front of the train.

'Ah, I thought she wouldn't hold out long,' said one passenger, calmly.

'You have had much of this?'

'Thirteen times. Thirteen times out of the train into the fields. At last they will hit the train and it will be finished.'

The party were mostly wives of officials. They had been in the train, hungry and thirsty, for forty hours. Yet the children were jolly and unaware of danger. They laughed as they scampered back to their seats. The windows were broken, the woodwork splintered as the train resumed its journey to Luck.

Indeed, every train leaving Warsaw had been bombed, especially those carrying government officials and their families. Many trains, packed with refugees, were bombed twenty times a day, with strange to report, comparatively few casualities.

I drove off and was soon passing companies of Polish soldiers, fresh, untouched with their supply waggons unscratched, who

35

having made their way across open country had seen no fighting at all.

'You're marching in an odd direction,' I suggested to an officer.

'Why, no, mademoiselle,' he replied taking my offered cigarette. 'We have orders to move . . . eastwards.'

That meant the Russian border, an apparently pleasing alternative to facing German mechanised divisions. Beneath an outward conventional show of loyalty, these officers were extremely critical of their immediate superiors whose wives and families were being evacuated towards Rumania in staff cars heavily loaded with personal possessions and sometimes even supported by army lorries carrying furniture and petrol.

Luck was in the last stages of complete evacuation. There was no food but I managed to buy a bottle of wine to keep me company for the road ahead. Scores of cars had been abandoned through lack of petrol. Some had crashed into bomb craters.

An air-raid alert greeted me in Krzemieniec and there was unusual alarm. Wardens literally flung themselves in front of my car. Terrified faces peeped from windows and doorways. I soon realised the reason for the near-panic atmosphere in a town housing neutral diplomats.

The afternoon before German bombers had attacked the defenceless town, skimming the rooftops, machinegunning and bombing. In half a minute sixty people died. Owing to the presence of foreign diplomats, the raid became known as a *bombardement célèbre*, an early Hitlerian affront to the world designed to stun and daze incipient opposition with one bloody blow to the face.

Krzemieniec presented a pitiable scene. The main street was blocked, the ballet-set broken, balconies sagged, roofs open to the sky, houses heaps of rubble.

At the Hotel Bono, the British Embassy staff were in conference so I talked with the English announcer of Polski Radio who had fled from Warsaw to Lvov where his regional station had been silenced by bombs and internal sabotage. He warned me not to stay in Krzemieniec because he thought the town would soon be cut off when the Germans made their breakthrough to Ternopol.

In the middle of these deliberations, I encountered the most interesting piece of secret diplomacy of the war, which was confirmed later by the British and the French. Since their departure from Warsaw, the foreign diplomats had lived closely together and established an almost intimate fraternity. In this ambience, Francis Biddle, the US envoy, developed great authority and became the unquestioned chief of the neutrals.

Biddle had been popular in Warsaw not because he was rich, handsome and came from an old Virginian family but because he blended cool, considered diplomacy with a deep sense of humanity. He was accessible and with everyone he offered informality and consideration. It was natural, therefore, that the Russian ambassador should consult him on a point of some delicacy the day before the air-raid on Krzemieniec.

Biddle was invited to the Russian Embassy – opposite the Hotel Bono – and shown into a dark room which served his Russian colleague as a bedroom and a *salle de réception*. To his surprise he saw, spread on a grubby table-cloth, bread, vodka and masses of caviare. After sampling these delicacies, he asked the Russian how he came by them. The Russian explained that with the Soviet frontier nearby he had merely ordered them to be sent across. And then his reason, his remarkable reason, for inviting Biddle to his embassy emerged.

Would the American Ambassador ask Col Beck, the Polish Foreign Minister, whether the Polish government cared to invite the Red Army into eastern Poland to keep order and prevent the Germans from occupying it? Biddle was startled. He pointed out that the Polish government was unlikely to do any such thing and he preferred not to mention the proposal to Col Beck even privately. But since the Polish Foreign Secretary lived only a few yards away why could not the Russian Ambassador ask him personally?

Later that day, the Russian envoy called at the American Embassy. Yes, he had seen Col Beck who told him that there was no question of Poland asking for Russian help. The Russian said he must contact Moscow as soon as possible and this would mean crossing the border to find a suitable telephone. The entire Soviet staff left the next morning. Two hours later came that devastating air raid.

A few hours after the attack, the Papal Nuncio called a meeting amid trenches dug on a football field. All the diplomatic mission chiefs were invited and Biddle was asked to take the chair. The Nuncio proposed that all present should send identical telegrams to their governments protesting against the bombing of civilian populations. At that very moment there was an air-raid alert. The diplomats took cover, tail coats and top hats rolling together into a trench.

'We crawled out when the all-clear sounded,' the Swedish minister told me, 'like dirty and naughty schoolboys trying to look as though we were not afraid.'

The meeting resumed and Biddle put an appropriately-worded protest to the group which approved it – almost unanimously. Bulgaria voted against the protest but then as a Balkan state she was in a difficult position. The only other dissenting voice came from the Swiss envoy, representative of the 'good works' nation, home of the Red Cross, habitat of the League of Nations. At that time Switzerland was telling neutrals that they alone could carry out relief work in war-time. Biddle half lost his temper and addressed the Swiss envoy in strong, undiplomatic terms.

Subsequently, I reported to the British diplomats on my vain journey north. They, too, had heard of the attacks on refugees but these accounts, although reported to London, had never been announced. This underlined in my mind at that time a suspicion that the British government had made a tacit agreement with Germany not to disclose such details in return for an understanding that the Nazis would not attack Britain. Our indignation changed with news of an impending German thrust towards Ternopol. Evacuation was planned for the next day and I found myself packed into a car with Frank Savory, Consul-General in Warsaw.

Savory, the most cultured of the embassy circle, had left behind in Warsaw his prized collection of Persian pottery and oriental paintings. He loved Poland and had turned down promotion to remain in the capital. He spoke the language fluently and knew more about their literature than most Poles. We drove for twenty-four hours, a long, exhausting trip over roads, tracks and fields. We reached the villa, which was to serve as the British Embassy at Ternopol, at breakfast-time to be offered by the military mission a real breakfast: toast, marmalade and real coffee!

After a rest, we motored on to Zaleszczki in the extreme south-east of Poland where 15,000 refugees were jammed into the last corner of escape into Rumania. They appeared to have eaten everything in every shop and restaurant. I entered one labelled 'Café Klub' where I addressed a Jewish girl in German, asking for a meal. She was quiet, smart and smiled sweetly.

'I 'ear there's something wrong. Wot did yer wonter order?' The accent was the most beloved Whitechapel.

'Could I have some lunch, do you think?'

' 'Course. These people don't know wot they're doin' of. Hier! Fritz!' She gave an order in bad German.

There she was, married to a Pole, living in a remote cranny of central Europe and still buoyed up with the cocky smartness of the Mile End Road. (A few weeks later I saw her arguing with all the confidence of a Cockney in the British Legation in Bucharest for a visa to return to her parents. She got it.)

The authorities handed over rooms in a military hospital to the diplomats and I was allocated one with windows overlooking the River Dniester – hidden in its valley – to the blunt hills of Rumania.

On the hospital lawn there was a crowd of diplomats, legation clerks, embassy servants, chauffeurs, officials, soldiers. Poles, Asiatics, French, Scandinavians, Russians, Latin Americans, British, Slavs: they talked, walked, gesticulated. Some were journalists and a good many were gatecrashers with no connection at all with the diplomatic world.

There was a good deal of concern among the British fraternity for the Ambassador who was missing. He and his staff had left Krzemieniec after my departure and there had been no news of their progress southwards. It was not until the following morning that I heard that they had reached Kuty on the border to the west. This village was the last 'home' of the Polish government.

The retreat south had brought scores of reporters into Zaleszczki from Bucharest in a string of taxis. And among them I was delighted to find my *Daily Telegraph* 'boss', Hugh Carleton Greene. He urged me to go with him immediately into Rumania and file my story.

Greene and I walked down to the long wooden bridge, which crossed the Dniester on the Polish border. His taxi was waiting on the other side: I could not use my car because it had no international papers. We must have looked an odd sight, Greene hugging a huge standard typewriter and I with a dirty pillowcase full of clothing. The Rumanian customs officer refused to let us through, but luckily Thwaites appeared and took over. A bank note vanished into the Rumanian's pocket. And we entered Rumania.

We drove to Cernauti about thirty miles away and I filed my story to London on the war situation and the escape from Poland. The German army was marching on Ternopol, leaving Lvov untaken, which had become the centre of heavy fighting on their left flank. A pincer movement was closing around Brest–Litovsk and this would cut off eastern Poland.

Warsaw was almost surrounded. The date: 14 September. The next day, the British diplomats arrived and disclosed that the Ambassador had decided to remain in Kuty. Greene and I then agreed that it was time to interview Sir Howard. Sonia Tamara of the *Chicago Tribune* joined us for the trip back to Poland and after the usual difficulties involved in crossing the frontier we reached Kuty. It seemed to be unconscious of war with people going about their normal business. The shops were open and fully stocked. With tree-lined streets and white timber houses, Kuty was almost like a small town in America.

We found Sir Howard lunching in the back room of a dirty restaurant – reputedly the best in town but that did not prevent flies, cheese and bottles sharing the same counter in the front shop. Sir Howard sat me down at his side and offered bread and tomatoes. He and his two companions, Clifford Norton and Robin Hankey, had become rather tired of each other's company on their journey south: they were tired of struggling with their radio and they knew nothing of the real war situation. They begged for news.

Sir Howard declared that so long as there was a Polish government on Polish soil he would not leave the country. And we learned that the Poles were launching a counter-attack in the south and the weather had changed. Rain was sweeping the countryside raising hopes that the invaders would soon be bogged down. Those hopes were indeed short-lived. We returned to Cernauti the next day – 16 September – while back in Kuty Sir Howard received a summons to the Polish Foreign Office, which was occupying a farmhouse. Col Beck sent a motor-cycle and sidecar to fetch the British envoy. Sir Howard had never before ridden in a sidecar and with his long legs one understood why.

At the farmhouse, Beck greeted him with the words: 'My

dear ambassador, I must tell you that the Russian forces have crossed our frontier and are marching into our country. There will be a complete and speedy breakdown. I advise you to leave immediately.'

Sir Howard returned to his embassy, packed his belongings for the last time on that long exodus from Poland and left with his staff for the Rumanian frontier.

At noon that day, Major Colbourne, American military attaché, was driving between Ternopol and Zaleszczki when he came face to face with an enormous 60-ton tank. 'I wondered', he said, afterwards, 'how on earth the French had managed to get these new tanks into Poland.' It rumbled towards him and he left his car to take a closer look. The upper deck opened and a soldier's head popped out. He wore a curious flat cap decorated with the star, hammer and sickle. Major Colbourne got into his car and drove off.

At about the same time an old friend, police chief Colonel Zoltaszek, was sitting in Ternopol after working all night. He had marched across Poland with his police force. An orderly interrupted him. 'Beg pardon, sir. Radio message that the Russians have crossed the frontier in force.'

'Crossed? You mean, invaded Poland?'

'No, sir. Message says no fighting. Russian forces moving in a peaceable manner.'

Colonel Zoltaszek hurried off to tell his senior officer, who, already encouraged by reports of Poland's counter-attack, felt that good fortune was at last on their side. At about 10.30 that morning I wandered out of my hotel in Cernauti and realised at once that something was wrong.

People were bunched together in groups all around the square. The narrower streets were filled, the corner pavements impassable. I edged into a group. 'What is it? What has happened?'

'The Russians have invaded Poland.'

I raced back to the hotel and told Greene. 'Nonsense,' he said.

But by noon confirmation arrived with stories of the welcome given to the Red Army men as saviours from the German invader. That afternoon I was driving down the main street and saw Sir Howard's Rolls-Royce drawn up in front of the consulate. I ran in and encountered a somewhat bad-tempered group of British diplomats. They had had a rough trip.

41

The long bridge at Kuty was packed with refugees and when the British party finally reached Rumanian soil, the frontier guard refused them entry. Sir Howard sat like a monument in the Rolls-Royce throughout the hot noon-day sun while refugees swarmed closer together around his proud car. Women and children fainted from hunger, heat and fatigue. The Ambassador remained stolidly determined not to move as the dispute with the frontier guard continued and telephone calls were put through to Bucharest. Rumours claimed that the Russians were approaching the frontier and panic scattered the refugees. Then suddenly Bucharest signalled that the British party could proceed and, as impervious as ever and without even a backward glance, the British Ambassador to Poland entered Rumania.

It seemed to Greene and me that the Polish government itself would soon be following the British example. We drove to the frontier and met hundreds of refugees, including soldiers, fleeing from Poland and, in the air, planes were flying south. The Polish Air Force was on the run.

Amid the rout was the British military mission from Katowice with lorries carrying staff and luggage.

As they were waved through, we saw headlights in the gathering dusk on the north bank of the Dniester. A line of cars stopped at the far end of the bridge. An elegant young man ran over and plunged into talks with the Rumanian frontier guards. He went back and then a car approached. Two bare-headed men in raincoats stood on the running-boards. The car stopped, documents and automatic pistols were handed over to the guards. One of them looked into the car and then saluted. On the back seat I glimpsed a dark figure, a blur of white hair. Then President Moscicki drove into Rumania and exile. In the car behind was Col Beck with his wife and daughter. Car after car and lorry after lorry, packed with baggage, crossed the bridge and slipped away down a hill following their President.

After a few uncomfortable hours of fitful sleep in the car, Greene and I prepared for a final visit to Poland. We crossed at noon after considerable arguments with Rumanian frontier officials. Kuty was quiet but tense with few people on the streets. At a cross-roads, a lorry was drawn up with two machine-guns mounted on it covering approach roads. Polish soldiers scanned the roads and countryside through binoculars while others squatted nearby. A group of villagers, some wearing air-raid warden armbands, regarded the scene. 'Are you expecting the Russians here?' I asked one of them.

'Yes, we were told that they would be here at noon.'

'Are you preparing against them, then?' Greene gestured at the machine-guns. The warden was astounded.

'Against the Russians? Why? No, no! We are afraid the Ukrainians will break in and kill us all before the Russians can get here.'

On the far side of a ridge came a crackle of shooting.

'Would you prefer the Russians or the Germans to come?'

Again, the villager looked astounded. 'Of course we prefer the Russians. We don't want the Germans, by God!'

There was more shooting. The soldiers trained their machine-guns on the approach roads. As we watched, a grey mass bulged into sight over the opposite ridge.

'The tanks! The Russian tanks!' cried the villagers.

It seemed time to be going. 'Good luck,' we said and shook hands all round.

On the drive back to Cernauti we encountered the inevitable refugees, mainly families of soldiers and airmen threading their way into Rumania as Polish warplanes continued to fly out of their defeated country. I counted seventy-four and then gave up.

We drove into Cernauti and continued our journey to Bucharest reaching the capital after two days of travelling. By then the harried Polish government was in exile. The three weeks war was almost over. But for Britain and the rest of the world it had hardly begun.

4 Bucharest . . . King Carol's Abdication . . .

In Bucharest there was but little time to rest and reflect on the triumphant Nazi victory over Poland and the ease with which those pincer columns cut the Polish Army into pieces. How was it possible that the strongest second-class power on the Continent had collapsed in only three weeks of war? The Poles offered two excuses: their inferiority in war-planes and lack of support before and during the conflict from the Allies.

It is often said by historians that the German Air Force disabled all Polish aerodromes in the first days of the war. This is not true. I myself saw the Krakow airport in use after being bombed during those first days. After a week, Lublin aerodrome was still in action. I saw many war-planes under camouflage on temporary airstrips. Reports that hundreds of German bombers raided Katowice were also untrue: there were never more than twenty over the city at any one time. Normally they hunted in threes.

Lack of fuel was the reason why those Polish fighters were so seldom seen over the battlegrounds. The Poles neglected to establish fuel dumps in different parts of the country for swift distribution and they failed to import adequate reserves. The Germans, too, took early action to knock out key roads and railways to prevent oil supplies reaching the Polish Air Force. Failure by the Polish government to prepare for war was compounded by British policy.

Britain failed to appreciate the Nazi menace. It was only after the Munich crisis that Mr Chamberlain and Sir Nevile Henderson viewed the Germans more realistically. They therefore concluded the Anglo-Polish Pact but this was a bluff with no hand to support it. Poor Poland. She was in no position to withstand the German onslaught with or without British help and I suppose the Whitehall conscience over her plight – if there was one – was soon swamped by the perilous situation facing Britain.

I had already seen war at close quarters and in Bucharest its effects were saddeningly evident in the thousands of refugees pouring into the capital. In the surrounding countryside they slept in cars or in the open fields, the rich buying food in the villages, the poor begging their way through a poor country. In Bucharest, they flooded into the legations and consulates of the allied and neutral powers, as well as into their own. They got drunk and quarrelled with the civilian population. The situation that followed each of the Nazi invasions reproduced itself with nightmare exactitude.

In any refugee exodus the great problem is always the children. In Bucharest they were fortunate. One of the best-known names in the capital was that of the Princess Caragea. More than half a century before she was kidnapped as a tiny child by agents of a rival Rumanian family. For ten years nothing was heard of her; then her father traced her to an English orphanage. As an adult and wealthy woman, Princess Caragea established one of the best foundling homes in Europe. A new wing had just been completed when I arrived in Bucharest.

When the Princess heard of the Polish children's plight, she offered to receive them. I found the children in a splendid modern building with sun rooms, nurseries, balconies and washing facilities and kitchens as good as I have ever seen. One half of the block was divided from the other by a 'secret' door. On one side, the new arrivals were washed, de-loused and given medical treatment whenever necessary. On the other side, they settled down as regular residents.

As I accompanied the matron on a tour of the orphanage, a scatter of children ran to her skirts shouting confidences. I talked to several. Then to one, a boy of three or four, I was incautious enough to mention his parents.

'All gone,' he said. He was quite composed.

45

'Where to?'

'There was a bang. Mummy went like that.' He gestured. 'All in bits. Daddy, too.'

My enquiries about Polish refugees convinced me that they were being well looked after in Bucharest, but there were disturbing stories emanating from Hungary.

About this time it became apparent there was no hard news in Rumania apart from local information that was supplied by the 'stringer' and refugees. So, just before Christmas 1939, I gladly accepted the offer of a journey on the Simplon Orient Express with Frank Savory, who was acting as a special King's Messenger escorting scores of Polish diplomatic bags to London via Paris. Many contained documents from the Embassy in Warsaw but others I knew belonged to the Polish Government. They were eventually handed over to the Polish Government in exile in Angers, France.

Shortly after we reached London the editor of the *Telegraph* received me with warmth but admitted that in this period of phoney war there were few openings. I wrote a few pieces on Poland and Rumania. I was then asked to go to Hungary to help organise the distribution of food to Polish refugees. Again I did something that none could envisage today; I set off on an assignment to Budapest to write for the *Telegraph* – if there was anything to write about – and assist refugees. I had been to Budapest before and I described how pro-German almost all my friends had become, but not, of course, the British Ambassador who was best known as the husband of Ann Bridge, who had written the book *Peking Picnic*.

The thousands of Poles in Hungary were in a bad way, due largely to the breakdown in the distribution of relief supplies. I was delighted when Peter arrived with her own convoy of trucks. With incredible energy she cut through red tape, upset local fund officials, and organised the distribution of food and medical supplies to the outlying refugee camps, many of which were disused factories. I met the former Chief of Police from Katowice living in squalor and he told me fresh stories of the Polish war together with the pro-Nazi line the Hungarians were putting out.

I returned to London in time for Christmas in order to spend the festive season partly with my parents and partly with my in-laws. I was still on friendly terms with my husband Van but he was growing a little restive about the time I was spending abroad.

However, in a curious and somewhat contradictory manner he encouraged me to consider further jobs in journalism. He was supported by our friend Terence Donovan, who was by this time well known as a skilled King's Counsel and Parliamentary Labour candidate. Terence arranged for me to meet several important newspaper proprietors and editors, including Lord Beaverbrook. I was offered a job on the *Daily Express*, but having worked so hard and so long for the LNU I hesitated. Thus I found myself in Paris in late February 1940 with various offers open to me from British newspapers and magazines, all interested especially in coverage from the Balkans.

High officialdom in London and Paris was already aware that the struggle in France was near its end. The Maginot Line was so far untouched, but the Germans were penetrating rapidly nearer and nearer to Paris from the lightly fortified Belgian frontier. In Ciro's and the Ritz Bar, where Kim Philby was a frequent visitor, gaiety had reached that peak of feverishness which reminded me so much of the atmosphere in Warsaw just before the Nazi invasion. The Paris shops were full of new summer models. British, Czech and Polish officers strolled along the boulevards. Englishwomen had been evacuated long before: those who remained were journalists, refugee workers or women in uniform. Plans were being made to evacuate children to the country. No one imagined that within weeks the cafés of the Champs-Elysées would be occupied by German officers. Few appreciated the gravity of the situation.

I grew increasingly anxious to return to Eastern Europe. I knew that it was desperately important for me to be east of the 'divide' before Italy entered the war. In fact, Italy declared war on Britain and France on 10 June.

By the time I had decided to leave Paris it was clear to me that a deadlock of many months would follow the German conquest of France. I never believed in the probability of the invasion of England, but it was obvious that it would be a long time before England would be able to counter-attack effectively across the Channel, which would become the new Maginot–Siegfried Line of Europe.

In those early days of the war, the Balkans were obviously

in Germany's direct line of south-eastern expansion. Rumania with its oil reserves was an obvious target and any thrust in that direction would involve Britain in counter-measures. Russia, also interested in extending her influence over the Balkans, was liable to appear as the champion of pan-Slavism, and Italy, following her occupation of Albania, was on the look-out for further aggression-without-tears. So I bought my ticket for Bucharest.

In the dim light of the Gare de Lyon, friends including Peter Norton gave me all their French money so that if I were not allowed to enter Switzerland I might have enough to return to Paris.

During the journey, German bombers flew over; the train stopped, passengers were alarmed but no bombs were dropped. When we arrived at the Swiss border everyone without a diplomatic visa was thrown off the train. Except me. Although my Swiss visa was not diplomatic – it was issued by a Legation and not by a Consulate – I managed to bully the frontier official to let me in. I reached Lausanne where I found the Swiss more depressed than the French, largely because trade was so bad with the large luxury hotels empty. They also feared that Germany might disregard their neutrality and invade.

Northern Italy was even more depressing and the train attendants treated me like dirt as they talked openly of entering the war within a few days. The hotels of Milan and Trieste were full of Germans complaining about the poor food.

Officially, the border between Italy and Yugoslavia was closed but it was possible to cross over on foot via a narrow bridge between Susak and Fiume that was still accepting local traffic. At each station on my way to Zagreb people were buying newspapers, and little groups of peasants collected around men wearing collars and ties who were able to read and explain what was happening in France. Every newspaper had a map with a black bulge indicating the German advance, which increased in size every day. Within the two months since my last visit, Yugoslavia had changed.

Always an indication of popular feeling and trust, the black market for money had fallen and while I had previously bought dinars at three hundred and sixty to the pound sterling I could only get the official rate of two hundred.

There were real fears that the Italians would invade Greece, taking Salonika and cutting Yugoslavia off entirely, but Belgrade firmly refused to make any military agreement with any other Balkan state. There was little admiration among the Croats for the Serbian head of state, Prince Paul, who was acting as Regent for the young King Peter.

Prince Paul, a sad specimen of Oxford-educated humanity, was playing hard on both sides. As the brother-in-law of Princess Marina, Duchess of Kent, he was in close touch with the British royal family. He convinced the British Minister in Belgrade, Ronald Campbell, that he held the reins of government firmly and used them in a way which would only benefit the allied cause. But he was saying the same to the Germans. A nobody in Yugoslavia before the assassination of King Alexander in Marseilles on the morning of 9 October 1934, Prince Paul had befriended artists and Leftist politicians. As soon as he became Regent after Alexander's death, the only artist of note he met was Mestrovic, a man of international reputation, whose works Prince Paul bought but never paid for. He had the look of a man without charm or reliability, a man whose unstable habits, not so much of physical as of mental disloyalty, caused his wife great unhappiness. He enjoyed being Regent and had little intention of giving up his power when the young king came of age. He was not only unreliable but a bad ruler in the technical sense. His secretaries were inefficient; he allowed them to keep papers from him. He once told me that although he had ordered *The Times* his secretaries often prevented him from seeing it. When I looked surprised, he said he was too busy to make a fuss.

He also disclosed that his programme was often mishandled and that some important English guests had been turned away without reference to him. Like other rulers and politicians in the Balkans at the beginning of the war he was playing for time. He retained a close friendship with Chips Channon.

Few people realised as France was about to fall and Italy to enter the war the extreme dangers facing the Balkan nations compounded by the close co-operation, which was still maintained between Berlin and Moscow, and the chronic lack of political stability everywhere.

The German–Soviet co-operation, which at the time was vital to Hitler, was later confirmed by Sir Stafford Cripps, who was by then Britain's Ambassador in Moscow. Earlier, the moves on the European chessboard had been fascinating for an objective observer to follow with Hitler forcing the game through Vienna, Munich and Prague while Britain and France responded with guarantees to Turkey, Rumania and Greece – guarantees that became perilous liabilities when the French débâcle revolutionised the whole position in the Mediterranean.

During the dreadful week in June that opened with the Italian declaration of war and ended with the first French appeal for an armistice, the centre of gravity of the war moved from the western battlefields to the whole area between the Danube and the Nile. It was also apparent that Britain could do no more than play a waiting game, holding off the threatened attack on that vital waterway – the Suez Canal – until reinforcements reached the Middle East from Britain, New Zealand, Australia, and most important of all, India. Then and only then could Britain hope to take the offensive.

Meanwhile, Germany was in a position to strike directly across the desert into Egypt and from their advance base in Albania into the Balkans. The Axis seemed to have every card in their hands, for their general advance across the Balkans was sweeping on, with Albania under their command, Rumania likely to fall as a result of military infiltration and disintegration, and Yugoslavia on the brink of economic collapse and virtually encircled by enemy forces. For a time Hitler came up sharply against the resistance of the Greek people but eventually the Nazis took Greece just as they had conquered every small country that had stood before them.

None of these portents had made any impact on Bucharest in June, 1940. There was some depression over the impending defeat of France, but social life continued to sparkle. Every evening the restaurants and night clubs were packed with diplomats, journalists, oil magnates and politicians. The bar of the Athenée Palace Hotel before lunch was the international meeting-place. There, Walter Duranty, 'king' of the journalists, held court on the events of the day and everyone crowded around to hear his comments. Princess Elizabeth Bibesco, daughter of Lord Oxford and Asquith and wife of a Rumanian aristocrat, came in every day to hear the news. Junior diplomats collected there the information for their despatches, which were sent by secret cipher but which arrived actually two or three days after the same information had been printed in American and British newspapers.

Behind this light-hearted atmosphere it was obvious that things were going wrong. The British Minister, Sir Reginald Hoare, had lost a great deal of his power. Before the war began he had been an intimate friend of the prime minister, Armand Calinescu, who was assassinated just after the downfall of Poland. Indeed, shortly after leaving Poland in 1939 I filed a story on the murder in Bucharest.

I was on my way to lunch when I was held up by a crowd, who explained how a farm cart had blocked the route of Calinescu's car on his way home. As the car slowed down members of the pro-German Iron Guard – a hated secret society – opened fire and riddled the prime minister and his private secretary with bullets.

The gunmen were hunted down, arrested and taken in a lorry back to the scene of the assassination and shot one by one, with thirty minutes interval between each execution. Their bodies sprawled in the dust for forty-eight hours as a public warning: news vendors, orange sellers, gypsy fortune-tellers and sellers of hot food did a great trade. Parliament passed a law permitting any policeman recognising a member of the Iron Guard to shoot him on sight.

Calinescu became a public hero. His body was laid out in state dressed in purple velvet and surrounded by candles. He was buried amid great pomp and ceremony. Not only was the prime minister dead but the Anglophile influence over King Carol was ended and the intimate contact which the British Legation had had with the cabinet through Hoare was over.

Hoare, who had been able to telephone Calinescu at any time of the day or night to obtain advice or information, made no attempt to become friendly with the new men who surrounded the king. He remained in contact, however, with Grigore Gafencu, the foreign secretary, a most attractive man. He married when young a Frenchwoman who, it was said, was brought to Bucharest as the mistress of an elderly rich industrialist, who tired of her. She then became a cabaret dancer and was carried every night naked on an ersatz golden plate into one of the night clubs. Here Gafencu met her and married her. She made him a lively and charming wife.

Gafencu liked to keep in touch with American and British diplomats but he had let Britain down badly over the planned destruction of Rumanian oilfields. Long before the war began, Rumania and Britain agreed that the oilfields should be destroyed if threatened by a Nazi invasion. Sabotage plans were drawn up by the General Staffs and oil experts of both countries.

Into this murky operation came a mysterious man known as Sindbad the Sailor, who produced a brilliant if ill-conceived plan for blowing up the Iron Gates, which were a shallow, narrow area of the Danube where the water flowed over a solid rocky surface and on through a dam. Destroying the Gates would prevent barges taking oil up the Danube to Germany. The plan was for three or four barges carrying a cargo of concrete with a crew of British sailors to sail up to the dam and blow it up or, failing that, to sink the barges and block the river for several months.

A team of British naval personnel was recruited – men with a knowledge of Rumania, a few who could speak the language. They all thought the escapade was rather a lark. At various ports along the Black Sea they were kitted out with old trousers and sweaters. A motley crew, indeed, that finally sailed up the Danube with explosives, ammunition and concrete.

All seemed to be going well until a so-called British agent let it all out while drunk and surrounded by pretty women in a run-down night club in Giurgiu on the Danube.

The British Embassy, of course, was the focal point for the operation and when it started to go wrong, Hoare, luckily for him, was in London for a high-level conference on policy in the Balkans.

It was also in Giurgiu that the daring British seamen stopped to refuel. This took longer than expected and the crew made themselves rather conspicuous by drinking beer with the local girls, causing such a rumpus that the local officials decided to take a closer look at their barge.

Undoubtedly, the careless chatter of the British agent earlier in Giurgiu had been picked up by German intelligence. And so the cargo was discovered and the expedition came to a sudden end.

Certain pro-German members of the Rumanian cabinet were delighted and Gafencu, who had been consulted over the affair from the beginning and given it his consent, did not have the courage to stick up for the British, who found themselves in an extremely delicate position. The British seamen were hastily sent back to Britain and so a pre-war and badly managed attempt at sabotage was relegated to a diplomatic pigeon-hole. Two years later a highly expensive bombing raid was organised by the Americans on the oil city of Ploesti but little damage was inflicted.

Gafencu did not last long, however. On 1 June 1940 his resignation was announced and this was the beginning of military preparations. Troops were mobilised. Permits were needed for any journey, even a walk in the mountains. Government and Press became openly pro-German, but this was eased somewhat by a visit from Sir Stafford Cripps. Gafencu was appointed as Ambassador to Moscow at the same time as Churchill sent Cripps to Russia as part of a general movement towards *rapprochement*. I had met Sir Stafford only a few days earlier in Istanbul where the British naval attaché had to arrange a special ferry to carry him across the Bosphorus to the European side. The attaché disapproved of Sir Stafford who, sensing this, talked freely to me of our mutual friend Terence Donovan.

We discussed the political scene and lunched at a Turkish restaurant. People who only months previously would have called Sir Stafford a Bolshevist and a Red were clamouring for invitations to meet him. Indeed, he made a profound impression on all those diplomats and officials who talked with him. Later several commented patronisingly, 'He cannot be such a Red after all.' Sir Stafford was optimistic about his mission to Russia although he felt he had been sent there two years too late. Germany and Russia were still working very closely together.

Two women dominated this particular scene: Princess Marthe Bibesco, wife of the head of the Bibesco house, who were once the ruling princes of Rumania, and Madame Magda Lupescu, the most powerful woman in the country.

Princess Marthe, sister of Prince Antoine Bibesco, who was dismissed from the Rumanian diplomatic corps where he had been the main contact for the British and French embassies, turned her social attention to the Germans and Italians. An extremely adroit woman, she had managed to keep on good terms with the Germans in the First World War, although she owned a house in Paris. Now she dropped the English for the numerous Germans who arrived every day. Princess Marthe was reputed to have been the intimate friend of King Carol's father; she was now a handsome woman of middle age who ran her house on model lines and whose garden, on which only Bulgarians worked because she had little patience with Rumanian peasants, was the finest in the land. Not only was she on excellent terms with all the officials, but she was known to be a friend of Madame Lupescu. In fact, one of the most sensational exhibits in Madame Lupescu's house, which was opened to public view after King Carol's abdication in the following autumn, was a letter from Marthe to Magda, in which she said: 'You are, in fact, the Queen of Rumania.'

I always think of Madame Lupescu as I last saw her: a tall beautiful woman of forty-five with blazing red hair and a hot temperament to match. Although a Jewess, she did not exercise an anti-German influence over King Carol as one might have expected. Born in Sulina the daughter of the local chemist, she was an extremely bright child and learnt English quickly from the then large British colony in the town. Her vivid personality soon enabled her to get a job in Bucharest where she met the monarch and came to influence his life greatly and subsequently the history of the country. She had a house in a smart suburb of Bucharest but had all her meals with the king and played poker with him almost every night, a game at which she was particularly skilful.

Her house was full of treasures; she had beautiful clothes and jewellery. On a patch of land outside the town close to Baneasa aerodrome she was building herself a large country house when the Germans invaded Rumania. Pillars for the courtyard were imported from an old palace in Italy, doors were opened and closed by electricity, sunken baths and beautiful terraces were created in the best of taste and there was a kitchen equipped to cook for at least two hundred people. There was a secret path from the house to the airport where King Carol's plane was always ready for take-off at a moment's notice if he needed to flee from his country.

The loss of the northern province of Bessarabia to Russia at the end of June, 1940, was not only the beginning of the end of greater Rumania and its independence but it set alight the powers opposing the king. There were about 150,000 Russians in Bessarabia, most of them peasants, who were settled there during a previous period of Russian government. There were also Germans, Bulgars and Turks. This mixed population had no say as to who in future should govern them. It was on 26 June 1940, that Bucharest received a demand from Moscow that within twenty-four hours Rumania should agree to the Soviet occupation of the province.

The language of the demand was not even diplomatic. This was the moment of supreme opportunity for the king. He telephoned Berlin and spoke to Hitler. The Führer said no help would be forthcoming from Germany if Rumania decided to resist the Soviet claim. He advised King Carol, whom he had never liked, to surrender to the Moscow demand. At this moment, King Carol could have threatened to destroy the Rumanian oilfields because Hitler could not have allowed them to fall into the hands of the Russians or, even worse, risk their being blown up. It was a trump card for the king but he lacked the guts to play it; he feared that war on Rumanian territory would be the end of his personal fortune.

In this he represented the great majority of his countrymen, who would have taken the same decision. They would not have dared to destroy the great oil wealth of Rumania, not believing that England could possibly win the war and fearing the truth of German gossip that any damage to the oilfields would result in the worst bombing on Bucharest that the Third Reich could produce. In the background, too, there was a substantial Fifth Column, which Rumania had never dared to challenge. The Ministry of the Interior had said that there were no less than 91,000 Germans in the country and the German military attaché claimed continually to neutral colleagues that the German minority was in a position to take control of Rumania at four hours' notice. King Carol knew, too, that if he took the risk of fighting the Russians (at that time no one was aware of the strength of the Russian army except that it had put up a poor show against Finland) Hungary and Bulgaria would attack him unless the Germans stopped them. Unfortunately, King Carol was only half English and even before the cabinet ministers arrived at his palace for talks on the sudden crisis he had decided that Bessarabia and Northern Bukovina should be returned to Russia.

As the cars swept into the palace yard, Russian planes were flying over the disputed territory. Tension was high in Bucharest as the Crown Council went into session, which ended tamely enough with an announcement that a Rumanian-Russian commission would sit at Odessa to arrange the handover.

King Carol knew that he was in disgrace after his many high-sounding speeches, in which he had said that not one foot of Rumanian soil would ever be lost. General mobilisation was then declared, adding enormously to the tension and fears of the masses and so a new government was formed to try to calm everyone. This was not at all successful since the new government was composed of men who had never been respected as they were all well-known swindlers. Maps of Rumania swathed in black crêpe appeared in many shop windows. Three days of national mourning were imposed and all places of amusement were closed for this period. Restaurateurs were told that their orchestras must not play.

On 27 June Moscow issued a communiqué declaring that Bessarabia must be evacuated within four days and on 1 July the Rumanian government renounced the British Guarantee of 1939 and stated that in future Rumanian policy would orientate itself towards the Axis. This really only confirmed what everyone knew but it was in effect an appeal to Hitler for protection against the future demands of Hungary and Bulgaria. But Hitler was not interested and he told King Carol in no uncertain terms that Germany was unable to offer a military alliance to Rumania.

Confusion, which never really began to sort itself out until the Germans occupied the country, reigned in all departments of state. Refugees poured into Bucharest. Hundreds of people with homes in the two northern provinces applied for permission to return to them.

Horia Sima, the Iron Guard leader, went to King Carol and demanded without much hope that an Iron Guard government should be formed. The king refused and the three Guardists in the cabinet resigned. But the men who remained in office were, on the whole, more fascist than the Guardists themselves.

At the height of the crisis, Hungary demanded that Rumania should hand over the province of Transylvania, a move that contributed greatly to King Carol's abdication and the carving up of the Rumanian nation. It was arranged that a Hungarian delegation should have talks in Turnu Severin, a small port on the Danube, with Rumanian officials on this latest threat.

I covered this rather farcical conference and on the opening day the two delegations were so much at loggerheads that it was impossible for them to begin their discussions as they could not settle the simple questions of procedure.

By this time I was working for the *Daily Express*. I resigned largely because the *Telegraph* 'stringer' in Bucharest was resentful of me, uncooperative and pro-German.

I was also offered a job on an American radio station but failed in the test because of my English accent.

It was obvious that Transylvania was a non-story but nevertheless I had to file a piece to the *Daily Express* in London. Thirty reporters were fighting for possession of one telephone box. Being small I pushed my way quietly through the crowd and then, dropping to my knees, I crawled between various legs to the kiosk door. From the floor, I reached up and grabbed the receiver from flailing hands and wrapped my arms around the mouthpiece so that nothing short of dislocating the entire apparatus could pull me out of the box. I put the receiver to my ear to be told by a girl operator that there was a call waiting for one of the reporters. I know that I should have handed the instrument over to whoever wanted it in that mad mêlée but I also knew that if I did so I would never see that telephone again. Quietly and calmly, I refused the call, which had been put through from Rome, and, huddling on the floor of the kiosk, asked for the number of my contact stringer in Geneva. I dictated my story for onward transmission to London, replaced the receiver and my day's work was over.

I returned to Bucharest. The Turnu Severin talks lasted ten days with predictable results that led to the transfer of Transylvania to Hungary and control of this corner of the Balkans by Germany.

For me the big story was still in Bucharest. In fact, six weeks before King Carol abdicated on 6 September he arrested General Ion Antonescu, the man to whom he had to turn at the last moment to save him. The king knew that his own job was extremely insecure: he knew that at any moment he might be shot by the Iron Guard or, if he were lucky, he might merely be asked to abdicate. Many Rumanians at the time of the abdication had so much respect for the general that they could not believe that a great deal of his anti-Carol activities were, in fact, inspired by personal venom against the king.

Antonescu, a former military attaché in London, was a little, round, fat man, not at all paunchy, but fat all over. Like Gafencu's marriage, his own was, socially speaking, catastrophic, as he married a manicurist whose manners were ill-bred and morals indiscreet. She did, however, dress rather well as she had once worked in a hat shop.

When the king ordered Antonescu's arrest, the general was brought from his country villa to prison in Bucharest. He was charged with plotting against the State. Few people outside Rumania had ever heard of Antonescu and those who had regarded the arrest as another clear example of King Carol's pro-German tendencies. During the weeks he was in prison, Antonescu built up a network of communications to keep himself in touch with the political situation outside. The king was becoming desperate to form a government and had even invited the Iron Guards to serve in one. They refused, saying they could not serve under a man who had lost Transylvania although their own organisation was known as the Rumanian Nazi Party. But they seized the opportunity posed by the loss of so much Rumanian territory to organise protest riots all over the country. They even shot some officials known for their sympathy and support for the king.

At this moment, the atmosphere in Bucharest was highly charged. Anger against the king built up in night riots with troops firing on crowds. He was loathed particularly for the money he spent on extending his palace which he wanted to be larger than Buckingham Palace; had he remained king it would have been bigger than Windsor Castle. New buildings included a theatre to hold more than one thousand people, a church for four hundred worshippers and enormous salons, still unpainted when he abdicated. In a pique of royal one-upmanship, the king had brought a man from Waring & Gillow to Bucharest to design the interiors. The no-expense-spared palace did him more harm than any political hatred. Any peasant returning to his village from the capital told his friends about the houses being pulled down around the palace so that the king might have a vista; the peasant could not be expected to realise that this vista was really a good sweep for machine-guns.

In those days, Rumanian peasants earned twenty lei a month when the official exchange rate was six hundred and twenty lei to the pound sterling and the black market rate was anything from 1,500 to 4,500 lei.

I hold no brief for the king: he was a swindler, a traitor to his country, a disloyal friend and a murderer, but he seemed no worse than the men who followed him. Transylvania was lost through him and Antonescu came in on the cry of saving it. Britain was happy to see the departure of a pro-German monarch who would be replaced by a sympathetic, if not exactly pro-British, dictator. No one apart from a few who were making money out of him wanted King Carol to stay. The Iron Guards hated him for ordering the murder of their leader, Cornelius Codreanu, and the Transylvanian Peasant Party, led by Maniu, condemned him as a dictator. So a sacrifice was needed and the most obvious one was King Carol.

He released Antonescu and asked him to form a government after failing to persuade all the other political leaders to help him to end the crisis. Antonescu accepted the task and immediately sacked his arch enemy Urdarianu, Minister of Court and intimate friend of the king. The general's accession to power was acclaimed as a *coup d'état* and certainly he acted as though it was. He made no great attempt to create a government: his aim was the king's abdication.

He knew that the king desperately wanted to retain some strands of power but when the final hours arrived on 6 September with ferocious crowds held back from the palace gates by machine-guns, Antonescu acted. Alternately, he bullied and cajoled the king to agree to abdicate, finally leading him to a window on the first floor of the palace to look down on the mob. When the people saw King Carol, they hissed. Antonescu quickly drew him into the room.

'I cannot be responsible for your life if you stay on,' he told the monarch. 'But if you leave I will guarantee that you and Madame Lupescu will arrive safely on the far side of the frontier. In one hour the soldiers will be unable to control that surging mob, the ammunition will run out, the palace will be broken into and your body will receive the same treatment as those of the Tsar of Russia and the King of France.'

King Carol walked across the room and stood for two or three minutes with Madame Lupescu. He returned to the general. 'Yes, I will go,' he said. 'There are two things I want: one that you should help me to persuade my son, Michael, to come with me, and two that you should realise that I know you could have formed a cabinet and prevented this situation. I know that you are a good enough soldier to have had the military under sufficient control to make this last melodramatic threat superfluous.'

Prince Michael was brought into the room. The king appealed to his son to leave Rumania with him and Madame Lupescu pleaded too. But it was in vain: Antonescu had won over the confused young man before his father decided to abdicate.

Madame Lupescu made a desperate effort to have the prince accompany them for their safety for she was far more alarmed than the king. She felt that the mob would never fire on the boy. She may, too, have experienced a feeling of feminine jealousy at the boy's going back to his mother. It had taken her years to win Prince Michael's affection and, probably, she quite genuinely did not want to lose it again.

In pompous phrases, the young prince told his father and his father's mistress that he would stay and become king. The draft of the abdication was swiftly drawn up, strangely enough in the presence of one or two of the more respectable Rumanian politicians such as George Bratianu as well as of the gangsters who were in office. Those of us who had been waiting up all night wondering how King Carol would withstand the storm were quite suddenly informed that the deed of abdication would be issued in a special communiqué at 7.30 a.m. The king had had two hours in which to answer Antonescu's demands.

At 9.30 a.m. on 7 September, Prince Michael took the oath as the new king 'to preserve the integrity of the Rumanian frontiers'. He signed decrees for a political amnesty and for the limitation of his own prerogatives. Then he drove through the streets in an open car and the emotional crowds applauded him.

It was also announced that the Queen Mother, King Carol's former wife, was returning to Rumania. Britain was delighted, feeling that as a friend of Princess Marina and sister of the King of Greece she would have a pro-British influence at court. These hopes were quickly dashed despite messages of warm congratulations from the British royal family.

I remember feeling rather sorry for the young king as I saw him standing on the palace balcony receiving the cheers of a curious mob. He looked lonely and unhappy as well as young and beset by bovine stupidity. He came out on to the balcony at 8.30 a.m. and appeared every half hour, hatless and alone. He was now king of a country with neither government nor constitution. In the centre of the crowd was a contingent of orderly Iron Guards who marched with flags and a picture of Codreanu under the leadership of the slain party leader's father.

Their demonstration meant little and, for foreign correspondents King Carol remained the centre of interest. He delayed his departure for two or three days. A special train with all his baggage and jewellery was sent on ahead of his departure on 10 September in great secrecy.

No sooner had his train lurched out of Bucharest station than van loads of police arrived at Madame Lupescu's house. They took no notice of six enormous Blenheims, which were chained in their kennels, and, while neighbours were being disturbed by the barking of the dogs, one hundred and sixty-four packing cases were carried out to waiting lorries. Madame Lupescu had meant to take them into exile but obviously had been forced at the last moment to leave them behind. The house was later ransacked by hooligans.

The return of Queen Helen, too, was held up for some days. And the spirits of sorrow, rejoicing and tension merged into one another so the shopkeepers of Bucharest hardly knew whether to laugh or cry. The nation was supposed to be weeping for the loss of Transylvania. The famous gypsy bands in the restaurants were silent, cinemas and nightclubs were shut. Even hotel bars were not allowed to open and restaurants were closed at the highly inconvenient hour of 11.00 p.m. In Bucharest where one normally does not have dinner until 9.30 p.m. or 10.00 p.m. it was irritating to be thrown out into the streets without one's coffee. The Rumanian national flag, swathed in yards of black crêpe was flown from every window. Official mourning was put on in a big way, yet there was supposed to be rejoicing at the Queen's return to her dismembered State.

The looks of this perfectly ordinary woman were described as though she were some fairy princess. Shops brought out from their storerooms pictures taken of her at the time of her marriage to King Carol some twenty years previously. Photographs of Prince Michael from the day he was born almost until the abdication of his father were also shown, draped with the Rumanian colours. The King's photographs, which had occupied the focal points of every shop window, were now relegated to the toilets, just in case he might return. Every Rumanian householder had a nail on which he hung the photograph of the Head of State and, once out of office they were invariably consigned to the wc.

The air of sadness in the city did not diminish as flags appeared in the streets. Many state employees, humble and important, feared the future. They had only kept their jobs by becoming at least nominally supporters of the king and members of the National Renaissance Front. They prospered during what was described as 'ten years of tyrannical government'. Many were corrupt and afraid of imprisonment. Already, Tatarescu, former prime minister, and Stavitski Melaxa, the great industrialist and friend of King Carol, had been arrested as well as large numbers of minor politicians.

While the king was in the process of abdicating and leaving the country, the Iron Guard were stirring up riots and disorders across the country. The Germans were also active. They set up an elaborate organisation along the Danube valley, which was to transfer the German minority from Bessarabia back to the Reich.

The German Commission, which had previously worked in .Poland, arrived in the disputed State with the full consent of the Russians. They built large camps in Galatz, and Zemun, a town in Yugoslavia just north of Belgrade. Several hundred German army lorries with soldiers and nurses in uniform arrived with the Commission to examine the German minority in Bessarabia and to carry out the evacuation speedily. It was stated officially that the number of Germans in uniform was so great that this operation could be accomplished in six weeks.

With all these developments, officials were genuinely relieved when General Antonescu formed a stop-gap government. The reaction in Bucharest was that the new leader had earned and deserved support from the populace. Feelings against King Carol remained bitter and deepened after his departure when it was revealed that he had ruled the country like a businessman, regarding himself as the managing director anxious to make as much money as possible out of the nation. During his first exile, which ended in 1931, he lived in Paris and in Kent as a poor man with an expensive mistress. Although he did manage to keep his seat on the Rumanian throne for ten years, the entire period was one of great uncertainty, in which he expected to be thrown out at any moment.

The king began in a small way by saving his money and buying a factory here and a factory there until he was introduced to the Greek-born Rumanian, Melaxa, who had started life as a humble mechanic on the Rumanian railways. Melaxa had charm, dynamism and initiative. In 1923, he started a small company to manufacture railway trucks and chose as his partner a businessman, who the following year was appointed Under-Secretary of State for Railways. Melaxa at once secured a ten-year contract for locomotives from the Rumanian government and, as his capital increased from about £5,000 to the equivalent in lei of £250,000 he was able to join the court circle and become a friend of Madame Lupescu.

Both she and the king were fascinated by this clever little man with big ideas for making money. Melaxa suggested to King Carol that the railways should be electrified, a proposal quickly accepted by the cabinet. The king sent Melaxa to Germany to buy a patent in order to carry out the project and when the patent was sold to the Rumanian State at an enormous profit, the king, Madame Lupescu and Melaxa shared in the rake-off.

Urdarianu was the fourth member of the palace quartet that formed one of the greatest swindling organisations of the century. A minor bank was declared bankrupt by the State. It was bought by the quartet – the names of the king and his mistress were never mentioned – at a very low price and they sold it after a few months at three hundred per cent profit to the National Bank of Rumania.

The quartet also bought a textile factory, which made uniforms worn by the only legal party in Rumania, the National Renaissance Front, to which every person holding any kind of job from a tobacconist to a Permanent Under-Secretary had to belong. If they did not join the Party they had to revert to their peasant holdings – the horror of all humble labourers, who always aspire to white-collardom. Impoverished officials in the country saved frantically to buy these vital uniforms. The design of the uniform was being changed constantly much to the distress of the humble workers, who had to save up again to buy the new mode. Perhaps King Carol, who went off to live in South America, owed his life to the fact that these workers never knew that he owned the textile factory which made the uniforms for his own national party and that whenever trade was slack the monarch changed the design.

No other firm could compete with the king in the textile or any other business as he alone could buy foreign currency at the official rate. For example, the official rate for the pound sterling was about 620 lei, but if a Rumanian wished to buy sterling he could do so only on the black market. The national bank would not consider selling him any – and to buy sterling on the black market in 1940 cost anything from 1,250 to 4,500 lei. So the king was the only man in Rumania who could and did buy lei at the official rate and with his pounds he imported raw materials free of duty, for which other people paid not only the duty but the higher price caused by purchasing goods outside the country with money bought at black bourse rates. The king, in fact, ran the black bourse, which was strictly illegal and very much against the interests of his country.

With King Carol exiled, Rumanian concern focused on the Germans, whose arrival was something of an anti-climax since they had been infiltrating into the country for many months. From the time of the German occupation until the severing of diplomatic relations in February 1941, everyone expected that there would be a complete breakdown of the Rumanian state and that Germany would declare a protectorate.

The German Minister Fabricius was recalled soon after the arrival of the troops to be replaced by Von Killinger, who was well known as the ruthless German Minister in Slovakia.

Fabricius, a tall good-looking man with a pleasant manner and little brain, had probably maintained his job because his wife was Goering's sister. He had two mistresses: Edith von Kohler, a beautiful smartly-dressed blonde who drove around in high-powered cars, and drank champagne freely, and Madame Butculescu of no particular significance. Edith, like her lover, was recalled to Berlin as I understood there was some difficulty about the large sums of money that passed through her hands and for which she could not account. When she was finally flung into prison she accused Fabricius of having siphoned off the cash but he maintained his innocence.

The real German behind the scenes was the sinister Neubacher, a cripple, who wheeled himself around in his own special invalid chair. His face made the Rumanian urchins, who pestered one so much for money, run away at the first glimpse of him. His deformity had so poisoned his mind that he liked nothing better than to see others suffer. His spare-time hobby was designing torture chambers for concentration camps. During the Spanish civil war, he paid several visits to Franco's side to see what effect could be obtained on political prisoners by revolving discs and triangles of varying colours; the prisoners were forced to watch until they went mad or made a confession.

Neubacher visited the prisons of Rumania when he first arrived but the bug-ridden dirty buildings were not enough for him. He devised methods of twisting arms and slowly pulling out toenails to obtain information, tortures that were practised on British officials arrested in the oilfields. Where his basic power came from in Germany is unknown but rumour had it that he was a personal friend of Hitler. He was the advance guard of the Gestapo, looking over the land and reporting on the organisation and numbers of men he was likely to need. The German army and diplomats were as afraid of this evil-looking man as if they had been Jewish refugees themselves. He seemed totally devoid of any human kindness; unlike so many murderers and torturers he had no soft feeling for dog or cat, no daughter or wife to love. He was never known to smile and rarely went out into society. He lived in a lonely villa on the side of the Carpathian mountains between the German headquarters at Sinaia and Predeal – and it was there that I saw him on brief occasions, from a distance. General Hansen, the German commander, paid a daily visit to the crippled Gestapo chief. General Antonescu went to see him at weekends.

The Germans admitted that Neubacher was the most powerful of them all in the Balkans. He arranged in October that the Gestapo should take over the buildings which had been used by King Carol's secret police, and I saw German lorries bring out filing cabinets and thousands of loose files.

When the Germans were planning the attack on Russia, it was Neubacher – and not the Minister or Field Marshal von List – who entertained General Antonescu and his nephew, Michael, to dinner to tell them that Rumanian soldiers would be needed in the German invasion of the Soviet Union. He told General Antonescu that he must find the troops: there were plenty already trained by the Germans who would make excellent shock troops for the re-taking of Bessarabia by Rumania. General Antonescu said he wanted Bessarabia back far less than Transylvania or the Dobrudja, but his Gestapo host promised that if Bessarabia were taken he would ensure that Transylvania would be restored to Rumania.

Before Neubacher arrived in Rumania he had been running a minor Gestapo within the Rumanian police force quite unknown to the king or any other statesman. Now like so many evil men he was in the open, in fear of his own life and generally went out with a bodyguard of about ten German soldiers. One became quite accustomed to Rumanian leaders being unaware of what the Germans were doing in their country. The Rumanian War Office, for instance, was rarely informed of the fresh arrival of German troops and the Rumanian chief-of-staff often had no idea how many German divisions were in the country. So they were quite unaware of the men Neubacher was recruiting to spy on them. They were well experienced, having worked in the camps of Polish refugees.

These refugees, most of whom were soldiers, marched into Rumania at the end of their three weeks of war and went straight into internment camps where they lived in vile conditions. The braver ones escaped, but the cowardly were influenced by Neubacher's men to return to Germany. Reliable refugee workers I knew informed me that they had often seen Neubacher in the camps.

The British Legation in Rumania always appeared to be full of

Poles until we broke off diplomatic relations in February 1940.

When Beck was interned in Rumania Gafencu was either too weak or too mean to take any risk to help the former Polish foreign minister to escape. But General Smigly-Rydz, Polish army commander, got away, crossing the frontier dressed as a woman. Beck was kept prisoner in an isolated villa on the banks of Lake Snagove, about thirty-five miles north of Bucharest. He had seven guards and, having once tried to escape, his daily exercise of rowing across the lake to a restaurant on the far side had been stopped. I once visited him there, entering the villa by the back door and made my way to his room striding past the guards with implied arrogance as though I were 'their' boss. Beck saw that I had a packet of cigarettes in my hand and he grabbed them without asking my pardon as a hungry man might snatch food.

Despite his height he did manage to elude his guards and drove off in a car with a German number plate. He had grown a moustache, obtained a British passport, bribed everyone in his path and was well on his way to the frontier on a fine Sunday afternoon when Neubacher's men stopped him and took him to Bucharest. There he was put into close confinement never to be seen again as far as I know. Beck's imprisonment was the greatest success that the Germans achieved in Rumania at that time, especially as their consul at Constanza had to sit and watch hundreds of Poles leaving the country and to know that it was from that port that Polish gold, which had been so dangerously smuggled out of Poland, passed into British hands.

Throughout this period of tension and uncertainty, the Iron Guard had been active at all levels of administration as I experienced myself. The relationship between General Antonescu and Horia Sima, the leader of the Iron Guard, was one of the most mysterious in modern Rumanian history. The general knew that he could not rule without their help and he feared that about one fifth of his army had become converts to the movement, the most dangerous section of which was led by the father of the murdered leader, Codreanu, who was believed to have been slowly strangled to death on King Carol's orders.

Codreanu's father was certainly mad, his particular form of insanity consisting of a pagan mysticism woven around his son's life and introduced into the policy and doctrine of the Party. There is little doubt that the old man thought he ought to have been chosen as leader. He was always willing to be interviewed by foreign correspondents although it was almost impossible to record anything he said since he never uttered a single, coherent sentence, went off at tangents and frequently rushed frantically about the room, screaming, 'My God, my son, leaders of my time, St Michael and the Angels!' It was suggested by those who claimed to understand him that he maintained that his son went one day to the chapel of St Michael on the archangel's feast day. Kneeling in front of the altar, he had a vision in which the Saint appeared before him, begging him to rise up and lead an Iron Guard party similar to the Nazi Party in Germany. That St Michael was ever so indiscreet I do not believe, but I do believe that the family – the son was never the same after his supposed encounter with the Saint – thought it was all true.

Indeed, throughout the period of their suppression, the Guard-ists met in a village in the foothills of the Carpathians where there was a chapel of St Michael. There at full moon, the inner circle cut themselves and exchanged blood from the wounds, after which they drank *tsuica* – the Rumanian vodka made from plums – and drew lots to decide who was to carry out the murder of their next victim. However, they mixed up God, Hitler and *tsuica* in such a curious manner that they were entirely unpractical and, apart from the assassination of Calinescu, they never did much damage. But they did form a strong minority within the Guardists, which Horia Sima found difficult to control.

On 15 September, the eve of St Cornelius's Day, the name-day of the martyred Codreanu and the day on which he was supposed to have experienced his vision of St Michael, some 40,000 Guardists staged a rally in Bucharest.

They reminded me very much of the fascist processions organ-ised by Oswald Mosley I used to watch unwillingly on Sunday afternoons while waiting for a bus on the King's Road in Chelsea. In Bucharest as in Chelsea the longer the procession, the pimplier the youths. I was not invited to attend the ceremony because the head of the Press Bureau had virtually declared me to be *persona non grata*, by saying 'We know she is very Left and we thought she might cause trouble.' Other British and American correspondents

68

were invited. But I was known to be strongly anti-Nazi as a result of my refugee work. At this time I was living on BBC news and was a strong supporter of Winston Churchill and his government.

I was soon to encounter the Guards personally. On 1 October 1940 three days after five British subjects had been arrested in the oil city of Ploesti, two policemen, a Guardist and a nasty-looking plain-clothes man arrived at my flat and said they were going to take me to the Prefecture of Police. I knew only too well what happened to British people who went there: they were tortured and frequently forced to confess sins they had never committed. I knew, too, that the only real objection the Rumanians could have against me – apart from being English – was that I had fairly consistently, sometimes subtly, sometimes quite openly, avoided their censorship for two months. It would not have been difficult for the Press Bureau to have produced a copy of my daily story for the *Daily Express*, which had passed the censor and had his stamp on it, along with a gramophone record of the actual story I had dictated over the telephone to Geneva, the two being in no way the same. Had they done this I suppose they would have been technically justified in expelling me; but as the censorship was entirely anti-British and pro-German one would have thought that they would wish to avoid making such a conspicuous gesture as to expel an Anglo-Saxon reporter. They refused to explain the reason for expelling me.

I was absolutely determined not to go with them to police headquarters. And I told them so. Speaking fast and furiously, I telephoned the British Legation. Robin Hankey was on the line, thank God. I explained my predicament – and he arrived at the flat within minutes and literally rescued me from a very dangerous situation.

The British Legation continued to give me every possible support and, in the end, my visa to stay was prolonged for seven days. For six weeks it was extended again and again: for being ill, for having a car accident, for having lost my passport, until I could think of no more excuses. Finally, the Rumanian government said that in no circumstances whatever would they allow me to stay any longer. So I wandered around, staying one night in one friend's flat, another night in an apartment I had decided to rent. This went on until the Greek war began and the *Daily Express* ordered me to the front. At this point, the Rumanian officials refused to give me an exit visa and kept me waiting for five days while the Legation pressed my claims.

There were, admittedly, several awkward moments. One evening I arrived about midnight at the entrance to the block of flats where I lived. Two Guardists grabbed my arms. 'Miss Hollingworth?' I jerked myself free, pushed them aside, jumped into my car and drove madly off in the direction of Giurgiu, and spent the night quite comfortably sleeping in my Ford on a by-road a few miles outside the city.

On another occasion, I had dinner with *The Times* correspondent, Archie Gibson, who took me out for a stroll afterwards. At the gate of his house, five men pounced on him and beat him up. They refused to let him fetch his passport and papers from his home and dragged him off. I was elbowed out of the mêlée but telephoned the British Legation as soon as I could. Gibson was released and soon afterwards was appointed assistant press attaché at the Legation

These incidents were symptomatic of the increasing state of anarchy in Rumania, which worsened after a devastating earthquake on 10 November that caused widespread damage and panic. I was on my way to the Greek war front at the time and I was disappointed to hear that those all-important oilfields had escaped the shocks that affected every building in Bucharest.

In the confusion that followed the earthquake, members of the various sections of the Iron Guard began to shoot at one another in the streets. There was an abortive attempt to kidnap Sima himself. The Jews became automatic victims of the prowling Guardists. They were frequently beaten up and their household goods stolen because the police were afraid to take action against the marauders. The Jews were sacked from their jobs and quickly the economy of the country began to crack.

The worst incident occurred on 27 November when a group of Guardists broke into a prison just outside Bucharest and murdered sixty political prisoners. The gang of murderers stole several cars and drove to the jail where they overpowered the warders. Then they started to kill the prisoners by slow and unpleasant methods. Two of the elder statesmen imprisoned there, M. Madgrearu and Professor Iorga, were well known outside Rumania and the death of the latter especially aroused much adverse comment in the world press.

General Antonescu was almost powerless in the deepening crisis and failed abysmally to track down those responsible for the prison massacre, although he did manage to prevent other assassinations, which he heard were being planned.

During these somewhat dangerous days, the most amusing place I lived in as I moved from flat to flat was one of King Carol's apartments which he had used as a love-nest, not for Madame Lupescu but for young girls who took his fancy. It was on the sixteenth floor of a skyscraper in the centre of town; the passage to the lift was dim and generally full of people. He had spared no expense in the furnishings. There was a cocktail bar and enormous plate-glass french windows opening on to a roof garden which had a small pool. There was inadequate kitchen accommodation as the flat was not meant for serious eating. The whole place was furnished like a yacht with liner-style rails at the edge of the garden. The lighting came from pseudo-searchlights, the beds were super-luxury bunks, the stairs were transplanted from a ship. The pictures were all poor ones of nude women in compromising attitudes. In the bathroom was a slimming exercise machine, which the servants told me the king used regularly.

When I finally obtained my exit visa, I drove to Giurgiu accompanied by Adam Watson, then a bright young third secretary in the Legation.

The harbour zone was forbidden to any traffic except that which was crossing on the Danube ferry to Bulgaria. We showed our passes to the German sentries and they let us continue. For a mile we drove through a German military camp where the soldiers were preparing their evening meal. I thought they were anti-aircraft troops for I certainly saw several AA guns, some covered and some being greased with their camouflage covers off. The Germans in the custom shed only made a fuss about my car leaving the country; everything else went quite smoothly and it was nearly dark when I drove on a zig-zag course over a few hundred yards between AA guns until I reached the boards over which one had to drive in the dark since there was a blackout. We felt a little embarrassed that German soldiers should guide us across to the ferry where Iron Guard police had arrested three Poles who thought they were safely outside Poland. I and other passengers protested but could do nothing.

Crossing the Danube from the dark hidden port of Giurgiu to the brilliantly lit town of Rustchuk in Bulgaria on the other side I little thought that within ten weeks, after a spell in Greece, I should return again to Rumania and cover the civil war there.

5 Diary from Rumania 'Revolution' . . . Evacuation to Istanbul . . .

During the Rumanian civil war I was the only British reporter in the country. This was fortunate but I was completely cut off; filing stories to the *Daily Express* was virtually impossible. All telephone lines were cut, there were no cable facilities, airports were closed and trains remained in their sidings. So I kept a detailed diary of those bloody days and once communications of a sort were reconnected I managed to telephone a story to London. It was splashed under a streamer headline: 'Revolution!' and ran:

'The civil war began with a round up of Jews by the Iron Guard, who had finally decided to topple General Antonescu. They picked up about 500 Jews from one of the poorer quarters. They did not choose them selectively – they seized the first men, women and children they saw. These people were taken to the slaughter-houses and killed in the manner in which Jewish religion demands that cattle should be slaughtered. Middle-aged women were hung up by chains, their throats were cut, and they were allowed to bleed to death while the jeering crowd imitated the prayers of the rabbi. After 50 people had been killed in this way the crowd got tired and shot the rest.

'On Monday, 20 January 1941 Antonescu's life was threatened three times by Guardists. A man dressed as a messenger from the Ministry of Foreign Affairs arrived with an important note, which he said he had to deliver to the general personally. As the

73

general came out of his bathroom, the man drew a revolver from his pocket. The general bolted into his bedroom, his wife shrieked and gave the alarm panicking the gunman, who fled.

'Twice during the evening, two plain-clothed Guardists tried to enter the general's home through the kitchen. They were both arrested and found to be carrying revolvers. Both said they were on a mission to save Rumania from Antonescu.

'These plots followed the dismissal of 10,000 Guardists, who controlled all the leading factories, mines, shops, docks and hotels. They earned 50,000 lei a month compared with a policeman's pay of 1,500 lei and a bank manager's salary of 30,000 lei a month. Antonescu decided to sack them all as part of a clean-up campaign and it was this move that brought the Guardists on to the streets.

'Antonescu, confident he would receive full German support, ordered his crack regiment to march up and down the main boulevards with machine guns. Field artillery was positioned in several alleyways near the palace and the headquarters of the Guardist movement.'

Then, as more and more German troops flooded into Rumania ostensibly to meet a rumoured Russian invasion, the long-expected civil war broke out. My diary recorded the events of those crucial days:

'Wednesday, 22 January. The Iron Guard is fighting General Antonescu and the civil war rages in Rumania. On Tuesday morning, General Antonescu again paraded a regiment of soldiers but they made no effort to take key buildings held by the Iron Guards. By the afternoon several isolated incidents, in which about seven people were killed, took place. Their dead bodies were exhibited in the yard in front of the Prefecture of Police in Bucharest. The population drank their coffee and crowded, out of curiosity, into the special streets where traffic was forbidden.

'But the Guardists were not idle; the crowds were given hurriedly printed leaflets accusing General Antonescu of being in the power of the British. The Bucharest radio was quiet except for a short and rather weak appeal by the general that order might be restored without loss of life. After his appeal marches of the Iron Guard were played. A curfew was called at 10 p.m.

'The police guarding the various legations decided life was too dangerous and went home. Odd rifle shots were to be heard throughout the night and it was impossible to drive from one end of the town to the other owing to the cordon of tanks around the barracks held by the Guardists in the residential part of the town and the Ministry of Foreign Affairs, also held by the Guardists. General Antonescu was confident of German support if necessary but rumour said that Horia Sima had already gone to Berlin to bid for the support of Hitler.

'During the night fights in Ploesti and Giurgiu resulted in those two important towns falling into the hands of the Guardists. The army, however, said they had taken over the Prefecture of Police in all important towns with the exception of Jassy and Bucharest.

'This morning, no newspapers, no trams, no buses; a few shops were opened but they kept their shutters down so they may close at a moment's notice. Taxis become few and far between as they run out of petrol, unable to buy further supplies. In the early afternoon, the Iron Guards, who had been parading the streets singing their songs without interruption, set fire to the synagogue and Rumanian officers watched without making any effort to prevent the outrage. At 4 o'clock, following minor efforts during the morning, a determined effort with heavy artillery was made to take the Guardist barracks. Noise of guns and smoke frightened a large part of the population, who retired to their homes.

'7.30 p.m. Noise of machine-guns, rifle fire and heavy artillery can be heard all over the town; crowds of enthusiastic Iron Guard supporters rush through the streets shouting, 'Up with Horia Sima'. The soldiers are now only managing to hold a few streets in the town. It is impossible to telephone to the Ministry of Foreign Affairs and few private telephones are working, although Rumanian officers hold the base of the telephone building; all the rooms filled with apparatus are held by Iron Guards. Only Iron Guard newspapers are on sale in the streets. Everyone feels that the general has lost, as the situation rapidly deteriorates and the noise of the shots increases. No one knows the number of dead or wounded but the total must now be well on five thousand. General Dragalina, in command of the Third Army at Brasov, has gone over to the Guardists and is bringing his men by means of forced marches to Bucharest. The 38th Infantry Regiment at

Braila is also marching on Bucharest, and the 4th Army Corps at Jassy have joined the Guardist cause.

'Petrol waggons used by the army to barricade streets in Bucharest have been set on fire by the Guardists. There is a general feeling that the Germans will not allow this state of affairs to last for many more hours, and as it seems unlikely that General Antonescu can re-establish order, the German military mission may take over by tonight. They may form another puppet Rumanian government or establish a protectorate; they themselves do not yet know.

'12.30 a.m. Thursday, 23 January. General Antonescu received General Hansen and arranged for German support. German troops were stationed during the night outside Bucharest ready to meet any army coming into the capital.

'I awoke from my couch in the drawing-room of the British Legation to the sound of heavy artillery. What remains of the British community in Rumania has concentrated into two or three houses. Until 10 o'clock shots could be heard in all directions and it was impossible to decide who was shooting at whom from where. At this hour General Antonescu spoke over the radio assuring the nation that he had the army with him but reminding people that they must defend their own homes against the thieves and odd hooligans who were still at large. 'Call in the army to help you,' he said. How people were to call in the army when wild, armed Guardists were on their doorstep, and no telephones were working, is difficult to say. At 10 o'clock also appeared a statement by Horia Sima, in which he ordered all Guardists to stop firing and resume their normal life. (This is now known to be bogus.) He said that the continuance of the civil war was against the interests of the Axis and the Guardists must surrender the buildings that they were holding immediately. Planes dropped pamphlets giving General Antonescu's speech, and planes dropped papers with Horia Sima's declaration. The German planes flying low zoomed ferociously around the town and for a time it seemed that the firing had stopped. General Antonescu issued a communiqué saying that they had control of the entire situation. Large lorries went into the scenes of action, coming out laden with the dead. I myself saw six enormous lorries packed high with corpses.

'Before lunch, however, it was apparent that the civil war

was not over; the Guardists had not given up the buildings they were holding and firing more furious broke out around the Prefecture and the Foreign Office. This was continued for five or six hours, heavy artillery being brought into play, and the normal life of the town, which had started during the morning, again ceases. At 5 p.m. about 50 German light tanks and 50 German armed motor-cycles and sidecars with attendant camions drove purposefully to the field of action. After two hours many of the streets where the fiercest fighting had taken place, had been cleared. And now at 7.45 p.m. there is still a little fighting for the German army to subdue around the Ministry of Foreign Affairs.

'General Antonescu says it is only the bad elements in the Iron Guard that are disaffected. He makes every excuse for the burning of Jewish shops and the many hundreds of deaths that have been caused. He has, rather pointedly, throughout the whole course of the civil war not wished to squash the Guardists entirely. The Germans will soon have stopped the fighting and now no one knows whether they will take control of the country or not.

'Friday, 24 January. Today is a public holiday in Bucharest, not, however, to celebrate the termination of the civil war, but one of many years' standing, still cynically celebrating Greater Rumania. Shops and factories are all closed. The population has had plenty of time to take stock of the situation and to see the many marks of blood on the dirty snow of the streets. Over 2,000 people are reported to have been killed in Bucharest and between 11,000 and 12,000 in the country as a whole.

'Many of these were innocent onlookers who were shot down by the army's machine-guns in an effort to oust the Guardists. Two sections of the town are still closed to traffic and Rumanian tanks are roaring around these areas cleaning up the last pockets of holders-out. This morning the leader of the Iron Guard student movement, who published the pamphlet specifically stating that the British Intelligence Service had organised the shooting of the German officer, Major Dietrich, was shot. Mystery surrounds Horia Sima; rumour says he may be shot too. In any case there seems little doubt that he was behind the whole plot.

'The German officers who took over the Prefecture of Police, which the Rumanian army had failed to take from the Guardists and the Ministry of Foreign Affairs are still standing by with tanks and twenty or thirty 4½-inch guns and ten 6-inch guns, but the town is quiet and the shooting has stopped. General Antonescu, having made himself head of the Iron Guard movement, now proposes to form a government within two days. There is no doubt that the government will be a military dictatorship and the only under-secretaries will be civilians. This government can last only if the Germans give massive support to General Antonescu. General Antonescu lacks the usual attributes of a dictator, and, although a good soldier and an honest man, he has by no means a strong personality. Under German direction he is calling up more recruits in an effort to occupy the younger and more unruly sections of the population.

'Walking around the streets of Bucharest looking at the many houses which have been destroyed or badly damaged by gunfire one sees that there is noticeably a stronger anti-British atmosphere than there was before the civil war. The Germans, on the other hand, are more popular; those Rumanians who resented their presence here now feel that a lengthy and uncomfortable war was stopped by German action . . .

'I had a narrow escape. A stray shot was fired from near my flat on a company of soldiers in the street. They immediately opened fire. Not a single window in my flat is whole; the walls are pockmarked three inches into the brick with machine-gun fire, mirrors broken, bookcases destroyed, curtains hanging in tatters; some shots even went through the wall. Luckily, the soldiers soon discovered that there were no Guardists inside the house and made no effort to enter. As yet no policemen have reappeared in the streets. They were the first to run away at the beginning of the disturbances, and order is still being maintained entirely by the army.

'Monday, 27 January. During Saturday and Sunday, General Antonescu has made many emotional appeals to the Rumanian people to be calm and to accept the new order which he is about to inaugurate. The public has, however, been shocked by the extent of the damage during the civil war. Visits to the Jewish quarter revealed the complete wrecking of houses and shops from which all the goods have been looted by Guardists. Many more people were cruelly shot than was at first supposed. Jews were strangled in public outside the burning synagogue, Jewish children were killed by Guardists while their houses were being looted, elderly bearded Jews were slain in the street, and I have seen their bodies lying naked in a yard after the Guardists had stolen their possessions.

'Others were packed into lorries and taken ten to fifteen kilometres out of the city on the way to Giurgiu where they were thrown out of the lorries and shot, about 100 metres from the roadside. A reliable witness describes this horrible scene in which about six hundred people were shot together and the Guardists going around afterwards shooting with revolvers those who moved. Perhaps 1,500 people were killed in this way, and are still lying unburied by the roadside.

'A strict curfew is imposed at 10 o'clock and all restaurants and places of entertainment are closed at 9 but the rioting is not yet over. On Monday morning between 3.30 and 4.10 a.m. Rumanian soldiers fired continuously with rifles from a garden below my window over one of the widest roads in the city. Where the fiercest fighting took place flags are now being unfurled and a stand put up on which lie the coffins of those soldiers who died fighting, covered with wreaths and wrapped with the Rumanian flag. Meanwhile, the public of Bucharest are being searched and are ordered to show their 'legitimation' papers (identity cards) every hundred yards. There is a serious house-to-house search for arms being made and no one can go in or out of the capital, nor may anyone travel as only military trains are now running. General Antonescu is ill, and the new German Minister, Von Killinger, who arrived a few days ago has not yet decided what Rumanian puppets shall be employed in the new government.

'News continues to percolate to the capital of what happened in the countryside. At Constanza the Iron Guard only surrendered at 1.30 p.m. on Friday to the German Consul and two German officers. They firmly refused to surrender to the Rumanian army before that time, even after three ultimatums had been issued.

'Throughout the civil war the British Consul, Mr Kendall, had a nasty time. Although no shots were fired, there were continuous hostile demonstrations outside the British Consulate, and a special pamphlet was produced by the Iron Guard against the British, mentioning Kendall by name. The Rumanian army have now disarmed most of the Iron Guard in Constanza but the leaders of the whole outrage are still walking about as free men and proud of themselves. Mystery still surrounds the fate of Horia Sima, who was arrested in his house and had in his possession 3,000,000 lei which had been pilfered from the Jewish shops in the city. Many arrests have taken place in Bucharest, but the Iron Guard are by no means smoked out. Tanks are still being used on houses containing nests of them. Four divisions of the German army remain outside Bucharest to quell any Rumanian troops or Iron Guards who might march on the city.

'Wednesday, 29 January. Some days ago General Jacobici, Minister for Defence, gave a dinner party and had as one of his guests General Hansen, head of the German military mission in Rumania. As the general was leaving he expressed the wish that he might return the invitation to Jacobici in Athens, where the British were supporting the Greek army, at Easter.

'A large quantity of arms has been found in the trams and taxis. I had a curious experience when my taxi was stopped and, to my horror, police found a rifle in the back luggage container, but although they examined me and the rest of the car very carefully, they did not arrest the taxi driver nor make any difficulties for me; in fact, the taxi driver and the police parted on the best of terms.

'Two Americans arriving here from Italy reported that they had seen German troops in Milan and Trieste but "nothing like as many in Bucharest". They believed the Germans there were technical experts. Many of the Germans now arriving in Bucharest have motored through from France and Belgium, and were dissatisfied that some of their colleagues already here were motoring back to Italy. This is a fair grouse as travelling is extremely difficult in Rumania. The recent snow has entirely blocked the road from Bucharest to Giurgiu and vast numbers of German soldiers are busy with spades trying to clear it. There is still a cordon around one of the streets at the back of the Foreign Office and the 4th Army Command is reported to be against the general and with the Guardist movement.

'Saturday 1 February. Horia Sima is hiding in the Italian Legation which is heavily guarded by Rumanian soldiers. Sima was first given sanctuary in the German Legation until Fabricius left; then he was transferred by a German army lorry. Everyone here asks why the Germans, who knew of Sima's plans to throw out Antonescu's government, gave their support to Antonescu only on the third day of the revolt, and why, after the revolt, they protected the leading Guardists and prevented Antonescu from taking serious measures to suppress them. An Iron Guardist ex-minister told me yesterday: "You cannot have a Nazi state without a Nazi Party. We are the Nazi Party and in the end the Germans will support us. Only because the wrong section of the Guardists was in power in some districts, allowing the industrial and economic life of the country to go to ruin, thereby endangering the success of Hitler's Balkan blitz, did the Germans come in on the side of the general."

'Every decent Rumanian feels that he ought to support the general, but many are disgusted by the flattering telegrams he exchanges with Hitler. Maniu has decided not to hinder the general in his efforts to keep order. He has made it clear in a manifesto, which, though unpublished, has been widely circulated, that he disapproves most strongly of the foreign policy of the government, especially of "marching hand in hand with the Axis".

'The Russian Ambassador stated yesterday that the communists took no part in the revolution.

'The revolution is not yet over. On Friday evening a Rumanian captain was stabbed at the Gare du Nord by a young woman Guardist. This evening a colonel and two junior officers were shot, again by women Guardists. As I write a searchlight flashes up and down the road in front of my window, looking for Guardists who are holding out on some nearby roofs. There are cordons still around large sections of the town and diplomats of the great powers have been carefully examined to make sure that they carried no arms when they entered the Foreign Office this morning. I was searched for arms five times within half a mile this evening, and there are three soldiers with loaded rifles every fifty yards in all the main streets.'

This concluded the entries in my diary dealing with the fighting in the civil war but the crisis, of course, was not yet over. The Germans were in no hurry to remove the military equipment in and around Bucharest as it provided an ever-present warning to extreme Guardists of what would happen if another revolution broke out.

The state funerals of those who had been killed went off quietly enough. Trials began of those who had organised the civil war or assisted in it in a big way. Rumanians and foreigners were equally surprised by the light sentences imposed on Guardist ringleaders even while the corpses of their victims were still being removed from the cellars of houses and shops in the main streets. The curfew was rigidly imposed although on several occasions, not wishing to spend the evening from 9 p.m. onwards in my flat, I dined at the Athenee Palace with colleagues, who were staying there, and then walked home by myself, a matter of over two miles. The snowy streets were absolutely empty save for the guards walking up and down. Surprisingly enough, they never asked me for my pass. My policy was to walk down the centre of the road in order to avoid being shot at by an over-zealous sentry should I suddenly emerge from a shadow. I heard afterwards that all the soldiers had orders to shoot at sight anyone they saw walking in the square in front of the Ministry of Foreign Affairs. I heard this only after I had crossed it at least half a dozen times. In this square there were four or five searchlights which every night were used after the curfew to help the sentries pick out people walking about the streets, or judging by the way they were used, climbing around the rooftops.

There was a clear increase in the number of German soldiers; there were reputed to be altogether eighteen divisions in the country and it was evident that as soon as the roads thawed Bulgaria was going to be overrun. The social life of the English in Bucharest at that time became rather limited as few Rumanians were brave enough to be seen with them.

I suddenly began to get to know more English people. There were parties in restaurants for Legation staff, which were great fun, but they had to stop because the restaurants were filled almost entirely by Germans who, after food and drink, were liable to cause incidents. However, this problem was overcome by the Legation Counsellor, M Le Rougetel, who gave two parties in his roomy flat. He imported a Russian band from a nightclub and the musicians were glad of some work since their establishment had been closed. The parties had to go on until 5 a.m. because until then no one could go home. It was a curious huddle of English people drinking, dancing, singing Russian songs and being very light-hearted while outside there was a tense atmosphere of anti-British antagonism.

The last of these parties took place two days before Britain broke off diplomatic relations with Rumania. Everyone there knew that it was really a farewell gathering but no word or expression betrayed the situation. I remember driving home through snow-covered streets and being stopped at a crossroads by troops. Three machine-guns were aimed at my car while officials looked at the papers of my diplomatic companions. We were allowed to drive on but the hatred shown on the faces of those soldiers for the British was very plain indeed.

Due to their own stupidity and the clever German propaganda, the Rumanians believed that the British intended to bomb their oil fields any minute although it was obvious that such a strike would not take place while a British diplomatic mission remained in Bucharest. However, an attack on the oil installations at that moment would certainly have caught the Germans by surprise and caused the maximum of damage. But the fate of the British in Rumania in such an event hardly bears contemplation.

It would have meant certain imprisonment and probable death for all of them. Critical as I am of officials, I can find no fault with the conduct of British affairs during those last anxious weeks. They all behaved with kindness, courage, resolution and efficiency.

At this time Rumania had become the auction-room for the sale of large quantities of loot from France. Early in February, notices appeared in the streets of Constanza announcing auction sales of valuable goods. At the appointed time, two large German army lorries appeared, packed high with stolen property. Then the sale began in the square where the statue of Ovid stands forlornly miserable, recalling his exile there in the days of Augustus. Mr Kendall saw gold coffee spoons, silver coffee pots, silver teapots, made by famous French firms and embellished with the arms of noble French families, being sold with German soldiers looking on anxiously to see what prices their loot would fetch. But the Rumanians were poor and so the Germans were disappointed. Linen sheets embroidered with the crests of dukes and ex-prime ministers were selling for 300 lei, which at the existing black market rate of exchange was the equivalent of not more than two shillings sterling.

Never until these last weeks in Rumania had it been possible to buy in Bucharest French perfume bottled in France. Previously it had always been sent in bulk and bottled in Rumania. But now the shops were full of French-bottled Guerlain, Lanvin 'Pretexte' and Patou 'Cocktail Dry' and French talcum powder from the more exclusive houses. One ironic sidelight of this strange situation was that Berlin had cut the pay of German troops in Rumania knowing they could well make up the difference by selling French loot.

By this time, Rumania was a country that had lost its soul. Partition, foreign occupation, earthquake, rebellion, civil war had entirely broken the national morale. All her leaders, honest or otherwise, could only wring their hands and bemoan the evils of the age.

One of the ways in which this was manifested was in the treatment of the Polish troops who still remained. Many had escaped from Constanza and other parts of the country, but those who were still in Rumania at the beginning of 1941 were simply sent back to occupied Poland in the course of the first five weeks of the year. Subsequently, all Polish women were returned to their homeland. There is, I believe, no precedent in history for sending interned soldiers back to enemy territory. The Rumanians made the excuse that they needed the food and accommodation for the steadily increasing number of Germans in the country. British and American protests were of no avail. The Rumanians endeavoured to make many of the Poles sign certificates saying that they wished to return to German-occupied territory. I never heard that any soldier had actually signed such documents.

In those last weeks in Rumania, although there were stringent regulations against carrying firearms and the police were continually searching civilians for them, it was not safe to go about without a revolver because armed bands of hooligans were always liable to attack solitary individuals if there were no German soldiers in sight. It was forbidden for more than three people to walk together, which simply aggravated the evil it was designed to cure. I carried a revolver lent to me by a friend in the embassy and slept with it under my pillow.

After I left Rumania when the Legation was evacuated to Turkey, it took me three weeks to grow accustomed to living without a gun. I was fortunate in that I never had mine taken from me.

Decent Rumanians were sick and tired of the disorders, but they saw no way other than a complete and proper German occupation to prevent their children from being beaten up in the streets. The Germans kept the fear of Russia so cleverly to the fore that everyone with a decent suit of clothing feared communism. They felt relieved, too, that their country would not be the battleground of a new Balkan blitz; it would merely be the Axis from which the blitz was to be organised. The tears and emotion so much in evidence before the British left were largely stimulated by the fear of future air raids, a fear that was cleverly played up by the Germans in the Rumanian press and over the radio.

Many Rumanians were genuinely sorry that their country had, as they thought, backed the wrong horse when they heard over the BBC of the British successes in North Africa. Secret societies sprang up all over the country to listen to the British radio broadcasts but the Rumanians were too dispirited to criticise the Germans in public, which was in any case quite understandable. Equally, the more sinister secret societies of the Iron Guard flourished despite the many communiqués breathing fire and slaughter against them issued by General Antonescu. Such was the prevailing Lewis Carroll atmosphere that the general was trying to win back support from the Guardists by avoiding the imposition of the severe punishments, which he and his government were almost daily proclaiming against them.

I was in a position to know. After Britain broke off diplomatic relations with Rumania, I was asked to help with the transport and evacuation of the Legation staff and those Britons who had stayed on until the last minute hoping that His Majesty would pay for their journey to some nearby sanctuary. Never have I had a piece of work which I enjoyed more. The Legation staff were all working under great pressure and strain but they were all unfailingly helpful. My lack of knowledge of internal Legation red tape must have been most tedious for them all. Only once was I charmingly and gently reminded by the First Secretary that the ministers of Allied governments really must not be treated as though they were German Jewish refugees. At the last moment, the Belgian Legation staff, a few Dutch and masses of semi-diplomatic Poles, who had been left behind by their Legation, all wanted to come with us. Of course, they all expected sleepers on our special train and first class cabins in the ship.

The Belgians were the worst. They produced two babies unexpectedly at the last moment. Few of the staff had time for
personal packing and no time for last-minute purchases. The
Americans were splendid. They took over British interests but
they also did any odd job to help our diplomats. And what a
tremendous send-off they organised! Our special train was due to
leave at 10.30 p.m. and as the curfew operated from 10 p.m. any
Rumanian who came to say his farewell not only risked imprisonment in the future for being pro-British but immediate arrest.
The station was so heavily guarded with German and Rumanian
troops that only people who shouted at them in English could
approach the train.

At the last moment I had to put five children in one sleeper
– that was all that was available – because an English woman,
married to an Italian, arrived at the consulate late in the afternoon
demanding to be evacuated. All her eight children had British passports, having been born in Soho over the small café they ran there.
We had to take them. The Consul insisted on this as the two eldest
boys were of military age. And like many other British subjects
in Rumania this large family could not speak English with any
fluency.

Princess Elizabeth Bibesco stands out in my mind as the tragic
heroine of this stage. Although her friends were leaving her in a
land of enemies, she gave everyone a charming parting gift. She
stood in the dark station, her white face no longer animated with
smart repartee, but mask-like and shrunken with misery.

I had arranged for a dining-car to be attached to the train
and, having checked everyone on I made straight for it. As we
sped across German-occupied territory, a gramophone played
the latest dance tunes, providing a rather bizarre element to our
dramatic situation. At midnight I went to bed and thanked God
that I was not a diplomat. Poor devils – they had done nothing but
say goodbye in different ways to men they knew to be scoundrels
and liars.

When we woke up, we were in Constanza station. I dressed
and rushed out to give the list of passengers to the consul. There
was no question of leaving the station. Thirty-five German lorries
and about six tanks were lined up in a siding. We could see
the Turkish ship in which we were to sail, the *Izmir*. Then we
heard that there had been a diplomatic hitch in London over the

departure of Rumanian diplomats there for Bucharest. It was all highly melodramatic.

We enjoyed our breakfast, we were wonderfully light-hearted, but I must say we wondered whether we might return to Bucharest that evening looking rather foolish. With some difficulty, our Minister was allowed to leave the station to go to the consulate where a pile of telegrams were waiting to be deciphered. We waited. German troops looked over the railings at us as though we were already interned.

At last the order came that we could embark. We left Constanza, leaving behind one Englishman who had been arrested by the Germans during the course of embarkation. As the ship moved from the quayside, the barriers to the docks were raised and hundreds of German soldiers rushed to the waterfront. Most watched silently as our ship slid away. A small group shouted, 'See you in London.' In the midst of the crowd of grey-green uniforms, one small man in black stood waving a large white handkerchief – the American diplomat who came to see us off. We waved until the ship turned out of the harbour.

The diplomats were satisifed with their cabins, but all the other passengers – especially the Belgians – complained about the accommodation for a single night. The Minister provided champagne for dinner, which stopped all the moaning. We landed in Istanbul the following evening. It was one of the happiest journeys I remember and I wished it could have lasted longer.

While we were being evacuated, the Germans were pushing ahead with their invasion of Bulgaria, an operation master-minded in the casino at the mountain resort of Sinaia, once the favourite holiday town of Queen Marie. The German General Staff in Rumania covered the gilded and red plush roulette tables with maps and telephones as they planned the next phase of the Nazi conquest of the Balkans.

The German invasion of Bulgaria in force took place at the beginning of March but this represented only the culmination of a long period of infiltration on a scale that was quite unrealised by the public in Britain at that time. By early February the penetration had been a matter of common knowledge at the British Legation for some days but during the civil war it was impossible to leave

Bucharest or telephone to frontier towns to confirm the latest German ploy. On 5 February, however, eye-witnesses testified that about one thousand German troops a day were crossing into Bulgaria by train. They took with them vast quantities of military equipment.

The technique had changed since the days when Hitler's soldiers marched into Vienna and Prague. In the Balkans, the 'tourists' arrived first and displayed their zeal for holiday-making near points of strategic importance. After that came the technical and economic experts, then troops in civilian clothes and, lastly, uniformed soldiers. Exactly the same method was used in Bulgaria as had been exploited in Rumania. By this time there were eighteen German divisions in Rumania and the equivalent of three in plain clothes in Bulgaria. As the Danube was still frozen, many Germans crossed by the land frontier of the Dobrudja from Constanza. The German aim was to conquer the Balkans by bluff rather than by blitz. That had always been Hitler's way: demoralise and then – if necessary – fight. The plan was clear enough. While the camouflaged invaders continued to enter the country, the Germans would delay their main invasion until the ice melted and pontoon bridges could be placed across the Danube.

It was naturally extraordinarily difficult to confirm news of the German troop movements. They had blocked all the roads on both sides of the Rumanian/Bulgarian frontier for a considerable distance and allowed only peasants who lived in the forbidden area to pass through. However, telephone lines eventually opened up and I was able to get a call through and spoke to three peasants who had seen lorries crossing the frontier. All this time, large quantities of anti-aircraft equipment were being shifted across the border to guard the new aerodromes being built in Bulgaria and the stores of food and fuel which had been stock-piled there since the previous September. Much of this military equipment was French and it was possible to see the old French signs beneath the newly painted German labels. I recall seeing at this time a bus-load of German soldiers passing along the main street of Bucharest in a vehicle which carried a board indicating that Brussels was its normal destination. Similarly, all the equipment used for the Danube pontoons was of French workmanship, much of it having been built by them for their own use in crossing the Seine after the bridges had been destroyed by German bombers.

Simultaneously, the German units at Constanza were practising embarkation and disembarkation. These units had arrived from Le Havre. Opinion at that time was divided between those who took this as evidence that the Germans had temporarily given up the idea of trying to invade Britain and those who thought that these units had been brought to Rumania for the express purpose of making us think that they had given up the idea of invasion. Few British diplomats believed that the secret war in the Danube delta was a prelude to an attack upon Russia. But Robin Hankey did – and he was absolutely right.

6 From Athens to the Front Line . . .

During the ten weeks between my departure from Rumania and my return to cover the civil war, I watched the developing disintegration of the Balkans from Athens, Sofia, Istanbul and Belgrade. The tide of the general fascist advance across the Balkan peninsula swept on with the German infiltration of Rumania and economic penetration and encirclement of Yugoslavia. The Italians had taken over Albania shortly after the war began. The German advance was blocked initially by Greece but eventually triumphed there, too, just as it had overwhelmed every small country that had stood in its way. The Greek campaign was an epic and fought out amid the mountains in terrible, sub-zero conditions in Albania. Although no effort by Britain could have materially affected the outcome, I firmly believe that British policy before 1939 could have helped to unite Greece in presenting a more democratic front against the enemy. The failure to do so certainly contributed to the weakening of the Greek resistance to the final German invasion in April, 1941.

I arrived at the Greek frontier at 5.30 a.m. on a dark, cold November morning on my way to cover the war. I walked across the border carrying just a rucksack and typewriter and found myself in the God-forsaken border town of Pythion. It took fifty-six hours to reach Salonika via Alexandroupolis in a filthy train that crawled along, stopping at every station to pick up conscripts and without any possibility of obtaining food on the way. In Salonika I found an hotel and then set out to assess the war situation. The Mediterranean Palace Hotel had been largely destroyed and there were a few bomb craters in the streets. Then an air-raid siren sounded and actually hurt my ear-drums.

Hysterical screams, cries and a stampede of what seemed to be the entire population carried me into an underground shelter. Here, sitting on benches or standing with bowed heads as the roof was very low, the Greeks waited for an hour and a half while three Italian bombers flew overhead doing no damage whatever. Women crossed themselves, men wept. I felt as though I were in a submarine and that any moment the oxygen would give out. I staggered over the sweaty and exhausted bodies to the door to try to get out. But it was locked from the outside. When the 'all clear' went off I rushed into the bank above but no sooner was I free than the warning sounded again. This time I took great care not to be caught in a crowd. But I went outside into the open air to find every restaurant and shop was closed.

I wrote a brief story of the scene in Salonika and went along to the censor, who refused to pass a word except a line saying where I was. I begged, stormed and tried every trick I knew but he would not yield. I tracked down his assistant and by bribing him I got a telephone call through to my contact in Belgrade and asked him to inform the *Daily Express* that I was still alive. He did not have the wit, however, to understand that it was the pernicious censorship that prevented me from filing stories.

Trying to obtain permits for the front became impossible so I caught a train to Athens and endured another slow, uncomfortable and dreary journey broken only by arguments with officials demanding permits to travel from one station to another. I refused to get off and when I finally arrived in the capital at 4 a.m. I was interrogated by the police, who finally agreed that I could stay. Surprisingly, I found a taxi and was driven to the King George Hotel, the Grande Bretagne having become the headquarters of the British military mission and the Greek general staff.

It is interesting to note that as in the First World War, when the French made the British pay rent for the trenches they occupied, so the British were made to pay full hotel rates for the rooms the mission occupied in the Grande Bretagne in Athens.

Even with a war on, Athens was delightful. It was warm and sunny; the oranges were still ripening on the trees opposite my hotel although it was mid-November. I breakfasted on the terrace. Most of the foreign correspondents were staying at the King George Hotel and they were all fighting for permits to go to the front. Days of total frustration followed as we battled with censorship and officials, who failed to understand that with their army beating back the Italians front-line coverage would mean front-page news in the democratic west. The *Daily Express* ordered me to leave Athens since there was little news available but I decided to make one final effort.

Thanks to the support of the British military mission two or three small parties were given permission to leave Athens for the border. It was, however, badly organised and I found myself in a car with Henry Stokes of Reuters and his Athens stringer, Mr Drossos, who was reporting all our movements to the Greek secret police.

We had a gruelling journey spending the first night in Lamia and then travelling through the mountains to Larisa where we reported to the base camp general, from whom we were to receive our papers for proceeding to Kozani. He briefed me on the war situation and said I could go anywhere on the front, but advised that the Koritza sector in the north would produce the best stories because the Italians were still putting up some resistance there. First stop was Kozani, a small town with nothing to recommend it apart from Mount Olympus nearby. My bed was damp and although bugs do not generally worry me much there were too many to kill or to allow me to sleep peacefully.

I made an early start but was annoyed to see Henry Stokes dressed as though he were out for a walk in Hyde Park in early spring. I made no pretence of an elaborate toilet – I was too eager to get on and see the fighting. We joined a convoy of army lorries heading north and drove along a narrow road into the mountains. In Kastoria I met the first troops who had been to the front. They were a fine crowd. They gave me Albanian money, changed Albanian for English cigarettes – the best of the bargain! – provided a vivid description of the rapidly retreating Italians and the hundreds who surrendered – 'faster than we could take them' as one soldier said.

The road to Koritza was appalling, cutting through a mountain pass where barbed-wire entanglements trailed up the slopes which were topped by pill-boxes. The mud was deep and twice our car had to be pulled free by bullocks. Here and there were the white skeletons of a horse or donkey which had been shot by the troops, probably because they became lame. Every particle of meat had been stripped from the bones, leaving the entrails to stink beside them.

With the Union Jack flying from the mudguard of the car, I arrived in Koritza, the first British subject to step on to Axis territory. British bombing had been extremely accurate and the airport was badly damaged. In the town itself, there were plenty of air-raid shelters, sandbags and the usual impedimenta of war but not one house could I find which had been damaged by a British bomb. The town was as packed with people as the King's Road on a Saturday night. All the shops were open and doing a roaring trade with Greek soldiers. At the military headquarters, a colonel – no generals had reached Koritza – fell on our necks when we offered him Greek cigarettes. In return, he gave me a huge Italian flag, as many fascist caps and badges as we wanted, Albanian cigarettes and – most important of all – a permit for me to visit the front as often as I wished. Immediately I went in search of Wellington boots.

I like towns where the cobbler makes his own boots and the baker his own bread, but especially I liked it in Koritza because one member of the family who owned each of the principal shops had at some time visited that mecca of the Balkans – America. 'You English girl! I Albanian boy! I live Chicago – bootblack five years. What do you want?'

I explained that I needed a pair of Wellington boots or riding boots. They showed me some truly magnificent riding boots which had been made for the wife of an Italian general who had left too hurriedly to collect them. Albanian money was changed greatly to the disadvantage of the Greeks at the pre-war rate of exchange (7 drachmas = 1 lek). This made everything absurdly expensive. A night in the hotel in Koritza cost as much as the best hotel in Athens and the price of my badly needed boots was completely Bond Street. They cost about £20.

Koritza, compared with other Albanian towns I visited, was a very bourgeois place. I saw typewriters for sale in one shop window and the latest shade of Elizabeth Arden lipstick. The prices were exorbitant. In a bookshop I lost my head and bought an enormous map of Albania which cost £3 and which I had to give up with a patriotic smile when I returned to Athens as the British military mission recognised it as the latest Italian map of Albania. I deeply regretted this as I have a passion for maps and always do my best work in a room lined with them.

There were many pleasant villas with gardens of their own, generally occupied by former Chicago bootblacks, who having made a fortune of a few thousand dollars, had returned to live in retirement in the place of their birth.

Early next morning, a party of foreign correspondents, including Richard Dimbleby of the BBC, set out for the front. I was wearing all the woolly sweaters and scarves I could find.

As it grew lighter, we saw naked corpses at the roadside, many of whom had been shot in the back while endeavouring to escape from their deep trenches as the Greeks advanced. Corpses on battlefields are always naked as the conquering army, whatever its nationality, relieves them not only of watch and rings but of warm coats, vests and trousers. The photographers got busy on the corpses. I merely looked at them, saw they were young Italians and felt rather pacifist-minded.

There were surprisingly few signs of battle so we drove on to the base of the Morava mountains where there was still some action. The troops obviously thought I was pretty odd when I emerged from the car wearing a long sheepskin coat and padded with scarves and woollies plus my boots. They were all most friendly without being in the least forward or unpleasant. They embarrassed me by offering me bits of dirty food. But the only time my life was in any danger was when I produced a packet of cigarettes in front of about fifty men. They had not seen any for days. I could only throw them into the air and leave them to fight for them.

Several were from Salonika and had been educated by French nuns so although they looked like a crowd of rough brigands they spoke French. I asked them how long they had been in the mountains.

One giant about six foot six with no teeth and villainous tattoo marks over his neck and hands replied in delicate Parisian drawing-room French. 'I was up there for six days.'

'Did you do much fighting?'

'No, we could never find the Wops to fight them. It was very difficult up there. We were generally above the cloud line.

They fire wildly, killing but few Greek soldiers. But we couldn't be sure how many were hidden behind the boulders.'

'Wasn't there any real scrap at all?'

'Oh, yes, on a plateau; they are fighting there still. But my bright officer wouldn't let me stay. Thought I was too delicate to stand the mountain air much longer.'

He proceeded to demonstrate his strength by knocking down a few of the smaller soldiers who were standing around him, listening to him speaking a foreign language. I withdrew before any more of the Greek army should be knocked out and inspected the camp myself. There was no sleeping accommodation for the men, or stabling for the horses or donkeys. They all lay about on the wet ground in what had been the orchard of a pleasant largish mountain farmstead. The farmhouse, which had been fitted up with extremely inadequate field telephones, was occupied by four staff officers. They were in a tremendous muddle trying to move some units to an advanced position without having any means of issuing orders except by pigeons, which work only over special terrain, or runners, which over the muddy mountain passes were a contradiction in terms.

Had it not been for the blessed supplies of macaroni, which the Italians had left behind, I was told, the Greeks would have been unable to continue fighting. Their supplies, which had to come through the narrow pass, in which I had travelled, were not arriving. The first convoy of ambulances either became bogged down or simply ran out of petrol, which was in short supply. So there was no hope for the wounded. They just died.

The Greek commanding officer ridiculed the fighting ability of the Italian soldiers and asked me if I would like to see some prisoners. He introduced me to ten Italians who were held in the stables where they were eating macaroni and grinning from ear to ear. I asked if anyone could speak English.

'Rather!' said one. 'I'm a Cockney, I am. My father had a little restaurant in Soho but when I was five we moved back to Trieste as mother didn't like the English climate. But I still remember my English.'

'Why are you fighting now?' I asked.

'No choice for the likes of me,' he said. 'We were just given our orders and had to obey them. I hate these bleeding hills and I was to go back to Trieste but it's better to be a prisoner than scrambling about rocks all day. I wasn't born to be a mountain goat.'

'What do you think about Mussolini?'

'I used to think him a silly old bastard, trying to make us all prompt, hardworking and unnatural-like. But since he sent me to this bleeding place, I know he's the devil incarnate. Why, the man needs seventy people to take him to the water-closet. Otherwise somebody would put a bullet through his back.'

'Aren't you rather disloyal speaking of your own country like this?'

'Perhaps I am disloyal but me and my pals didn't want to fight and now we are taken prisoner we are not going to pretend we love the old bastard.'

'What do you think of the king?'

'Oh, he's all right,' the young man said, contemptuously.

'What sort of government would you like in Italy?'

'I don't care about governments,' he said. 'All I want is to live with my wife and children, keep a little restaurant and sit and look at the ships coming into Trieste harbour.'

'How do your mates feel?'

'Oh, less than I do. They aren't educated like me. They can't speak any English.'

'What were they before they joined up?'

'Dock labourers. They're all beef and no brains. That's why they were sent to haul guns about these slopes.'

'What are you going to do with yourselves now you are prisoners?'

'Oh, we've got a pack of cards and I expect we shall soon enough be given some work to do. I don't care where they send me so long as they send me away from these wet hills.'

With this I departed, suggesting that he might try to educate his fellow-prisoners by teaching them some English.

A single file of slowly-moving donkeys, mules and men were arriving from the mountains. They were all exhausted. One donkey or mule carried the equipment for three soldiers, who were far tougher than the animals. They had not shaved or washed for about ten days. They looked tough and, despite the low temperature, they rushed to the water supply. Unlike Englishmen under similar conditions they failed to consider the animals at all and, only after they had eaten, slept and drunk did they think of watering the donkeys. What really amounted to grim cruelty was the way no donkey was ever relieved of its burden. The saddles, night and day, were never removed. Such treatment threw an unfavourable light on the Greek character but I admit that the Turks behaved equally badly to their animals and probably any Balkan people at war would not have been much better.

I began to walk to the front for no car could proceed far in eight-inch deep mud. It was heavy going. Open boxes of Mills bombs were scattered beside the track along with empty tins of Italian food which had been taken by the Greeks from corpses of prisoners and eaten on the spot. Walking through a deep ravine edged with a stream of blood-stained water, I saw an Italian wooden hut built to house five or six officers. Everything had been removed from inside except the dog which piteously awaited his master's return.

I took him up the mountains with me, feeding him on biscuits and had no difficulty in finding a Greek soldier to adopt him. The troops coming down were armed with pre-1914 rifles and not one of them had any ammunition left.

At last I arrived on the battlefield. The Italians must have had some heavy artillery, but they were shooting wildly with their rifles as they retreated and many of them were giving themselves up. I had been at the front in Poland and seen the German attack crush Silesia. But this was no front of blazing guns, of well-uniformed marching men. In the Polish campaign and the worst part of the retreat I saw more formal order among the Poles than among the Greeks, who were under enemy fire. The Greeks were certainly brave, but mountain warfare was in their view not suited to modern methods and the people involved reverted almost automatically to the tactics of a century ago. This was a doll's house battlefield compared with Poland. When one could see through the mist there were the Greeks at their best, rounding up pockets of Italians still at large on the rugged heights above us.

Several times as I walked, unaccountable bits of slate slipped down on to my path indicating that there up above me there were probably Italians getting desperate for food and clothing.

The Greeks were very quick to rush to the dead when the mist cleared exposing any new corpses to relieve them of their uniforms. I am superstitious about this and I have never taken

97

anything from a dead body, but my morals on the matter are unsound as I gladly accepted a beautiful green cloak from a dead Italian officer which was offered to me by a Greek.

Tramping about in mud amid the clouds and unable to see what was going on seemed to be quite unprofitable so I decided to descend. And there at the military headquarters was a majestic car and Arthur Merton, who was known as 'General Sir Arthur'. He was surrounded with picnic bric-a-brac. There were camp beds, buckets and everything one would need at the front line.

'I decided not to get my boots dirty,' he said. 'You must be cold. What will you have to drink? Tea or coffee or perhaps a little drop of brandy?'

I chose coffee.

'Now what kind of sandwich? Chicken, *foie gras* or sardine?'

I chose sardine and was given a large block of milk chocolate to round off my meal. I always think of 'General Sir Arthur' whenever I see an elaborate picnic basket. As one of the senior officers in the British mechanised division which took Benghazi said to me: 'Any bloody fool can be uncomfortable in a war. But it takes a clever and experienced man to be well provided.' 'General Sir Arthur' was just as well provided and just as munificent at the time of the evacuation from Greece a few months later. Christopher Buckley of the *Daily Telegraph* left Greece with Merton who was travelling with ten days' supply of food. He deposited a large part of it with the Legation for clerks and cipherers who were being hastily evacuated and with the remainder he was able to feed a considerable number of the ship's passengers on the voyage to Alexandria.

We all returned to Koritza at dusk just as Italian bombers were trying unsuccessfully to hit the new Greek headquarters. I visited the Café Munich, the local brothel, now deserted, which had housed fifty Italian women. It was divided into two sections: one for officers, one for other ranks. In the latter department, the men bought tickets from a woman behind a glass window as at a cinema. The equivalent of 2s 6d (about 12½p) enabled them to enjoy the company of an Italian girl for twenty minutes. On the officers' side, the price was more than double but it appeared that the time was unlimited.

I walked through the passages and looked into many of the deserted rooms. They were cleaner than I had expected, devoid of the pink lighting effects so noticeable in the brothels in Rumania. The women must have left in great haste. There were underclothes lying about, which no woman would willingly have left behind, and I saw two fur coats.

I looked at the gramophone records which seemed to be an essential part of the furniture in each room: I cannot think why. I was amused to notice among records of Italian grand opera there were those in English of 'Tea For Two', 'Sing To Me, Gypsy' and 'The Maid Of The Mountains'. An atmosphere of male sweat and lipstick stains made me feel hot and uncomfortable. The bathroom surprised me. It was large and airy, tiled and with every kind of modern American douching gadget and with two large white couches, perfectly clean. I could only assume that this was prepared for the defeated Italian commander-in-chief to forget his sorrows in the company of the lady of his choice. In the 'other ranks' part of the state-run brothel, the partitions between each couch were only about five feet high and as the couches were not provided with sheets I felt that this section was not as free from the propagation of venereal disease as it should have been. Suddenly, I felt the need for air and rushed into the street.

The local people to whom I talked were full of stories about drunken Italian soldiers, their orgies, their raping, their rapid departure at the approach of Greek soldiery. I discussed politics with the local chemist, who was so proud of his American passport that he carried it openly in his waistcoat pocket. I asked him if the people wanted King Zog to return. 'Perhaps 10 per cent, most of them those to whom he gave jobs, but the great mass disliked him.'

'But, surely,' I said, 'you don't want Wilhelm of Wied who is still painstakingly learning Albanian somewhere in Germany? I met his son quite recently staying with Alphonso Merry del Val, Spanish Chargé d'Affaires in Bucharest. He's a poor specimen.'

'No, we don't want that lot. In fact, these Albanians don't know how they want to be governed. Now we Americans . . . ' He then gave me a lecture on the American Constitution, which he had had to learn to take his Citizenship Examination.

Townsfolk who had fled from Koritza were returning with their few belongings when we left for the journey back to Athens.

99

Near Larisa there was an air-raid and the familiar sound of whistling bombs frightened Drossos, the Reuters stringer in Athens. He wanted to take cover and waste hours of our precious time hiding from a few Italian bombers which were unable to bomb accurately however low they flew. I resisted because it was very important to me to get my story off before the other correspondents who were in the car following us. It was impossible for us to file stories to Athens from such a remote area but Drossos put his copy over merely by producing his pass from the Security Minister. This infuriated me when I learned the head of the British military mission, General Gambier-Parry had been unable to get an important call through to a general in Larisa. Drossos was met by ingratiating officialdom wherever he went except the front line where army officers told him: 'We are the bosses up here and you damned secret policemen had better watch your step.'

Back in Athens, General Haywood, who was to take General Gambier-Parry's place as head of the mission, had just arrived from England. Both generals were anxious to know what I had seen at the front so over dinner I briefed them on the situation.

More than half of the Greek electorate were sincere Anglophiles so they were naturally confused by the British attachment to the dictatorship of General John Metaxas. How could Britain condone his Nazi-style rule with all the trappings of secret police, banishment of political opponents and beating up men and women on the elastic charge of 'communism' when the British people were engaged in a life-and-death struggle against Hitler? A fair question, no doubt, but answered by the expedient necessity of having friends and naval bases in the Eastern Mediterranean where defence of the Suez Canal was imperative.

General Metaxas assumed power on 4 August 1936, little more than a fortnight after the outbreak of the fascist rebellion in Spain, and proclaimed a dictatorship on the grounds of having to meet the danger of a communist revolution.

I met him on several occasions during my visits to Greece. He started with the great disadvantage for a dictator of being physically most unprepossessing. Metaxas looked like a tubby little elderly professor. He was obviously efficient and an admirer of efficiency. But equally obviously, the concept of liberty as an absolute political value never entered his head. Like so many political tyrants, he was in private life exceptionally courteous. He possessed charming manners. And, although he was probably one of the most distinguished generals in Europe, he never wore uniform. This was not, I believe, due to any desire to play down the military nature of his rule but because his squat, stubby figure looked frankly ridiculous in 'regimentals'. He was one of those men who seem to have been born in a bowler hat and short black coat. His régime, in fact, was a tyranny in the strictest sense of the word. Criticism was stifled. Leaders of constitutional parties were banished to islands where, if they suffered no actual ill-treatment, their living conditions were designed to cause them unhappiness and neglect, which were the cause of death for some of the more elderly politicians. Special Committees of Safety were formed throughout the country to try political prisoners against whom no charges could be laid by the ordinary processes of law. These resembled to some extent the Star Chamber in England during the seventeenth century. Some quite humble people were severely beaten up and, in some authenticated cases, tortured. Metaxas did not strike me as deliberately cruel so much as ruthless, and totally insensitive in the means which he adopted to secure his ends. In strict political terms he was supported by only 10 per cent of the population: the rest detested him.

He manipulated the press so that daily the newspapers published laudatory articles about him. His taste for the sycophantic led him to inspire features comparing him to Pericles or to the great Byzantine emperors. It was not unusual to see him acclaimed as 'John Metaxas, Founder of the Third Greek Civilisation'. Such adulation evoked ridicule from the populace. Equally inept were his attempts to interfere with the cultural tradition of Greece. He refused to allow public performances of Antigone unless the 'unauthoritarian' passages were cut and he banned Pericles' Funeral Oration from use in schools claiming that this speech, the high spot perhaps of the whole of Thucydides, was politically subversive because it praised democracy.

Metaxas also established a youth movement and insisted that membership was compulsory for all schoolchildren. They did little more than stage endless parades although there was a good deal of fascist ruffianism in the higher ranks. Everyone saw the organisation, which was known as the Neolais, as a budding Praetorian guard. Metaxas also created a secret police force, which for brutality and efficiency probably surpassed any similar organisation anywhere in the Balkans. They were Gestapo-modelled and Gestapo-trained and they came under the control of the Minister of Public Security, the sinister Constantine Manyadakis. His name was synonymous with the brutality of the Metaxas régime. I felt that he must have deliberately cultivated an unshaven, gangsterish appearance to enhance his reputation as the Himmler of Greece. Sitting in his office beneath a picture of the Nazi Gestapo chief, Manyadakis would toy with a revolver while giving an interview, a rather disconcerting habit. Such interviews were rare and always took place with two secret agents present throughout the proceedings.

It was odd that Manyadakis, whose instincts were sympathetic to the totalitarian system, should have been among those ministers who leaned towards Britain.

This was certainly not due to any ideological affinity but to the shrewd calculation that Britain would eventually win the war. He expressed a grim Goering-like humour, which was manifested in remarks that the Greek régime was not a dictatorship but 'a controlled democracy'. He once told an American journalist, who praised the courage of Greek troops on the Albanian front: 'After the war, it will be my business to arrest the heroes.' His one relaxation was to hold a late-night court in the lounge of the King George Hotel where he sat and listened to the gossip of the day. The composition of the circle never varied. There was a certain Greek journalist whose conversation Manyadakis found amusing and refreshing, whom he expected to be in nightly attendance as a sort of court jester. On one occasion, this unfortunate creature, during a period of exceptional pressure at his daily newspaper, absented himself for two successive nights from the gathering. Manyadakis's reaction was swift and characteristic. On the third evening, a police agent arrived at the newspaper office with orders to arrest the defaulter. The journalist spent two nights in gaol and was never again known to absent himself from the 'court'.

Metaxas and Manyadakis were the only men of note in the government of ageing hangers-on. They were soon to be enveloped in Nazi power play. Maybe Hitler was too sure of the support he expected from Metaxas. His German training, his sympathies with the Kaiser in the First World War and the nature of his rule should have made him an ideal puppet for Berlin. It was significant that while the British guarantee to Greece in April 1939, was played down and Greek Government spokesmen were instructed to call attention to its unilateral nature to foreign correspondents, every prominence was given to the worthless Italian 'scrap of paper' guarantee in June, 1940. Since the beginning of the war, Metaxas had repudiated positive Germanophile sentiments.

'I am not pro-German, I am not pro-English, I am pro-Greek,' he said. Then, with an excess of candour, 'I am not pro-German, but it is a question of finding a market for our tobacco crop.' Like other Balkan countries, Greek economic dependence on Germany had increased throughout the 1930s with exports to the Nazis rising from about 20 per cent in 1929 to about 33 per cent ten years later and imports over the same periods increasing from 10 per cent to 23 per cent. Manufactured goods such as typewriters and sewing machines, with which Germany repaid Greek produce were often valued at as high a rate as 25 per cent above that asked by other countries. Germany had outbid the US for Greek goods and she now turned the clearing system to her advantage.

Nevertheless, Germany was taking no risks. Despite being a spiritual Nazi, Metaxas was a patriot and Berlin wanted a pliable tool. It hoped to find this in Kodzias, Minister-Governor in Athens, an open admirer of Goebbels and Goering. The plot evolved mysteriously in the fortnight after the anniversary celebrations. With the moral support of Germany, it was intended that Kodzias should declare himself prime minister and then effect a coup backed by four pro-German ministers and university professors. Then on 15 August 1940, an Italian submarine torpedoed a Greek warship, *Helle*. The Axis Powers gambled on a powerful, anti-government reaction from the Greek people over this outrage but it did not happen. In fact, the opposite occurred and Greek allegiance to their government in the face of foreign aggression produced a slap in the face for Hitler and Mussolini.

Metaxas stood up to the Italian threats. He told Mussolini that Greece would fight against any invader. A bold decision since Greece was not ready for a war with her forces unmobilised, inadequate and scandalously ill-equipped. The general took a strong line with the timorous plotters in his cabinet and told them flatly that any attempt to launch a coup would be crushed and the leaders exiled to the island of Daphne where the best-known lunatic asylum in Greece was established. Kodzias faded from the political scene in the following weeks: no doubt he was lucky to escape with his life.

The torpedoing of the *Helle* was not the only provocation Greece had to endure from Italy, which had become an open champion of a Greater Albania after seizing that country in 1939 by naked aggression without any shadow of extenuating circumstances. In October, an Italian plane dropped three bombs on Greek territory, an incident hushed up by Athens which was desperately trying to avoid any action seen as a 'provocation' by Rome. Even so Metaxas strengthened his meagre troops along the Albanian frontier, hoping with the approach of winter Mussolini would delay any attack until the following spring at least. But Mussolini, encouraged by advice that the Greeks would never oppose his army, lobbed his ultimatum into Athens at the burglar's hour of 3 a.m. on 28 October. It demanded acceptance within three hours.

The ultimatum followed a dinner at the Italian Legation at which several Greek ministers were present. As they left each guest received a pamphlet containing an appeal: 'Greeks! Do not be misled and allow yourselves to become the tools of British Imperialism. The Italian nation wishes you nothing but well, and the Italian army is at hand to free you from your oppressors. Resistance is unnecessary and will be unavailing. Place yourselves under the protection of the great Italian State.'

Metaxas rejected the ultimatum immediately and explained why in these words. 'I had no alternative. The Axis asked me to co-operate. I was told that I must surrender the Tchamouria region of Northern Epirus to Italy and allow Bulgaria an outlet to the Aegean Sea. This was in addition to economic co-operation. Had I made these concessions I should have divided Greece into three parts – one part ruled by the Axis, a second remaining to us, and Crete which would certainly have been seized by the British. I had no alternative.'

Even during the three-hour time limit set by the ultimatum, Italian troops were moving forward in the frontier districts. Probably Mussolini hoped that the Greeks would put up some semblance of resistance since his prestige needed victories to set against the sweep of Napoleonic triumphs of Nazi Germany. It was hard for fascist Italy to have to include Guadalajara among her battle honours.

Far from seeing his troops march into Athens on 4 November as he planned, Mussolini suffered the humiliation of realising they were a spent force only ten days after he ordered the attack. It was the first defeat for the Axis Powers in the war and it finally pricked the myth of Italian military prowess, which was doomed to founder in the sands of North Africa and become a stock music-hall joke in wartime Britain. The Greek army stemmed the initial Italian thrust and, as early as 31 October, they were on Albanian soil after successfully counter-attacking. The Italian forces in the centre fell back in disorder from the Pindus mountains and triggered off a general retreat. By 18 November the last of their troops had left Greece.

I did not remain long in Athens mainly because of the lack of co-operation by the authorities with foreign correspondents. So I left for Istanbul on my way back to cover the civil war in Rumania. My companion on this journey was Lord Glenconner, head of the United Kingdom Commercial Corporation in Turkey, who had been in Athens to explore the possibilities of setting up an office in Greece. Christopher Glenconner still had the air of a playboy. He was tall, handsome and amusing. No one would guess that he was an astute businessman and a serious student of economics. The journey was uneventful until we reached Larisa where we had to transfer to an unheated wooden truck. Glenconner remained in good spirits throughout a night and a day, jumping out of the train at stations to fill our bottles with water, buying oranges and, on one occasion, even tiny bits of meat grilled on a skewer over a charcoal fire. They were delicious. Glenconner's secretary was not accustomed to roughing it. He was miserable, but sensibly drank a large quantity of wine and went to sleep on one side of the carriage while Glenconner and I swapped stories. This was difficult owing to the jolting of the train, the frequent stops and the fights I had with lice-covered soldiers trying to force their way into our carriage where we already had three Greek officers.

We arrived in Salonika at 4 a.m. and I took the party to the Hotel Luxe where the Glenconner charm produced a breakfast of boiled eggs, toast, butter and marmalade and coffee. At 7 a.m.

we were both occupying an old-fashioned telephone booth trying
to contact the British Consulate to obtain a car and drive to the
Turkish frontier, which would have saved at least a day on the
trains. The British Consul refused to co-operate. So Glenconner
hired a taxi – with a gold sovereign!

I bought some sweets to eat on the way, knowing how partial
his lordship was to chocolate. We drove past lakes to Stavros
and on beside the sea and crossed the Struma river feeling very
pleased with ourselves. Then . . . trouble. The engine boiled. We
stopped and had to search the mountainside for water, eventually
finding a dirty pool. We filled our hats with it but lost most in
returning to the car. After several attempts, we started the engine
and set off again. Very quickly the car broke down once more.
We knew that a consular official would be returning along this
road from Kavalla with a girlfriend so we decided to wait for them.

They duly appeared but were not the least bit helpful. They did
not want to turn around and drive us to Kavalla. At this point I
lost my temper and, supported by Glenconner, we forced them
to take us to Kavalla where without waiting for food or drink
we hired another taxi. We reached Seres, centre of the tobacco
industry and very much pro-German. We were ordering a meal
in the local taverna and imploring the proprietor to let us cook
it ourselves when word spread that three English people were
in town. Two Americans working for Chesterfield cigarettes
swooped down on us and took us out to their compound.
I think this was one of the most moving experiences of my life.

I have never had the sense of being so genuinely welcomed
even by my closest friends as I had from those two Americans.
One was young from New England and the other elderly from
Chicago. Both were longing to hear the sound of the English
language again. We were given innumerable 'Old Fashioneds' –
rye whisky, sugar, orange bitters and mixed fruit. I have a good
head for drink but certainly we all had a very good time. They
were anxious that we should stay the night and both Glenconner
and his secretary wanted to do so. I was also in favour of staying
but there was no time to be lost, so I pulled two very reluctant
men out into sub-zero temperatures at 2 a.m. to catch a train.
In fact, we had to board several on the next stage of the
journey, sometimes sitting in compartments with snow blowing
in through broken windows. I refused to stop for breakfast in

Alexandroupolis and when we finally reached the frontier we were very hungry indeed. We crossed into Turkey and I made my way back into Rumania.

I later returned to Greece and on my way I stopped in Istanbul. I was staying at the Pera Palace Hotel when a bomb exploded destroying the access to my room. The bomb was assumed to have been placed in the luggage of a junior British diplomat when he left Sofia after Britain broke off diplomatic relations with Bulgaria. At that point I decided to move into a flat.

7 'The Collapse of the Balkans' ... By Caique from Southern Turkey to Alexandria ...

'The collapse of Greece, Bulgaria and Yugoslavia followed the same pattern as Hitler's earlier conquests: economic pressure, infiltration, intimidation and, finally, the take-over either by bloodless occupation or force of arms. Political appeasement plus acute anxiety to avoid provocation provided Nazi Germany with easy stepping-stones to establish her forces in southern Europe. These schoolboy bully tactics paid off and proved again at international level as well as in the playground that once an aggressor finds a victim unwilling or unable to defend himself he will be encouraged to seek more prey.

'So it was in the Balkans in 1940–41. I had seen enough during my weeks in Greece to deduce what was likely to happen in the spring particularly if the German infiltration into Bulgaria continued. At the beginning of January, about eight hundred German troops a day were smuggled into Bulgaria across the easy flat route beside the Black Sea, on which Russia had her eye. Half a division of German troops was stationed near Constanza so not much notice was taken when hundreds of soldiers arrived nightly. I had stood at that station and watched them get off the train, walk off into the town and return in mufti to continue their journey into Bulgaria. At the frontier, convoys of lorries were waiting to transport the new arrivals by night to camps and aerodromes in the interior.

'As early as the summer of 1940, I paid a brief visit to Bulgaria, crossing the Danube from Giurgiu to Rustchuk. The

Danube even then looked like an inland German river. There was an enormous amount of traffic and each barge flew the swastika. The Germans had managed to obtain control of the port of Giurgiu by means of a Rumanian decree, which forbade people to enter the riverside dockyards. Men who had worked there for thirty years were suddenly banned. Giurgiu was famous only for the pipeline from the oil district of Ploesti. On the Bulgarian bank of the river German influence was just as strong.

'Even in June the three extremely bug-ridden hotels of Rustchuk were crammed with Germans and I had difficulty in obtaining a room. All the shops were full of German products. There were rumours, some undoubtedly true, of German mechanics and technical experts, probably soldiers, being landed from barges in a backwater up the river from Rustchuk. The cost of living in Bulgaria, as in Rumania and Yugoslavia, was rising fast and the paraphernalia of visas and certificates governing how much money one could bring in and take out of the country was increasing. As I wanted to stay only one night in this miserable town I had considerable difficulty in persuading the authorities that I was not a spy, as there was no British consul present. The local people hated the Germans and had watched them build a huge school, a road leading out of the town, and improve the docks. The average Bulgarian had far more affinity with the Russians, whom they regarded as their great Slav brothers, who had helped them in the past. But like everyone else in this corner of Europe they were so impressed with German efficiency and the overwhelming Nazi successes that they thought there was nothing else to do but follow the German line.

'Indeed, Bulgaria had been falling into the Axis camp since the rise of Hitler. After the First World War there was strong anti-German feeling in Bulgaria, which having backed the wrong horse in two previous wars did not wish to repeat the experience for a third time. King Boris had too much German blood to be able to think objectively about Germany and had married an Italian princess. Bulgaria found the Rome end of the Axis more respectable but she was the natural supplier of wheat, maize and tobacco for Austria and Germany. There were no other industries worth mentioning and it seemed a pity that the country was not content to remain an agricultural producer: the Bulgarians were probably the best farmers and gardeners in Europe and managed

all the large estates of Balkan royalty and nobility no matter how
much the different races hated each other.

'There was, for instance, an unofficial agreement between
Hungary and Bulgaria under which the Hungarians imported
about fifty market gardeners a year in return for fifty Hungarian
cabaret artists, who performed in Bulgarian theatres and night
clubs. At a time when currency restrictions became fashionable,
the members of both professions were preparing to depart for their
home country as it was impossible for them to send money home
to their parents or wives and children. So it was arranged that the
money earned by the Hungarian dancing girls in Bulgaria could
be used by the wives of the Bulgarian gardeners in Hungary while
the parents of the dancing girls in Budapest would be supported
by the wages of the Bulgarian gardeners.

'The Bulgarians always maintained that they were thrown
deeper into the Axis net than was necessary owing to the bad
commercial treatment presented by Britain. Dominion preference
and heavy import taxes in Britain hit Bulgarian trade extremely
hard. The Bulgarian Minister of Commerce, Professor Zagoroff,
worked hard to improve trade relations but he was a disillusioned
man when I saw him in Sofia in 1940. Educated at the London
School of Economics, Zagoroff was a genuine Anglophile. He
introduced me to other members of the Bulgarian cabinet who
were as pro-German as he was pro-English. "It is hopeless," he
told me. "I know I am fighting a losing battle and I can get no real
help from the English, who regard Bulgaria as very unimportant
whereas the Germans seem to think we are the most important
country in the world."

'King Boris, too, was a realist. He understood that the Germans
could easily over-run his country so he decided to remain a king
with Hitler's blessing rather than lose Bulgaria and become an
exile. That was the situation: an exercise in political and personal expediency. King Boris handed his country to Hitler on
a plate. He was among a number of Balkan monarchs who had
been backed by Britain and failed to support her in moments of
crisis. Only King George of Greece stood by the British and he
was, alas, unpopular in his own country.

'On 1 March 1941, Germany formally occupied Bulgaria
and within a month Yugoslavia signed "a treaty of adherence"
to the Axis Powers, which came as no surprise since it was the

culmination of a long period of close collaboration between the Regent, Prince Paul, and two successive prime ministers, Stoyadinovic and Cvetkovic. 25 March 1941, was Yugoslavia's own Munich representing a combination of timorousness and treachery. Yet within forty-eight hours there was a rebellion by the people. They took two days to force Prince Paul to resign and abolish the Regency.

'Yugoslavia like other Balkan nations had been infiltrated both economically and physically by Nazi Germany. For a year about thirty thousand husky Teutonic "tourists" had been arriving in the country supposedly to augment the 120,000 Germans in a camp near Belgrade who had arrived there from Russian-occupied Bessarabia. And at the highest level there was an ominous question mark over the role Prince Paul had played in the downfall of his country. He was certainly playing a double game. He was very much under the influence of the pro-German White Russians. He and Princess Olga, sister of the Duchess of Kent, visited Germany many times and during the winter of 1940–41 he was in close touch with Berlin. Hitler's secret agents always stayed at the palace in Belgrade.

'The Yugoslav government ignored the obvious threat and made no move to help Greece when she was attacked by the Italians from Albania. When the Belgrade coup, led by the air force, was staged, Prince Paul resigned and the young King Peter assumed personal power supported by wavering generals. For a few days Yugoslavia indulged in an orgy of defiance. The tramwaymen of Belgrade burned Hitler in effigy in front of the German Travel Bureau, centre of the Nazi propaganda drive. A distinguished Serbian general marched about the streets wrapped in a Union Jack. A car owned by the German press attaché was destroyed and he was publicly "de-bagged" in the street.

'But this spate of anti-German sentiment was far from welcomed by the new government of General Simovic, who was already negotiating a kind of pact with Berlin. He wanted to hold off Germany while seeking help from Turkey and, above all, Russia. Britain sent General Sir John Dill, a member of Churchill's kitchen cabinet, to Belgrade, to propose a close military alliance but it was turned down by the Yugoslav General Staff, which was still anxious to avoid "unduly provocative action".

'The German attack early on Sunday, 6 April, was swift

and devastating. Belgrade was bombed. So were other major cities including Zagreb. But the main thrust came from Serbia in the south where five hundred parachutists took Skopje within two days. There was some strong resistance in the north-west but by the next weekend Belgrade had fallen and it was all over for Yugoslavia by the following Thursday. The Germans were left to face a long guerrilla war with two partisan groups: the Chetnicks led by General Mihailovic, who operated in Serbia, and the National Liberation Front of Marshal Tito, who recruited his force in Bosnia, Croatia, Montenegro and Slovenia. When it was discovered that Mihailovic had co-operated with the Germans, the Serbian partisans joined Tito whose subsequent force of 800,000 men held down forty German and Italian divisions until the end of the war.

'The picture of Balkan defeatism was much the same in Greece. Anthony Eden, the British foreign secretary, and General Wavell, British Commander-in-Chief in the Middle East, had arrived in Athens only one month before the latest German expedition, to try to save some element of stability from a crumbling situation. The influence of King George was seen to stiffen the Greek general staff with the realisation that having gone so far with Britain, which was sending three or four divisions to Greece it was too late morally and technically to withdraw from the threats of war. Yet throughout this period there seemed always something a little amateurish, not to say naïvely ostentatious about the British moves. Eden's decorous journeying from Cairo to Ankara, and from Ankara to Athens, had somehow the smack of the old diplomacy. It was picturesque, it impressed, and yet it seemed remote from reality. It belonged to the age of Castlereagh and Talleyrand rather than to that of Ribbentrop and Molotov. Those communiqués stating that all was well, that complete unanimity of views existed between whatever governments Eden happened to be talking to – had we not heard them all before? One was reminded of that wet and gusty weekend between Bad Godesberg and Munich.

'After Eden's talks in Athens, Greece suddenly became totally and perhaps unexpectedly committed when George Vlachos, editor of the pro-British *Kathimerini*, published "An Open Letter to Herr Hitler". Obviously tipped off by the Athens government, he declared that if Greece were attacked by Germany she would fight and there was no question of sending away the British troops, who had recently arrived. Greece, which had given the world an example of how to live, would now give an example of how to die.

'The release of this letter in a muzzled press was a clear sign that Greece accepted the inevitable. The Germans had almost ostentatiously not participated in the attempted Italian invasion of Greece through Albania. And the war with Germany opened in the most ominous manner.

'At 3 a.m. on 6 April as Nazi troops launched their onslaught in Yugoslavia, an immense explosion followed at intervals of half an hour by two others shook every house in Piraeus. Eleven miles away in Athens doors were blown in and windows broken. A 12,000-ton ship heavily laden with TNT had been blown up by a delayed action bomb destroying seventeen vessels nearby. The work of unloading the ship had been suspended for the whole of Sunday which was inexcusable since an air-raid was expected that night. Additionally, the ship should have been towed out of port as a normal precaution in wartime, which was anyway just around the corner.

'The great explosion shook the nerve of the people in Athens and gave a foretaste of the thunderbolt quality of the German offensive, which had coincidentally been launched in Thrace and Macedonia. Athens, in fact, was not bombed in the ensuing conflict although the port of Piraeus was raided nightly.

'In the holding action in Macedonia, the Greek forces displayed extreme gallantry, repulsing German attacks with dive bombers, parachutists, heavy artillery and tanks. The Greek troops there were certainly not contaminated by defeatism, which was still rife in the High Command. A Greek junior officer, wounded in the fighting, produced a phrase which achieved considerable publicity in Athens.

' "These Germans", he said, "are all right as fighters in their tanks but once you get them out of their machines they are nothing but chauffeurs."

'Nothing but chauffeurs! It raised morale in Athens but this relative optimism was not shared by the Greek cabinet and still less by the general staff or the army commanders. The backbone in high quarters was rotten.

'The Nazi Fifth Column, believed in certain official British circles to be non-existent because it did not pursue the precise methods employed in Norway or in Holland, was very active during the early days of fighting. Rumours, good and bad, predominated and produced a menacing yo-yo quality to morale. Optimism was brushed aside by uncertainty and bewilderment. But because this was an entirely new Nazi tactic, certain British circles held pugnaciously to their line that there was "no such thing as a Fifth Column in Greece". One important Legation official petulantly refused to see patriotic Greeks who called with information about Fifth Column activities and yet in less than a week he was overwhelming the British Embassy's overworked First Secretary with the most inadequately authenticated rumours concerning the impending formation of a pro-German cabinet.

'Even the Greek Ministry of Information failed to kill rumours of approaching disaster and false reports that the British line had broken on the Olympus front and that the Australians had been cut to pieces on the Larisa plain.

'Certainly, German intelligence had pin-pointed our air bases and eliminated them in the early days of the battle on that plain. Again, air superiority was the key element in the German success and, as the US Air Attaché remarked at the time: "The British have sent a boy to fight a man."

'With the retreat falling back on all sides, the cabinet was on the verge of breaking up. The king and his prime minister, Korizis, were in favour of fighting on, but Korizis was a sick man unable to decide whether or not to order the evacuation of troops to Crete, which in itself might upset British plans for withdrawal from the mainland.

'The minister of shipping, Ziphos, was acting as the link between the British Legation and Korizis and he was charged with finding out exactly what the prime minister's plans were. Korizis procrastinated more and more as the young minister pressed him for a decision. "I must have your reply," he insisted. "It is essential that there should be no further uncertainty or delay in this matter."

'Korizis finally roused himself. He rose and walked slowly towards an inner room. At the door he paused and turned. "In one minute, Mr Ziphos," he said, "you will have your answer." The door closed behind him. A moment or two later, Ziphos heard the sound of a revolver shot. Korizis was the second prime minister to commit suicide as the result of the German drive through the Balkans. Count Teleki of Hungary was the first.

'The king immediately took over the premiership himself, a step advocated by the British after the death of Metaxas, and appointed Kodzias, Minister-Governor of Athens, as his deputy, an administrator well known for his pro-German sympathies. A strange appointment, which lasted for only one day. This large, talkative man was nobody's choice except the monarch's and, through the advice of Thomas Bowman, the British vice-consul in Athens, who was practically running the country, the king was told that Kodzias was not acceptable.

'A compromise was found in Tsouderos, former governor of the Bank of Athens, a Cretan, who failed to rise to the occasion by cleaning out the old-guard administration. The entire fabric of government was falling apart and things were not much better at the British Legation where a senior member of the staff had decided that the evacuation of British women and children at an early stage would upset the morale of the Greeks. As a result, ships bringing British troops from Egypt returned empty. I still fail to understand why the evacuation of British civilians in such a manner would have injured Greek feelings. Certainly there could not have been a more pathetic sight than the siege of the Legation by swarms of Britons on Thursday 17 April. The Legation, once the home of Sophocles Venizelos, the leading left-wing politician in Greece, was one of the most conspicuous buildings in the capital with its coating of sickly pink paint. What happened was sheer meat and drink to the enemy propagandist.

'Careful arrangements had been made the previous summer to evacuate the entire British colony had the Italian invasion proved successful but the ship chartered for this operation was handed over to the Greek government for use as a hospital ship. Now the British enclave had no idea whether they would be evacuated at all, or if so, by what means. The British subjects raging around the Legation forecourt were not an impressive sight. Had evacuation plans been ready, unquestionably the British residents would have been patient and co-operative as the British people, whatever their other faults, normally are in a crisis.

'It was greatly to the credit of the British director of publicity that he alone among other members of the Legation tried to explain to the minister the dilemma in which Britons found themselves. It was not, he said, as though the demonstrators were demanding "a couple of battleships escorted by half the Mediterranean fleet". They merely wanted to know how the Legation intended to ensure their safety. In the end, the Britons were evacuated over five days as the British and Greek forces were being routed by the Germans but the plight of the Cypriots and Maltese in Athens became a scandal. When the Germans marched into Athens hundreds of these members of the British Empire were grouped outside the British consulate still hoping for a miracle escape from Greece. The British civil servants had, of course, departed days earlier.

'The final stages of the campaign were a foregone conclusion. The last of the British troops had withdrawn to the Thermopylai line by 21 April, the day when the Greek army chief, General Tsolakoglou, capitulated on behalf of all Greek troops on the Albanian front. This left the British army to fight a rearguard action while their soldiers were evacuated, an operation that was more formidable than Dunkirk although fewer men were involved.

'The distance to Crete is far greater than the width of the English Channel and the Germans had secured positions in Greek islands and mined the Saronic Gulf outside Athens. And the Germans had mastery of the air.

'Within this daunting framework, the British forces combined to achieve a remarkable success in rescuing the hard-pressed soldiers making for the embarkation beaches in the south. The Royal Navy deployed six cruisers and nineteen destroyers, which co-ordinated their operations with eleven transport and assault ships along with many smaller craft. It was a night evacuation which began on 24 April and lasted for six days.

'During the first two nights some 17,000 British soldiers were brought out with the loss of two transports and the next night navy warships went into five embarkation points and saved another 19,500 troops. But there was disaster at Nauplia where another transport ship stayed too long with 700 British soldiers aboard. German dive bombers sank her and two destroyers, *Wryneck* and *Diamond*, moved in and rescued most of the soldiers only to be attacked and sunk shortly afterwards. Only fifty survivors were picked up. On the beaches of Kalamata 8,000 troops and nearly 1,400 Yugoslav refugees awaited rescue by two cruisers and six destroyers on the final night of the evacuation but only about 450 men were taken off after fierce fighting. However, more than 4,000 other soldiers were saved at Monemvasia by navy warships. The final tally of British troops rescued from Greece was more than 34,000 out of a force of 53,000. They left behind about 1,400 officers and men, many of whom thanks to Greek bravery and cunning were able to make their way in groups to Egypt that summer.

'This rearguard action was followed by the battle of Crete, a grim epilogue to the disastrous history of the twelve months during which Germany had eaten up the Balkans. The loss of Crete was the blackest moment since the fall of France. We had, after all, been in Crete six months, plenty of time for preparations against a German attack. But the British commanders were changed far too frequently, so perhaps they did not have enough time to set up their defences. Maybe the island was not regarded as being particularly important. Churchill had declared in the House of Commons only a week or so previously that we had every intention of holding Crete and Tobruk and yet we were not ready. The British high command knew the attack was imminent and we were still not ready. At least the government did not try to sell the press and public a story of yet another brilliant retreat and successful evacuation.

'No one would have accepted that. Again, air power was the winning factor in the German invasion of Crete. Our air forces in the Middle East were numerically totally inadequate. The dangers of the German drive to the Balkans were pointed out by Churchill in a brilliant speech in the Commons just after the Nazi occupation of Austria. So, owing to the loss of our bastions in central Europe and thanks to the "peace in our time" mentality of a prime minister and his advisers we found ourselves in a position in which we needed an air force not equal to but double the size of the combined Axis forces.'

These opinions were penned with Christopher Buckley, the most respected war correspondent of World War Two, in my book *There's A German Just Behind Me*, which was published in 1943.

I am still convinced that the original decision to hold Crete was justified, that we came near to success and that the battle was among those in which decisive success only just eluded us. With more warplanes and more guns it could have been a different story.

The one encouraging feature in this depressing episode appeared to be that the parachute bogey was largely exploded. High-ranking officers agreed that while potentially formidable in a sparsely inhabited country, paratroops would have had little opportunity in a country such as England. Even though they dropped on Crete from a much lower altitude than in Poland or Flanders they still took twenty seconds to reach the ground, a perfect target for crack infantrymen. 'We fire at their feet and we can be almost certain of getting them,' one New Zealand soldier told me. Moreover, during the period of a minute or two after landing the parachutist is still an extremely vulnerable figure.

When the Germans were about to take over Greece I was in Turkey where anti-British sentiment was strong. Many Turks felt a deep sympathy with the Germans if not actually with Hitler. This was apparent even in shops, and in government offices German correspondents were accorded facilities denied to Anglo-Saxons. I remember going to the telegraph office one day with my 'collect card' to send a press telegram to the *Daily Express* when the man behind the counter said 'We no longer extend "collect" facilities to British correspondents. You must pay cash.' 'Why?' I asked. 'Because,' he said, 'the Germans are going to win the war and win it soon and you don't think they will pay the bills for the anti-German propaganda you British journalists have been writing. Although there is no censorship in Turkey we have been disturbed by the untruthful rubbish that has been sent from here,' he added. After that one always had to carry enough money around to send a story.

It was with some relief I received orders from the *Express* to go to Egypt or, better still, Crete. So I set off for southern Turkey hoping to find some means of transport from there. By the end of May 1941 I was in the port of Mersin on the south-east coast where I stayed with the British consul and his wife, Mr and Mrs Terence Brenan. They were among the most helpful British officials I had met in the Balkans. They strongly advised me – obviously as a result of a general directive from Whitehall – not to attempt to cross the Lebanon which had been taken over by the Vichy French. In fact, I made a mistake in not going via Beirut as it would have been a splendid story and there was a handful of American correspondents there who survived in comfort.

The only subject of conversation in Mersin was the Battle of Crete and every morning the entire staff of the consulate came into the drawing-room to hear the news.

The British with Poles, Belgians and other allies found themselves in a virtual dead-end in Mersin. Few ships operated from the port since Turkish ships were not allowed to leave their territorial waters. Every day German warplanes flew over Turkey on their way to reconnoitre over Syria, which had closed her borders and stopped the railway system.

I was lucky. I discovered that the captain of a boat – a caique – flying the Palestinian flag had been visiting Mersin to make 'certain arrangements' which I interpreted as meaning a particularly profitable enterprise otherwise he would not have dared to make the trip. He intended to take the risk of crossing the Mediterranean to Egypt and he agreed that I could travel with him. There was, of course, no accommodation for passengers aboard this 150-tonner and no food or water. However, Mrs Brenan supplied me with cooked chickens, bread, water, wine and fruit.

The boat carried a small engine and six large sails. The lifeboat as well as the entire deck space was full of cargo. Unhappily, the cargo consisted of bags of nuts well covered with fleas and bugs, which scotched my belief that one never encountered the two together. I do not mind not washing for a week or more but I do hate getting fleas in my hair.

The other passengers were a German woman married to an Indian, two hearty Belgians determined to join the British army and a British officer who had been advising the Turkish army. They were all desperately dull. So much so that I gave up the idea of brushing up my French and learning some German. In a pit of dreary dejection, I asked the British officer what to him was the most enjoyable event in his life. He replied, 'The pub crawl I go on every Saturday evening when I am in England.'

I thought crossing the Mediterranean in a small boat would be something of an adventure and possibly enlivened by machine-gunning Nazi planes. Our tiny craft was not worth a bomb. We were shadowed by enemy aircraft but they did not attack.

When we left Mersin, the flag came down and the captain imposed a blackout. Although the sea was moderately calm, three of the passengers were immediately ill. Waves occasionally washed over the side, soaking all my clothes and luggage and ruining my only expensive garment, a Persian lamb coat. It was impossible to change or get warm so I just slept and let the fleas and bugs do their worst.

By day it was blisteringly hot; there was no shelter from the sun. Luckily I am dark-skinned and did not suffer but one of the other passengers was ill for a fortnight afterwards from the effects of sea sickness, cold and sunburn. It took five days and nights – among the worst I have ever endured – to reach Alexandria. But it was fun sailing into harbour among all the warships, many of them bearing scars suffered in Crete. It took all morning and most of the afternoon to get permission from the Egyptian officials to land although the British had completed their formalities in minutes. Dirty but cheerful, I hauled my luggage from the caique and took a taxi to the best hotel – the Cecil – where to my surprise they allowed me to enter.

I reported to the British Consul-General who promptly lent me £20 and invited me to lunch with some very interesting people who had just arrived from Crete. I met many familiar faces from the Balkans.

8 Egypt and the Desert War . . . Persia . . . The Surrender in Crete . . .

Egypt was a new and exciting country to me but I did not then realise that Alexandria was European and in no way typical.

It was hot and I bought a straw hat with a large brim – which in fact I never wore – before taking the train to Cairo. The journey was memorable for the brilliant flame trees which were then in full bloom. I took a taxi to the Hotel Continental and telephoned to Robin Hankey who was already working in the British Embassy. He immediately invited me to dine with his 'chums' who were sharing a flat in Gezira. Robin put me in the political picture and told me to make my number with Army public relations and the Americans. He also put me up for membership of the Gezira Club which throughout the war was a crucial meeting place. But for me the main attraction was the splendid swimming pool; during my first early morning dip I recognised General Sir Archibald Wavell (Commander-in-Chief of the Middle East Forces from 1939–41). He lived in a splendid house nearby. We developed a casual acquaintance and he introduced me to members of his staff at the evening 'get togethers' he gave in his garden. He even introduced me to his successor General Sir Claude Auchinleck. During 1941 the two outstanding generals exchanged command, Wavell taking over India from Auchinleck.

General Auchinleck personally assumed responsibility for the 8th Army when it appeared Rommel was but a few hours from the vital port of Alexandria and a day or two from Cairo. He stopped Rommel on that narrow strip of desert, which I had so often visited, between the Mediterranean and the Qattara Depression, a daunting, wind-scoured region of white sand and rock which was totally impassable to tanks and heavy artillery. It was Auchinleck who persuaded Churchill to dispatch with speed enormous quantities of arms and equipment to Egypt – via the Cape, of course. They arrived in time for General Bernard Montgomery (Monty) to deploy them.

The reaction among Egyptians was fascinating. Those who were pro-British were panicking over what would happen to them if Rommel's army reached Cairo, while those in the opposite camp were stocking up with celebration bottles of champagne.

My relationship with Monty was not good. He was something of a woman-hater and would not accept the accreditation of British women war correspondents although the Americans, with some difficulties, persuaded him to allow Clare Booth Luce and others to join the Press corps in the desert.

Monty certainly had charisma and the men loved him for wearing their regimental badges on his cap and for demolishing the 'them and us' barrier between officers and men. The troops, however, thought it odd that he did not drink beer. They appreciated his showmanship more than the diplomats and senior officers in GHQ in Cairo, who were amazed when during Easter, after the battle of Alamein, Monty returned to Cairo and took over the Embassy ballroom for a reception to those troops on leave as well as the Press. The curtains on a stage built for visiting theatrical groups were drawn aside and Monty popped out to give an 'I came, I saw, I conquered' type of speech. I never met him alone at this time and my contacts, who opened doors for me to report the war at close quarters, decided it was better for me not to do so.

Just as the men loved Monty, the officers tended to fear him. He treated junior officers harshly while senior officers found wanting – in his view – were summarily packed off back to Britain or some distant command. General Wavell said of Monty: 'He has one of the clearest brains we have in the higher ranks, an excellent trainer of troops and an enthusiast in all he does.' Though Wavell, too, criticised Monty's 'impatience and intolerance'.

The soldiers, however, saw in Monty a man who was trying

to ally himself with them by informing them of his intentions out in the desert, where there were no girlfriends to whom they could pass on highly-secret information. Certainly he inspired in the troops a zest for supremacy and victory over the enemy. Monty was firm in his religious belief and his faith gave him great confidence in himself, although he was hampered by his inability to compromise. These characteristics, noted by his contemporaries at St Paul's School in London, remained with him throughout his life. Like many other people, including myself, Monty never believed the Germans would win the war, but few optimists would have begun re-training troops – just back in Britain after the flight from Dunkirk and suffering two thousand casualties – for the next phase of the war. In his eyes re-embarkation for France!

When I was in Cairo I learnt to fly in order to help me understand air warfare and I flew with the RAF on bombing operations. Not only did I want to know more about air power but I believed – how wrong I was – that after the war it would be as important for people to know how to fly as to drive a car. I learnt to fly painstakingly at Heliopolis with Colonel Ralph Neville. Our instructor was an anti-Nazi Austrian pilot who had escaped in the hope of being able to join the RAF. I don't know whether he ever achieved this ambition.

The ability to pilot a plane became more useful immediately after the war when Richard Wyndham MC became the unlikely correspondent for the *News of the World* in the Middle East. He had his own plane – sometimes planes – and believed it was the only sensible way for a foreign correspondent to operate. I flew many times with him but only in the Middle East. So far as learning to parachute was concerned I was inspired by Leonard Mosley, who learned the art in order to be parachuted into France, ahead of the Normandy landings. I managed a few drops at Ramat David in Palestine, finding it a relief to jump out of a plane after the torture of jumping off lorries. Ralph Neville also took the para course and, alas, broke his leg and suffered some slight disability for the rest of his life.

When I first arrived in Cairo in 1941 just after the fall of Crete, I found little difficulty in visiting the 8th Army and attending official Press conferences and background briefings. By then I had left the *Daily Express* for Kemsley newspapers and so I became accredited for the *Chicago Daily News*.

They sent me to Palestine where I found Jewish refugees, recently arrived from Germany through various illegal channels, working on ships in Haifa harbour. I also spent over six months in Persia and travelled around Iraq as well as Egypt. I went to Tobruk, a British enclave besieged by the Germans, El Adem and many other battlegrounds.

At the end of the desert campaign after the British had captured Tripoli, Monty suddenly ordered me back to Cairo.

I was then sleeping in a truck at Castel Benito, the main airport just south of Tripoli. I suppose I could have obtained a room at one of the many Italian hotels and *pensions* in that city but I preferred to remain where the action was.

It seemed illogical that I should be ordered back to Cairo because I was a woman when there were thousands of other women in Tripoli. The town was full of Italian women who had not been evacuated and there were plenty of nurses based at the airport. Friends at the British Embassy in Cairo were supportive and so was Randolph Churchill, who was active in press relations there for a time. The Americans were downright angry, so it was not long before I was flying out of the Egyptian capital to join the US operations which were based in Algiers. Maybe no one told Monty that I was there but in any case I drew none of his usual wrath. By that time to his eternal credit, General Eisenhower insisted on having a few experienced women correspondents around, who – and this was vital – demanded no special treatment. It was essential to be able to go without washing, sleep in the open desert and live on bully-beef and biscuits for days on end. Many male correspondents got themselves sent back to Cairo because they could not take it.

Long before Monty appeared on the scene in the Western desert, the campaign had been a pendulum that had swung too often against the British. There were the 1940 successes against the Italians, who were overwhelmed by the British drive into Libya after Mussolini had entered the war. Something like one hundred and thirty thousand Italian soldiers were taken as prisoners-of-war and marched back to Egypt to be herded into improvised camps. The Italians always did themselves rather well with their supplies – good food and wine, flamboyant uniforms, crisp bed linen, ice-cream galore and brothels. In one of the first British offensives a mobile brothel was captured and posed a unique problem in disposal for Lieutenant-General Sir Richard O'Connor. He was fated to be captured himself in Rommel's first big attack across the desert with Lieutenant-General Sir Philip Neame VC and Major-General Gambier-Parry who had been a brilliant leader in the British military mission in Greece. It was always a mystery to me why these generals should have been travelling together in a dangerous area.

Rommel had been ordered by Hitler to take over from the effete Italians and with the Afrika Korps inject some iron and steel into the Axis campaign. He immediately introduced a new tactic: using the German 88mm anti-aircraft gun against British tanks which he did with devastating effect. The British lost half their tanks, some of which were to be repaired by the Germans and put into service for Rommel. He soon became a living legend, quite wrongly leading his troops in the forefront of the battle, and being criticised for spending too much time away from his headquarters. Nonetheless, he became the outstanding general of the Second World War, beloved by officers and men alike even though at times he was openly critical of Hitler for not according greater priority to the desert campaign.

War correspondents claimed they knew when Rommel was around or when he went away as the tone of the German radio always dropped when he left the battlefront and rose sharply on his return. Naturally, there was strict censorship in Cairo and elsewhere in the Middle East and because we were not allowed to write about how the British were fighting we tended to concentrate on Rommel until we had – rightly – built him up into such a hero that the censor was ordered not to permit his name to be mentioned.

Rommel landed in the Middle East when thousands of British troops and aircraft had been sent to Greece in an effort to stop the German invasion of that country. General Wavell, who was by this time chronically short of some types of equipment and troops, was humiliated by Churchill for failing to carry out his orders and break through Rommel's line with the new British Crusader tank. Wavell quite wisely resisted pressure from Churchill to launch an immediate attack in a situation in which both the Germans and the British had lost their punch.

The subsequent British attack succeeded initially only to find itself halted by another Rommel counter-blow. Rommel's offensive, known to the Allies as the Battle of Alam el Halfa, had to coincide with the full moon of 27 August 1942. When he was planning his breakthrough to the Suez Canal, the Field Marshal went forward to the minefields near the coast road and began giving orders to a motor-cycle recce company there. To demonstrate his ideas, he led a patrol into the few dangerous yards of No Man's Land in front of the British minefields.

Twenty minutes later he was back. 'What the hell are you doing?' he asked the commanding officer, a young captain. 'Nothing, Field Marshal, since you took command of my company,' was the reply.

Rommel laughed as he began briefing the officer on his new ideas. Then, a British bullet shattered his field-glasses as he held them to his eyes. Without flinching, the Field Marshal continued to talk, merely throwing away the now useless leather strap. 'To say my men would die for him is an understatement', the captain said later when describing the incident.

However, in August 1942, over a month after he had been halted at El Alamein by Auchinleck, courage was not enough to ensure a breakthrough. In German eyes this was to be the decisive offensive in North Africa and it was lost through the failure of Germany and Italy to supply sufficient petrol. The Italian General Cavallero promised six thousand tons of petrol and Field Marshal Kesselring guaranteed to send five hundred tons by air in an emergency. The Germans had no maps or any idea of the terrain before them so the moonlight at this time was essential for the opening phase of the battle. (I did not discover this until I returned in 1967 with Monty for the twenty-fifth anniversary of his El Alamein victory.)

At the time we all knew the British Minister of State resident in the Middle East, the Rt Hon. Richard Casey, who was also a member of the War Cabinet, had left Cairo secretly to visit Monty's headquarters at Alamein to hear why the battle was proceeding so slowly. Casey knew – but only he – that Monty had all the details of the German forces and the commands coming in from Berlin. Few if any other generals have ever had the advantage of such up-to-date military information about the enemy during the crucial battle.

The Italians were a terrible liability. So much so that German generals envied the British battle formation supported as it was by the Americans and Commonwealth troops.

Everything had been ready for several days when Rommel gave the order for the two Panzer divisions and the 900th Light to break out to the south in an attempt to turn the British flank and attack from the rear. It was an adaptation of the tactics which had been so successful in Tobruk: Rommel's famous 'left hook'. But the British had, unknown to Rommel, and even before the arrival of Monty, dug themselves into heavily defended positions on the Alam el Halfa ridge.

Rommel planned that his force should go about fifty miles due west by moonlight and then turn to attack the British troops on the ridge. But the German armour met with many unexpected natural obstacles – impassable stones and rocks and soft sand – as well as minefields, so Rommel lost the vital element of surprise on which the whole plan finally rested. At that moment he considered calling off the entire operation but his chief-of-staff, General Bayerlein, reported that he had overcome the British minefields and was pushing eastwards. In view of the danger to their flank and worried by the shortage of petrol, Rommel gave the order to turn northward earlier than he had originally planned. RAF strikes and artillery fire pinned the Germans down and they were unable to advance on schedule.

By 31 August Rommel had received no extra supplies of petrol and he was on the point of abandoning the offensive when Italy and Germany assured him that fuel was on the way – by sea to Tobruk and by air from Europe. It never arrived and from Rommel down to the German infantry venom was directed, probably for the first time, not at London but at Berlin and Rome. And so it was that Auchinleck was able to withdraw to the 'Alamein Line' – the space between the sea and the Qattara Depression – and withstand the ensuing forays and shell-fire from Rommel's army. The much-vaunted Afrika Korps was in a state of complete disarray with their tanks, which had drained all the ordnance lorries of petrol, now bogged down and immobile in the sands. With what was left of the German armour concentrated in the south, Rommel was wide open to attack from the best route along the northern coastal strip.

It was an immense relief to him that the expected attack from the British was postponed for several weeks. It gave him time to sow half a million mines in the path of the enemy.

Once he had completed his defences, Rommel handed over his command to his deputy, General Stumme, and flew back on sick leave to Germany. He was suffering from the aftermath of jaundice. It is interesting that Rommel contracted this illness, which must have had something to do with the desert and lack of fresh food. Hundreds of British officers and men suffered from this grim complaint, including myself, that caused deep depression and rendered it impossible ever to be a blood donor.

Back in Germany, Rommel met his former chief-of-staff and friend, General Alfred von Gausse, who was recovering from a war wound. When I met Gausse in Germany after the war he told me that they both had grave doubts about the sycophants around Hitler. Gausse's over-riding memory of Rommel, however, was the passionate loyalty he always received from all ranks whom he led in many actions in his own car, Mammut, a captured British armoured command truck. Gausse recalled that morale was high even after they had begun to withdraw from their positions at El Alamein. He emphasised that no petrol had been received for months from Italy and it was necessary to drain the petrol from one or even two tanks to fill up a third.

Throughout that crucial summer, Rommel battered the British line without effect although the ferocity of his attacks persuaded the British Embassy and GHQ in Cairo to burn their confidential documents. I remember war correspondents rushing back from the front, buying civilian cars and setting off for Palestine while others intrigued to obtain seats on aircraft for the Sudan or, better still, for South Africa. The Gezira Club was empty and the cooks at Groppi's were icing cakes with German and Italian colours.

Two officers stopped me in the Kasr el Nil, Cairo's main street, and said, 'Get out of the city quickly! Rommel has surrounded Cairo with two divisions we knew nothing about and they will be in occupation tomorrow.' But it was not so and Rommel's failure to break through towards Suez at Alam el Halfa was the turning point of the desert war.

It was in the tense situation before Rommel's el Halfa offensive that Churchill, accompanied by the Chief of the Imperial General Staff, Sir Alan Brooke, arrived in the Middle East and met Wavell and General Smuts, the South African prime minister, in Cairo. Churchill demanded changes in the command structure, insisted that a new spirit of enthusiasm and high morale should be introduced and demanded an early offensive – by September. Auchinleck refused to consider an attack as early as that but agreed that command of the 8th Army should be taken over by Lieutenant-General W.H.E. 'Straffer' Gott. He was killed in a plane crash the following day on his way out to Cairo. And so the second choice was informed. Lieutenant-General Montgomery arrived in Cairo on 12 August 1942, and took command in the desert war within twenty-four hours. At El Alamein he met his old friend, Major-General Francis de Guingand, who was chief-of-staff in the 8th Army. In the weeks that followed Monty exuded tremendous energy in his briefings with his senior officers and getting to know his troops. He wore their hats. He inspected every section of every line handing out cigarettes which he never personally smoked. Morale went up like a barometer in a heat wave.

In the higher echelons of military and civil power, there was far more criticism of this new bustling little commander than is realised today. His immediate entourage was thoroughly loyal to him and gave him their complete support. But in GHQ Cairo he was feared and disliked, no doubt the product of incompetence and complacency faced with a downright demand for efficiency and order.

There was similar disquiet among diplomats and civil servants. The general mood of criticism was expressed in feelings that 'The Auk', as Auchinleck was affectionately known to his staff, had made all the preparations for the next British offensive and Monty was basking in all the glory. The planning of the battle of El Alamein was certainly the direct result of Auchinleck's enterprise and vigour.

Monty waited until the night of 23–24 October to launch his famous attack. But he never successfully answered the question of why he failed to cut off the retreat of the German forces with an upper-cut thrust from the south. He had seven hundred and sixty seven tanks set against the three hundred German machines and for the first time the British troops used the six-pounder anti-tank gun. Further, Monty's communication line was a mere one hour's drive to the delta while Rommel's supplies had to be sent more than eleven hundred miles from Tripoli. For once the British had air superiority and yet Rommel and his Afrika Korps still escaped.

El Alamein will go down in history as one of the last set-piece battles. It was not the outright victory Monty and his loyal war correspondents claimed at the time, greater success could have been his with an earlier attack, but it was the most important single battle of the war, which catapulted Monty on the crest of a victorious wave across the deserts of North Africa and into Italy.

Monty often repeated this statement: 'Whenever I was given a free hand to fight the war as I thought right, success was complete and decisive: and the end of the war brought nearer – e.g. Alamein, Sicily, Normandy, the Ardennes, the crossing of the Rhine. Whenever my advice was not followed we got into grave difficulties.' There is some truth in what he said.

The 8th Army was a formidable fighting force that took the ebb and flow of defeat and victory very much in its stride. They appeared to be natural desert fighters and could have been easily melded into any of the warrior tribes of the desert. The French were equally adaptable and so were the Indians, Australians, New Zealanders, South Africans, Poles, Czechs and Greeks. The Gurkhas were perhaps the most outstanding for their ferocity and discipline. They are the only troops I know who as paras drop from aircraft at attention. I know this from experience as I passed one or two when I dropped with them near Ramat David in Palestine where they were training for operations in the Far East.

Cairo, of course, was the rumbustious centre of it all, a capital for leave from the front, a city for fun, a colourful mélange of smart hotels like Shepheards, night clubs, belly dancers and tarts, noisy trams and faded monuments, spies and intrigue, smells and disease, the Nile and the pyramids, all of them over-laid with the excitement and tension of war.

There were, of course, daily briefings in Cairo for war correspondents when we were brought up-to-date on the war situation or given just what GHQ thought we ought to have.

It was at one of these press briefings that I again met Christopher Buckley of the *Daily Telegraph*, who had been evacuated to Egypt from Athens aboard a cruiser which had taken part in the operations in Crete. I was staying at the Continental Hotel at the time. After a few weeks, Christopher found accommodation in a 'chummery', a delightful flat overlooking the Nile on one side and the Gezira Club on the other. After he had lived there for a few weeks one of the occupants – a Greek – moved out so I took over the empty room.

Christopher Buckley was then, I think, in his mid-thirties, slim, tall, but with a slight stoop that reduced his height. He wore thick glasses and, although he was basically good looking, few women noticed him. I remembered him from Athens where he had always been correctly but inconspicuously dressed. However, when I first met him in Cairo he was already in the uniform of a war correspondent. Indeed, he was very much the number two man on the *Daily Telegraph* to 'General Sir Arthur' Merton who went to Persia, Palestine or anywhere else where he thought there might be a good story, leaving Christopher to cover the day-to-day military developments in the Middle East. This he did with some distinction and, although he rarely mentioned the fact, he knew North Africa better than any other allied war correspondent.

After reading military history and strategy he became a school teacher for a time but when he realised the Second World War was on the horizon he decided – unlike most generals and experts at the time – that when Hitler's legions had overrun France, Holland and Belgium, Mussolini would persuade him to clear North Africa of any French remaining in Morocco, Tunis or Algeria. These operations would be carried out from Italian bases in Libya. This done the Axis would then launch an attack on the British in Egypt and Palestine before going on to Iraq.

Although Christopher's forecast was not one hundred per cent correct, it was better than most. At the time and at his own expense, he crossed North Africa to see the terrain for himself before he began his career as a journalist in Athens where, because he knew the language, he managed to obtain a job on a local paper.

I recall Christopher bewildering some of his colleagues and public relations officers by talking of the Mareth line to the west of Tripoli in what was then, Italy's Libya. But after he had spent a few months in Cairo it was generally recognised that Merton's number two 'knew his stuff'. Unhappily, Merton was killed in a motor accident on the road to Alexandria when driving with Randolph Churchill. At his funeral in Cairo Cathedral his brother turned up curiously wearing a little Jewish cap.

Following Arthur Merton's death Christopher took over as the *Telegraph* correspondent in the Middle East. He became friendly with Alexander Clifford, who was covering the region for the *Daily Mail* and his close friend and working partner, Alan Moorehead, who was working for the *Daily Express*. They had covered many stories together in the western desert and were only too happy to have Christopher with them as his background military knowledge was extremely useful. The trio were later to become famous but it always struck me as odd that they had but little to do with one another socially. I cannot recall Christopher having a meal with Alan Moorehead in Cairo and, after the war, when they were all in London they rarely met. But this does not detract from the deep professional friendship that developed when they were covering the 8th Army and, even more important, the war in Italy and the second front in France; indeed, right up to the unconditional surrender of Germany.

Alan Moorehead was married to Lucy, a pleasant, intelligent woman, who was the civilian personnel assistant to the commander-in-chief in Cairo, and Alexander Clifford married Jenny Nicholson just before the Allies crossed the Rhine. They stayed with me years later in Jerusalem when Jenny had already made a name for herself as a foreign correspondent. Christopher was in many ways a loner and I was surprised when he married later.

The life of a war correspondent in Cairo was pleasant enough. A majority lived in 'chummeries', which were pleasant flats with anything from three to five bedrooms, or in hotels. Everyone went each day to the briefing at the Press Centre in the Immobilia building in the centre of the city where there were reference books and it was here that the military and political censors operated. On the whole the military were more efficient than the 'Anglo–Egyptian' censorship as the political section was called. However, despite their over-careful attitude to the local scene they did allow, obviously by accident, a report about 'Tanks in Abdin Square' by Willie Forrest of the *News Chronicle* to be transmitted to London.

King Farouk, then a young man, had a government in power that was certainly not favourable to the British war effort and, indeed, may have had hidden sympathies with the Axis powers. Thus British soldiers training for their commission were used to surround Abdin Palace, where Farouk lived in the centre of Cairo, while tanks were moved into the square. The British Ambassador drove in an armoured car with his oriental councillor to the Palace to inform the king he must call on Nahas Pasha, leader of the Wafd, to form a government. After the ambassador had stated his case, the king refused to comply until the curtains were opened and the king saw British soldiers surrounding the Palace, and the tanks parked ahead in the square. After this the monarch changed his mind speedily and agreed to Nahas taking over as prime minister. For reasons best known to himself, the ambassador had wanted the whole episode to remain secret at least for a time.

It was one of the few occasions when a correspondent had a 'scoop' because official communiqués, handouts and briefings, combined with censorship, meant that the majority of correspondents filed the same story on the same day and the only difference was how they wrote it.

Correspondents were allowed to join Gezira Club where they could ride, play polo, tennis, golf, swim and enjoy relaxing meals. Despite the shortage of girls many frequently attended the nightly dinner-dance in the garden of Shepheards Hotel. There were, too, trips to Alexandria to make contact with the Royal Navy and visits to the Canal zone. Compared with Britain, despite the heat, life in Cairo was generally glamorous. There was plenty of petrol available, no food rationing and a wide range of social activities. Further, correspondents appeared to get on reasonably well together and there were fewer rows and rivalries than in most other capitals where large numbers of journalists have been based.

Much of my free time was spent with Christopher and he gave me invaluable help and advice when I was writing 'Germany Conquers The Balkans'. The publishers later changed the title to *There's A German Just Behind Me* (see Chapter 7), which irritated him almost as much as it did me. He taught me a great deal about warfare and introduced me to the works of

Clausewitz, the great German strategist. Maybe I helped him
a bit with journalism. I do remember wandering hand in hand
through the moonlit gardens of the Gezira Club and discussing
what we would do after the war.

We were devoted to one another in a way but it was not
an 'affaire' in the accepted sense of the word. His death in a
minefield during the Korean war was an unnecessary tragedy.

It is difficult for me to recall when I first met Geoffrey Hoare who
was to be my second husband. When I arrived in Egypt, Geoffrey
was editor of the *Egyptian Gazette* which then had a circulation
of around 300,000 but shortly after this in the summer of 1941
The Times, for whom he had been 'stringing' offered him a job
as their Middle East correspondent. Geoffrey was pointed out to
me at press briefings, however, as the best bridge player in Egypt.
I suppose we said the odd word to one another until Leonard
Mosley, who then worked for Kemsley Newspapers, took me
round to the 'chummery' where they lived for a drink. Geoffrey
was charming and, after this, whenever we met we discussed the
news and it is rather unromantic to add that we took a long time
to get to know one another well.

He was then tall, blond and thin with an impeccable taste in
tropical clothes and, far more important, a profound knowledge
of Egypt and its politics. He was not among the early morning
group of officers from GHQ and diplomats who rode their polo
ponies round Gezira Club before having a pre-breakfast swim.

In some ways Geoffrey replaced Christopher as an intimate
friend but it was a relationship that took a long time to develop,
perhaps because when I was in Cairo I had an enormous number
of friends there, many of whom I had known in the Balkans, such
as Robin Hankey who had been in the Embassy in Warsaw and
Bucharest before becoming First Secretary in Cairo.

While I was in the Balkans I had but few letters and those I
wrote home took six months to reach England – if they arrived
at all. However, in Cairo we were allowed to use the Army mail
and I soon learnt that my husband, Vandeleur Robinson, wanted
to marry someone else. Although the lady in question changed
from time to time he did, in fact, divorce me for desertion a year
or two after the war. It was a simple, uncontested case. From the
time of the civil war in Greece in 1945, Geoffrey and I planned

to live and work together and we were fortunate in being able to marry and 'live happily ever after'.

There was nothing really dramatic in the failure of my first marriage. From the time I went to Poland to work for the News Chronicle Fund for Refugees, Vandeleur could not make up his mind whether to support my career or urge me to return to London. Looking back, I feel he did support me, and he certainly encouraged me to return to the Balkans via France and Italy during the period of the phoney war when he must have realised there would be little chance of my getting back to London. He became taken up with Albania and would, doubtless, have worked there in some capacity had we renewed diplomatic relations at the end of the war.

The press briefings were always held at noon in Cairo. After one session, the director of Army Press Relations, Lieutenant-Colonel Philip Astley MC, announced, 'Oh, by the way, a French general has just arrived. I can't remember his name.' A junior officer whispered, 'de Gaulle.' Then Astley said, 'Does anyone want to see him? I don't think the man speaks English.'

There was a hush: obviously no French correspondents were present among the thirty reporters there. Finally, I broke the silence. 'Yes,' I said, 'I would like to see General de Gaulle.'

'When would you like us to wheel him around?' asked Astley.

Thus de Gaulle came to see me that afternoon in the cool, dark lounge of Shepheards Hotel. It was 4.30 p.m. He had an *aide-de-camp* with him and he gave me an excellent interview, speaking at length about French interests in the Far East and the Levant. De Gaulle told me that I could quote him and I did so – extensively – in a story I filed to the Kemsley group.

I felt rather pleased with myself so I was a little surprised when the *aide* telephoned me some days later to ask when the interview would be published. In those days British newspapers never reached Egypt but I was sure that the general would have been informed by his London headquarters about the story. The *aide* explained that Madame de Gaulle was particularly anxious to read my story.

I sent a service message to Kemsley enquiring just when the interview was carried and in how many of their newspapers. The reply, in fact, was sent to an older and more experienced colleague, Aubrey Hammond, who relayed it to me. The story had not been used because French-born Lady Kemsley did not like General de Gaulle. Moreover, there was no intention to publish it.

I was acutely embarrassed and offered some half-baked excuse to the *aide-de-camp* that pressure of space in newspapers of only four pages had prevented publication: that the opinion in London was that there was room only for active war news. The general never forgot the incident. Whenever I met him afterwards either in war or peacetime he would say, 'Ah, I remember you in Cairo.' But his words carried no rancour.

Years later when Geoffrey and I were living in Paris we were invited to receptions at the Elysée Palace when de Gaulle was president although the press was not normally invited to such functions.

Cairo may have been the nerve-centre for disseminating information, but for me the news was out there in the desert with the British troops. I made many trips with them, often behind enemy lines although frequently it was difficult to tell exactly just where the front line petered out so contact with the enemy was a real possibility.

One night I travelled with Colonel Ralph Neville, who was with intelligence – GSI 22 – and whose job was to round up enemy equipment from tanks to rifles. We took two trucks with drivers and a few men to see if we could find any discarded German arms among the dunes. After a couple of hours or so we stopped, having found precisely nothing, and dispersed ourselves. This meant digging a shallow trench and getting into it full-length and covering oneself up to the neck, rather like the game children play at the seaside, but for us it guaranteed warmth from the cold desert night and, we hoped, a hiding place from any wandering German troops.

I dozed off and in the early hours awoke to hear voices. They were quite clear. German voices. They seemed to be about one hundred yards away, a German recce party, which had stopped awhile among the huge sand-dunes. I literally sweated with fear. I had never been so frightened in my life.

I could feel that sand sticking with perspiration to every pore all over my body. I hardly dared breathe: a sneeze would have brought death to us all. They chatted away interminably and I wondered if my comrades were feeling as terrified as I was. I have no particular feelings about death. For me – that's it. There's nothing more. People who believe there is are fortunate. But that night I was certainly scared stiff at the thought of discovery and what might follow. Then the sound of an engine. Oh, what blessed relief! The distant crunch of a gear and somewhere over there they, that unseen Nazi threat, were moving further and further away. They would never know just how close they were to us.

Colonel Neville slept soundly throughout this dangerous episode and was rather amused – if a little frightened, I thought – when I related my experience. Why the Germans did not spot our trucks remains a mystery. I think Neville would have dismissed my story as a dream had not his driver and a sergeant confirmed it. They, too, were awakened by the Germans.

One of the prime factors behind the defeat of the German armies in North Africa was Hitler's obsession with his invasion of Russia. He certainly had envisaged his Afrika Korps capturing Cairo and sweeping triumphantly on into Arabia and Persia to link up with his armies in the south of the Soviet Union.

Churchill's apprehensions about the political situation in Persia came long before the battle of El Alamein. GHQ in Cairo received confidential reports from their agents of pro-German activities in that country and the Shah, Reza Khan Pahlevi, a Persian cossack officer, was openly pro-Hitler. The crunch came when, after the German attack on Russia, the Americans were anxious to send supplies of urgently needed equipment to the Soviet Union. The obvious route was by sea to Basra and then by road across Persia.

To secure the route the British, with a handful of men, entered Persia from north eastern Iraq. There were many amusing reports of the Persian army running away and there was certainly no resistance. The Russians, at the same time, occupied the north-western territory making their headquarters in Tabriz. I flew into Persia on 25 August 1941 only three months after my arrival in Egypt from Greece. Reza Shah had already abdicated under British pressure and gone into exile. He was succeeded by his son, Mohammed Reza Pahlevi, then twenty-one years old.

I went down to Basra where troops from the UK were suffering from chronic sunburn as they set up special facilities for the transhipment and transport of goods to Russia. At that time the only air-conditioning was in the bar of the Airport Hotel. There was nothing for the troops to do and the regulations forbidding them to go into local bars were relaxed.

On my return to Tehran I ran into Colonel Neville who with Major Dennis Moore, another intelligence officer dealing with enemy equipment, had been assigned to find the arms and ammunition dumps the Germans had hidden in various parts of the country. I was able to accompany first one and then the other on various trips and some arms were discovered in the foothills of the mountains of Darband. But before that find I went with them to Tabriz where I managed to get an interview with a Russian general, who greeted me in his hotel room wearing his heavily decorated jacket over his pyjamas. There was snow outside on his balcony. He gave me a cautious briefing on the military situation which added little to my knowledge, but the Chicago paper I was working for was delighted and they sold the interview to other American papers.

We left Tabriz and returned to Tehran passing through several Soviet control points. Back in the capital, I obtained an interview with the young Shah despite a general lack of co-operation from the British Ambassador. But at the embassy I found Nancy Lambton (later to become Professor Ann Lambton) whom I had known in London as Lord Cecil's niece. She was a young woman of character who hated debs balls and social life generally and reportedly took her Persian grammar book into the cloakroom to study while the rest of the world danced. She spoke excellent Persian, was extremely interested in politics and had many friends in Tehran. She kindly put me up and I am sure that it was through her that I became the first person to be given an interview with the Shah.

Filing copy from Tehran was totally frustrating, partly because the British spokesman had little to say and, above all, there was Soviet censorship. Every press cable had to be stamped by three officers – British, Russian and Persian.

When I saw the Shah he welcomed me in a small study in his palace where he had a range of bound books on military history and strategy, which we discussed for two hours – a long discourse partly due to the fact that he spoke little English. As my luggage had been severely limited, I was wearing what my future husband called 'your ill-fitting battle dress'. When I made a move to depart, the Shah said, 'Please, *do* stay for lunch. My wife is so lonely.' I accepted his invitation, of course, and was duly introduced to the Empress – King Farouk's sister. She was somewhat over-dressed and wearing long, heavily-jewelled earrings. 'Could I be mistaken for a European?' she asked. I did not think she could but refrained from saying so. In the clothes I was wearing I could hardly offer a comment on fashion! Rather cheekily I compared the 'flash' entrance hall of the palace to a Lyon's Corner House in London. While checking the quotes with me the following day for a story I intended to file, the Shah said, 'Do you really think it is as good as Lyon's?'

The Shah soon changed his image from that of a naïve young man to a pompous head of state ensconsed on the Peacock throne. In later years almost the entire bureaucracy was terrified of HIM – His Imperial Majesty – who used a solid gold telephone and tended to dismiss anyone who disagreed with him. But he received me several times when I visited Tehran later largely, I suspect, because I was a friend of Sir Denis Wright, a highly successful ambassador there for nine years. I also met the Shah in Marrakesh after he had been exiled by Ayatollah Khomeini in January, 1979.

After six months in Persia and Iraq I returned to Cairo, my base for the entire Middle East war. I followed the Americans across Libya into Tunisia and then on to Algeria staying in Algiers where General Eisenhower established his headquarters before the invasions of Sicily and Italy.

I recall a flight from Italy designed to drop British officers to join Marshal Tito, the communist rebel leader in Yugoslavia. We flew from an airport near Bari with the group, including a woman, who were all brave and glad that at last they were joining the guerrillas. We encountered no AA fire, nor did we see or hear an enemy aircraft. I recall the sad empty planes on the return journey.

Towards the end of the war, I joined raids over the Mediterranean designed to shoot up enemy shipping. There were only two of us on one particular mission, in which the pilot frequently and suddenly swooped down to within a few hundred feet of the target ship. Maybe we were occasionally under fire but one never heard the noise and apparently the plane was not hit.

It may seem strange to report that bombing raids could be extremely boring. It was always exciting to get permission to go on one and the briefing was generally interesting, but perhaps I was fortunate in that the actual raid was generally tedious. On a long bombing raid I just sat listening to the pilot's comments until the target had been reached. Tension rose somewhat then but after the bombs had been dropped there was nothing to look forward to but the long journey home.

In 1944 we were alerted to the expected collapse of the German forces in Greece following the Allied invasion. With three American reporters I boarded a troopship at Alexandria.

We crossed the Mediterranean and on the approach to the Greek mainland there were several small German naval boats wanting to surrender but they were ignored as our convoy headed for the port of Piraeus. Total disorganisation greeted us and we had to walk to Athens carrying our kit – in my case, a typewriter and a toothbrush. At the Hotel Grande Bretagne, the Germans had not long been gone. Their cigarettes it was said were still smouldering in the ashtrays in the bars. It had taken over a week to reach Athens and as I was having a drink in the bar who should arrive but Geoffrey then working for *The Times*. He had just flown in on the first available plane from Cairo!

When months later the news came through that the Germans were about to surrender in Crete, I could not wait to get there and obtained permission to fly in with Geoffrey. We arrived with a British officer to find the island packed with German troops – five or six divisions evacuated from Greece.

We tracked down their senior officers and told them that they would have to surrender. They did not like the idea at all. So we tuned in to the BBC German service which was carrying the announcement of the German surrender in Greece. They signed without fuss on the dotted line. We allowed them to keep their arms because communist rebels in the hills were getting out of hand and they had to be kept under some element of control.

Geoffrey and I commandeered two staff cars and for the next few days we drove around the island like lords.

The Crete surrender was at the time of the fall of Hitler and his Nazi régime but in the Middle East murder and mayhem continued with the worsening situation in Palestine. The war had brought a temporary truce between the warring Jews and Arabs, and Britain, which had been given the Mandate in 1922 to form a Jewish national home in Palestine. But hostilities resumed soon after the unconditional surrender of Germany. The Jewish terrorist organisation, the Irgun, which was led by Menachem Begin, who was destined to be a future prime minister of the State of Israel, smuggled explosives into the King David Hotel, the Jerusalem headquarters of the British administration. Begin's organisation was brilliant.

On 22 July 1946, Geoffrey and I were talking together in the car about three hundred yards from the hotel where we were staying while covering the troubles. Suddenly there was a tremendous explosion as the building was torn apart, collapsing into a mountain of rubble. Over a hundred people – Britons, Arabs and Jews – were killed; we could so easily have been among them. We both ran across to the devastation, appalled by the prostrate dead and the cries of the injured. Begin maintained later that warnings had been issued to the hotel and the public but they certainly did not arrive in time to save life and limb. It was, in fact, a diabolical statement by the terrorist leader that the fight was on again and the State of Israel would be created out of blood if necessary.

Certainly, blood flowed in Palestine before Israel became independent in 1948. During that period there were many atrocities carried out by Begin and his terrorists, such as the fate suffered by a group of British sergeants in an orange grove. They were hanged from the trees with wire. They were all in their twenties; it would have taken twenty-five minutes for those young, fit men to die.

When Begin rose to political power in the late 1970s I often found myself in his presence. But I never greeted him. I would not shake a hand with so much blood on it.

9 Paris ... D.H. Lawrence's Lover ...

Shortly after the German surrender Geoffrey and I returned to London to enjoy a vacation and confer with our various newspaper 'bosses'. At that time we decided to live openly together on a permanent basis. We took a pleasant flat in Earls Court and met old friends. Geoffrey was persuaded to join the staff of the *News Chronicle* which, in many ways, suited his own political inclinations better than the more prestigious *Times*.

In Greece at the end of the civil war Geoffrey had devoted himself to politics while I – generally accompanied by Stephen Barber who was then working for A.P. – went out each day with the paras as they cleared the city of communists and other rebels. Influenced by what he had seen personally and what he was told by such responsible people as Brigadier Barker Benfield head of Force 133 in Crete, together with Greek right of centre friends, Geoffrey was critical of government policy in Greece. Even Osbert Lancaster, who was sent out as press attaché to Athens, failed to change his mind. In fact, Geoffrey's attitude was mild when compared with all but one of the American correspondents and the majority of others there. *The Times* was loyal to Geoffrey although the editor, Barrington Ward, was 'reproved' for 'their very unhelpful line' as Harold Macmillan discloses in his War Diaries in the entry for 7 December 1944.

This background may have contributed to Geoffrey's move to the *Chronicle* but I think the salary offered was almost double what he earned with *The Times*. Further, although Geoffrey spoke reasonable Arabic and certainly enjoyed Cairo he did not wish to spend the rest of his life in the Middle East. He went back there for the *Chronicle* with the promise of a change in a few years.

We got along well because Geoffrey, like my platonic friend Hugh Carleton Greene, was a complete egalitarian. Further, as he had become deaf as a result of spending too much time with the artillery in the desert, my loudish voice attracted him. My father was deaf and I had been brought up to speak loudly and clearly; indeed, my sister and I were told almost every day 'Please speak up: it's rude to mumble.'

Geoffrey was anxious for me to continue with my career and gave me a great deal of help. When he wanted to play high level bridge I covered for him, while he covered for me when I went on trips to look at ruins or merely meet friends. Shortly after Geoffrey joined the *News Chronicle* I became correspondent for the *Observer* and *The Economist* and finished up back in Palestine, for a time, doing the same job Kim Philby was later to do.

In those days good friends did cover for one another, a practice that had the advantage of enabling a correspondent to leave the capital and see something of the country in which he was working without the risk of missing a major story. The *News Chronicle* were well aware that I wrote the odd report for Geoffrey and claimed they could always tell because I overdid his style. But when I requested them to point out the reports they claimed I had written, they always got it wrong.

Today it would be unthinkable for one correspondent to cover for another for even the most innocuous story.

Where there is a big news story there is never any problem about social life. Although there may well be shortages of food, drink or accommodation there is plenty of company. The social life in Egypt during the war was during the day at Gezira Club and in the evenings at private dinner parties and dinner dances in the garden of Shepheards and other hotels. The cheap wine came from Palestine, Turkey and Egypt itself and, of course, there was plenty of beer. I recall that the excellent orchestra at Shepheards played 'A Nightingale Sang in Berkeley Square' just before midnight. This for me was the signal to go home in order to be up shortly after six for my morning ride on Sim Sim a polo pony.

On operations, one naturally ate with the group and, although standards were not as high in Tripoli as in Cairo, by the time Algiers was occupied a new wave of culinary skills captivated the officers in General Eisenhower's Headquarters there.

During the so-called civil war in Athens we were on half rations over Christmas but, early in January when supplies of food were restored, we all celebrated what was called 'Scobiemas' after the pleasant GOC General Sir Ronald Scobie. Although he was ultimately responsible for the military actions taken against the Greek Communists and other resistance groups, many of whom had been in the hills fighting the Germans during their period of occupation, Scobie was far more popular than the British Ambassador Sir Rex Leeper. The latter was generally regarded as too far to the right of centre even for the Greek rightwingers.

However, conditions changed when my friend Sir Clifford Norton, who had served as Minister in Switzerland after Poland, was appointed as Ambassador in 1946. I made a point of getting back to Athens to meet the Nortons. With great tact, Clifford relieved the locally appointed staff of their power. For example, David Balfour who had been a Greek Orthodox priest in Athens before the German occupation had become Leeper's right-hand man. Indeed, he lived in the embassy and answered the telephone out of office hours, putting the calls through to the Ambassador only when he approved of the caller. The Nortons stopped this and began entertaining a wide variety of people naturally including Peter's artistic friends. I was proud to be able to introduce her to Ghika, whose pictures I had saved from destruction by British troops when they occupied Athens. The young soldiers, having taken over Ghika's studio, thought on that chilly December night the canvases would make a good fire. But I used my authority as a war correspondent to stop this until I could find an officer to give the order that the paintings were to be stored in safety.

The Nortons came over to visit us in Beirut when that city was the great free commercial centre, something like Hong Kong became later. In those days when almost everyone had exchange controls, Lebanon alone was free for bankers and traders. There was an underlying animosity between the Moslem and Christian Communities but it was not easy to trace as the tradition of a Christian President and Moslem Prime Minister appeared to work and all the religious communities were represented in the

Cabinet. The food was superb – whether French or Arab – so, too, was the local wine. People used to ski down from the hills above the city in winter and then take a tram to the sea for a swim.

Geoffrey and I had a base in Cairo but stayed in hotels when covering news in Baghdad, Beirut, Athens, Damascus or Ankara. During the two years we spent in Palestine after the future prime minister Begin had organised the blowing up of the King David with such success, we took a cottage – Spiridan Cottage, Upper Baka, near the Bethlehem Road. We had a large wild garden and it was here Geoffrey indulged his interest in watching rare birds, lizards and insects. I recall going on a long walk in the hills on Princess Elizabeth's wedding day in 1947 as we rightly assumed there would be no interest in Palestine that day. The cottage was small; we had a study, sitting-room and dining-room downstairs together with kitchen and a room for our excellent Arab maid. Upstairs we had three small rooms so frequently found ourselves putting up friends such as Elizabeth Monroe of *The Economist*, Alexander Clifford and his wife, Jenny Nicholson, together with relatives who made their way to Jerusalem.

Our maid never wore a veil but months after we left the cottage I met her in the town with her husband and she was veiled. She explained now she was no longer a maid, she had gone up in the social scale and could demonstrate this by veiling. Later, I found this practice common in Egypt. Women who had worked in the cotton plantations who went to the city wore a veil to demonstrate that they were now middle class. Generally, they did not stick to the veil for long.

In Alexandria I spent an interesting weekend with Azzan Pasha and his wife. He was then Secretary-General of the Arab League and they lived a completely European life. He did not drink but wine and whisky were around for anyone who wanted and, in that house, men and women were equal. I recall him mentioning the dangers of Moslem Fundamentalism and his wife expressed sympathy and sorrow for the women of Saudi Arabia. Times have changed dramatically since then with the fundamentalists leading the pack in Iran supported by Gaddafi in Libya.

Local leave immediately after the war was taken in Cyprus which was the most relaxing peaceful area of the Middle East as well as being relatively inexpensive and charming with several good hotels and splendid beaches. On later trips to Cyprus when defence correspondent first for the *Guardian* and then the *Daily Telegraph* I stayed with the general who commanded the British troops there.

Naturally, clothes are always a problem when moving from one part of the world to the other. I remember going to Algiers for one night from Paris to interview the President. While I was there I was ordered to Egypt. But with a typewriter, toothbrush and a couple of safari suits one can make out. I usually have an uncrushable long dress and rely on being able to buy cheap padded coats if suddenly sent to a really cold place such as Peking in winter. Once in Inner Mongolia in winter when the rivers were being used as roads, the heating more or less broke down in my bedroom and I slept in all my clothes including my fur coat turned inside out.

The big problem for journalists, I have found, is carrying around the papers and books needed for reference. If one is suddenly sent to, say, Australia one needs enough books to read on the plane and a large number of clippings and photocopies of recent articles. Although today typewriters are no longer necessary, some form of word processor and/or computer with a printer is essential. This equipment tends to be heavy.

Going home alone in 1948 I covered the Danubian Conference in Belgrade. I was both pleased to be going back to a place I had once known well but apprehensive about my lack of knowledge of the Tito régime and also the subject of the Conference – 'Navigation on the Danube'. However, when I arrived I found my old friends Denis and Iona Wright in the Embassy and the Ambassador, Sir Charles Peake, was extremely helpful. Shipping faded into the background as news of the split between the Soviet Union and Tito was leaked to the outside world. Four months before the Conference opened on 20 July, there had been semi-secret disagreements between Moscow and Belgrade in which Moscow complained that Russian experts in Yugoslavia were being given 'hostile' treatment. The basic issue was that Marshal Tito had decided he was strong enough to take his own line when it differed from that proposed by Stalin.

One of the excitements for me was talking to Mme Anna Pauker who was then Foreign Minister of Rumania. I told her secretary, with truth, that while I was working in Rumania during the war, Mme Pauker was in prison. I had tried to see her there but without success. She was now enjoying a few luxuries in Belgrade and who could blame her after all she had suffered at the hands of King Carol and others. She appeared to be confident and was obviously on good terms with Vyshinsky. I never knew what caused her later downfall. None would speak of it when I went back to Rumania but it was said she was manning a telephone line in one of the ministries.

In 1950 Geoffrey was offered the temporary post of head of the Paris office which he accepted with joy and was told it would be permanent if he did a good job there and if William Forrest, then in Paris, was promoted to be diplomatic correspondent. I gave up my job with *The Economist* in the Middle East and with the *Observer* and went to Paris with Geoffrey because I knew that city better than he and he was anxious to have my help. But I agreed to still spend at least three months of the year in the Middle East. Work was not hard to find in Paris. Darcy Gillie needed an assistant to file for the *Manchester Guardian*. At first we lived in various hotels which was useful in getting to know the city. Peter Norton visited us from Athens and bought abstract pictures and introduced us to groups of artists.

When Geoffrey's appointment was confirmed we took a flat; technically the address was rue de l'Université, but, in reality, it was in the Place Bourbon behind the Chambre des Deputées. Passing by there now it seems incredible that we could then afford to live in this splendid neighbourhood. Geoffrey's office was in the rue Reaumur and I sometimes worked there. We became friendly with the chief of the *Daily Telegraph* team, John Wallis, who had an office in the Place Vendôme. Gradually we discovered how different it was to cover Paris from, say, Cairo or Beirut. The office was far more interested, perhaps because it was near and maybe a majority of readers had visited France.

In those days correspondents usually gathered before lunch in the Crillon Bar – again unthinkable today as salaries and expenses have not kept pace with the ever rising price of a 'cup' of champagne. After lunch in a nearby bistro correspondents went to their offices unless the Chambre des Deputées was in session. They were the days of normal political disputes interrupted by someone bursting into the Marseillaise. At this point the debate had to stop and all deputées stand while it was being sung.

They were also the days when General Eisenhower was setting up Nato's military headquarters near Paris – Supreme Headquarters Allied Powers, Europe – Shape, while Lord Ismay was the first Secretary-General of Nato. I was fortunate in meeting all these people because the Chairman of the *News Chronicle* was Lord Layton who, as Vice-President of the Council of Europe, paid frequent visits to Paris. As Geoffrey handed much of the social political contact work to me, I used to drive Lord Layton around and join him for lunch with the VIPs. At that time they were an impressive group as international organisations multiplied.

We both enjoyed life in Paris and eventually made our home in a large rambling flat at 7 rue du 4 Septembre which had a back door on the rue St Augustin near to the Bibliothèque Nationale and within a few minutes walk of our Club, the Cercle de L'Union Interalliée, next door to the British Embassy. The flat was large and we shared an enormous study/studio as well as having guest rooms – so convenient in Paris. However, Geoffrey soon began to miss the country and his insects. (He kept dragonfly larvae and other insects in the Paris flat and I must be one of the few people to have used a fishing-net in the Bois de Boulogne to obtain mosquito larvae required as food for the young dragonflies.) I saw houses advertised for sale in the Loire valley at reasonable prices but they were all in poor condition. One wise agent advised me to go to 'the invasion route' east of Paris where I found a small modest house with a deep well in the valley of the Grand Morin in the Brie country on a 'dirt' road but only an hour's journey by car from Paris. There we spent extremely happy weekends, especially after one of the ministers gave an order for us to have the telephone installed.

At the rue de 4 Septembre we entertained politicians, diplomats and the corps of foreign correspondents who were either based in Paris or attending international conferences there. It was a pleasant time and a change from the hurly-burly of wars.

In the early 1950s a strange interlude occurred which after all this time brought me into conflict with my parents.

I was attending an embassy reception in Paris when I was

approached by a pretty young woman, who after the initial introductions, turned to me and said, 'I hear you come from Rutland. You must know Mrs Fred Heath.'

'Yes,' I replied, 'I do indeed know Mrs Heath.' The Heaths were near neighbours of my parents in Thistleton. A somewhat frailish woman, Louie Heath was married to a rich former boot and shoemaker and they assumed the appearance of rather stylish countryfolk. Before she married, her name was Burrows. She had been a teacher.

Then, my companion added, 'Mrs Heath is something special. She was not only the long-time mistress of D.H. Lawrence but his first mistress, who taught him English and manners and how to get around in the world. Their love letters must be extremely important.'

This is no great secret today but in those days few people knew of this remarkable liaison. My parents were living in The Old Rectory in Thistleton, which was then in Rutland – it has since been absorbed into Leicestershire. I loved that old, rambling house because it had so many rooms as well as four large attics. When I was next visting my parents I raised the subject. Over a Saturday night drink, I said, 'Have you ever heard anything about Mrs Heath? Did you know that she had a very important affair with D.H. Lawrence?'

Both father and mother were extremely shocked. The question evoked all their antagonism to journalism and my particular career. 'How could you have entered this ghastly trade?' father demanded. 'It isn't even a profession. It's . . . it's something connected with the tradesmen's entrance! How could you listen to any suggestion that Mrs Heath could have been anyone's mistress let alone the mistress of D.H. Lawrence?' He went on and on in this way for sometime with mother agreeing with him that it was quite despicable for their daughter to repeat such rumours and that they were ashamed to have a daughter working for any newspaper, apart perhaps from *The Times* which never dwelt on such innuendoes.

I was, therefore, slightly surprised when leaving church the next morning with the Heaths when my father turned to Mr Heath and said, 'Oh, Fred, by the way, did Louie ever know a man, an author called D.H. Lawrence?'

Fred Heath stopped in his tracks. He was perfectly still as his face turned pink. He was clearly horrified. 'Where on earth did you hear that?' he asked.

They both came home to have a sherry with us as they usually did after morning service and nothing more was said. However, after they had departed, father did say to me in a rather disinterested way, 'Oh, Fred was rather surprised that you or anyone else knew that in her youth Louie had some kind of a flirtation with D.H. Lawrence.'

I then made it my business to find out all I could about that *affaire*. From the girl who had first mentioned Mrs Heath to me in Paris, and Vence where D.H. Lawrence had worked, I discovered that Louie Burrows had indeed been his first love and had taught him how to write. She possessed a large number of love letters from him which she bequeathed to Nottingham University after her death in May 1962. I found them there. They had been entered lovingly in a book lined with tissue paper.

They provide an intriguing insight into D.H. Lawrence's first love. In one letter, dated 7 October 1907, he wrote, correcting a story she had written about a gamekeeper: 'Avoid bits of sentimentality like crusaders . . . Select some young fellow of your acquaintance as a type for your lover and think what he would do . . .' On 17 December 1910, he wrote a letter to her in which he said, 'Oh, you'll have to burn this paper. How I chuckle, seeing you doing it. Hell – or here – or you.'

In a letter dated 30 December 1911, to a friend, Edward Garnett, Lawrence described her without naming her: 'My girl is here. She's big and swarthy, and passionate as a gipsy – but good, awfully good, churchy. She rubs her cheek against me just like a cat . . .'

When he jilted her he wrote: 'The best thing you can do is to hate me.'

That was something Louie could not do. Neither did she follow his advice to destroy his letters. Even when this daughter of a country school headmaster became herself headmistress of Quorn Church of England School in Leicestershire she liked to carry the most tender of his one hundred and sixty-odd letters in a special pocket in her corsets.

When the letters began to deteriorate with the years she wrote to the British Museum for expert advice on the best way to clean them without damaging them. The museum suggested a special solvent. She had it prepared at a local chemist's shop and cleaned and ironed every letter. She then wrapped each one separately along with three manuscripts of early Lawrence short stories in blue tissue paper and kept them in a special file in a safe.

She always refused, possibly out of a mixture of pride and prudery, to discuss her relationship and fifteen-month engagement to Lawrence with any scholar or biographer. She was in her early fifties when she married Frederick Heath in 1940 after a medium in Leicester told him that his first wife wished it. I knew Louie as a woman with strong but quite conventional views, culturally pretentious, deeply religious, with an interest in spiritualism and astrology. She seemed to spend much of her time embroidering altar cloths for Peterborough Cathedral.

One would never have suspected that she was the 'Louie' of Lawrence's 'Kisses in the Train'.

When Lawrence died in 1930 she flew to Nice and then drove to Vence for the funeral. For the mourners she was a mystery woman, standing in the back of the church, alone and saddened. She left without revealing her identity. But she went back to visit his grave on at least two other occasions in the 1930s. Once she met Sir Herbert Read, who disclosed afterwards that although she still resented being jilted by Lawrence she had never lost her love for him. In the early 1950s she persuaded her husband to visit Lawrence's grave with her.

Just before her death Louie announced that she had decided to publish at least a selection of the love letters 'to show what a delightful man Lawrence really was'. Her husband, however, persuaded her against publication and, moreover, made determined efforts to comply with Lawrence's own advice and have the letters burned. Louie's family, fortunately, managed to have copies made during her last illness; one of the family actually tried to take the originals from the house as she lay on her death-bed. These she had bequeathed to her nephews and nieces, who in 1968 allowed them to be published by Nottingham University Press.

Louie died with a volume of Tolstoy at her bedside, in which Lawrence had written on 13 December 1907: 'Should you live to look at the blue binding and think of it, years hence . . . then give a sigh – or, better, give a smile . . . ' It was his first present to her. She was buried in the churchyard that abutted my parents' home.

As I had obtained all the background, I thought the letters would provide the basis for a book on Lawrence. I mentioned this to my husband's friend and literary agent, David Higham, who had helped to launch Geoffrey's book *The Missing Macleans*. I provided him with a synopsis but to my disappointment and anger he argued that the subject was not my *métier* since I was a correspondent writing on politics and defence. He passed the information on to another client.

10   The Algerian War . . .

The year 1962 opened ominously for France with President
Charles de Gaulle and his government facing the real prospect
of disaster over the worsening situation in war-torn Algeria,
which was then an integral part of France and not just a colony.
For eight years, the Fronte de Liberation Nationale, the leading
nationalist movement known simply as the FLN, had waged a
bloody rebellion for independence against the French authorities,
the administration in Algiers backed by the army and, later, the
renegade secret organisation – the OAS – of ex-General Salan,
the champion of one million settlers, who watched their way of
life being eroded daily by the bomb and the bullet.

The Algerian march towards independence was a traumatic
experience for France and demonstrated its extreme feelings
towards overseas possessions. Government after government had
fallen in attempts to try to solve the Algerian problem. It had
faced and resisted the 1958 revolt of the French generals, who
with the connivance of the former resident-minister in Algiers,
Jacques Soustelle, and the full support of the settlers – the
colons – refused to recognise the government of France. In
Paris, a Committee of Public Safety for Algeria under General
Massu was established and it proposed the return to power of
General de Gaulle. Thus on 8 January 1959, the war hero, the
man who represented above all the grandeur of France, returned
as the national leader once again.

However, de Gaulle's proposals for solving the Algerian crisis later astonished and angered both the army and the settlers, perhaps because they included the startling declaration that there should be full voting rights for Moslem women, enough schools for Moslem children within ten years, schemes for new industrial centres, housing projects and the restoration of farmlands.

Here was the recipe for the ultimate independence of Algeria and it was complete anathema to the army and the *colons*. In 1960, General Salan and three other senior officers had staged an unsuccessful coup attempt. For a time it was serious enough to provoke wild rumours in Paris itself that the city was about to be beseiged by an army of parachutists from Algeria. Nevertheless, for the first time since the French revolution of 1789 a military coup against a government in Paris had seemed possible for many anxious hours. General de Gaulle yielded not an inch. A member of his staff told me that the President went to bed early and disliked being disturbed after 11 p.m. But on the night of Salan's revolt – 24 January 1960 – the Defence Ministry woke him to report that a number of French squadrons at Maison Blanche – the airport of Algiers – were ready for take-off to bomb Marseilles, Toulon or Nice. 'Well, there's nothing to stop them,' de Gaulle replied. The warplanes never took off: they were grounded by a sudden *hamseen*, a severe storm. The threat had little chance of becoming reality since a military thrust across the Mediterranean would have loosened the army's grip on the Algerian rebels. The President acted quickly. He dismissed the rebel generals and Salan, stripped of his rank, went underground with his secret army to organise a campaign of terror against the Moslem rebels.

The President's riposte brought immediate riots in Algeria. Europeans, driven to distraction by years of terrorism, went on the rampage invading government offices, setting up, if only for a brief period, their own revolutionary organisation, and demonstrating on the streets by beating out the rhythm of 'Algérie Française' on motor-horns, pots and pans.

In January 1962, complete anarchy reigned with terrorist attacks, mainly by the OAS, becoming daily events. The casualties mounted and de Gaulle and his government no longer even pretended to control the situation. Secret negotiations between the rebel government – the GPRA – and presidential emissaries had practically reached the point of a peace treaty early the previous month but they broke down on one point. The rebels insisted that General de Gaulle should arrest Salan and the other former generals and colonels and then clean up the OAS. Without this, ultimate independence would lead to nothing more than a full-scale war between the two communities. As it was, Salan and his blood-stained cohorts ignored all orders from Paris to curb their hands and so nothing was done to counter their catalogue of bombings and shootings. The OAS often instigated attacks against the army under the guise of the FLN rebels, hoping that counter-action would be taken against Moslem areas. Many loyal police officers sent over from France to lead investigations into the murders were shot themselves.

The war between the French army and the FLN nationalist rebels was as good as over but civil violence followed and increased to terrifying proportions. From the very beginning of the Algerian troubles, the real problem lay with the army, which had brought General de Gaulle back to power because it believed that he would seek the military victory in Algeria which had eluded the generals for years. The army believed that de Gaulle stood for 'Algérie Française' but so far as is known he only uttered the phrase once, preceded by the word 'Vive'. Many of his intimate supporters denied this but John Wallis of the *Daily Telegraph* heard the President use the evocative words during a tour of Algeria, although he may have been carried away by the enthusiasm of the crowds.

When the army discovered to its shocked dismay that de Gaulle, the realist, intended to seek a negotiated peace – the only way of saving something from the ruin of French dreams of an empire – it turned savagely against him. He played for time. Even after two military revolts he never took really strong action against the mutineers. The President always argued that the mutineers represented a minute part of the whole and that the majority of officers and troops were loyal to him. Yet those who supported him – about three hundred thousand men – were still unable to arrest Salan and his accomplices. To have asked why would have produced unacceptable answers for the President. It would have disclosed the gigantic support for Salan among not only army and police but rank and file. And his refusal to look facts in the face where his army was concerned was his fatal, albeit temporary, weakness.

The result was that early in 1962 when I returned to Algeria peace seemed as far away as ever. The violence had spread into France with bombs exploding on the streets of Paris. The President ignored protests and took no action. After all, France was then more prosperous than it had been for decades, unemployment had all but vanished; industrial production was soaring; the franc had again become a hard currency; gold and foreign exchange reserves had reached robust levels.

The difficulties with the five partners in the Common Market were also close to a solution raising hopes of even greater prosperity from a new European association. Yet to revive his fading popularity General de Gaulle needed peace in Algeria. That appeared remote and unlikely. He was afraid to impose actual martial law in case the entire army went over to Salan. The OAS virtually controlled Algeria and certainly was the power behind all communications links on land, sea and in the air. No one could enter Algiers without their permission; none could leave without an OAS exit visa for some weeks. They were strongly, sometimes violently, opposed to the presence of foreign correspondents as I was to experience myself.

I spent many months in Algeria. Indeed, I visited the country countless times in the war and after 1954 covered the opening of the FLN's attack on the French authorities and *colons*. I had many good contacts among the FLN and the French. I was once escorted from Tunisia through the barbed-wire frontier of Algeria and walked through minefields to interview FLN leaders. The violence of those early days in Algiers and other main cities in the country also had its support in terrorist outrages in Tunisia and Morocco. But 1962 was probably Algeria's ugliest episode.

In February, European confidence in Salan was unshakeable even when reports circulated that a ceasefire agreement had been reached between France and the GPRA. I was lucky enough to get a scoop on the terms of the proposed agreement, which visualised the French army remaining in Algeria for a transitional period of three years and French citizens retaining their nationality during that time and then deciding whether to retain it or opt for Algerian citizenship. French property rights were to be safeguarded and French interests in the oil and gas fields of the Sahara would be recognised with prospecting remaining firmly under French control.

The terms offered no particular surprises and the OAS had already condemned any agreement as further evidence that General de Gaulle was a traitor. The European attitude was completely phlegmatic. When I asked a Frenchwoman, a strong supporter of 'Algérie Française', why she was unmoved by the prospect of a cease-fire, she said, 'We have every confidence in the General (Salan). He will not let us down and his orders are to continue living our normal lives until the cease-fire and our general strikes have been proclaimed.' A French taxi-driver, who was taking me from the Aletti Hotel where OAS agents watched the movements of all foreign correspondents, made a typical, if stupid, observation: 'Wait. Keep calm and just think that by this time next year we shall have President de Gaulle on trial as a traitor in a glass cage just like Eichmann.' The Moslem view was tempered with doubt that Ben Khedda, the GPRA leader, could accept a cease-fire when France was unable to control its army let alone the OAS. For the officers disloyal to de Gaulle operated without fear of arrest. When occasionally challenged by an OAS gunman, they openly admitted their identity and were allowed to pass on their way.

In anticipation of a formal cease-fire announcement, some forty thousand French troops were moved into the Algiers region but in Oran it was the OAS which openly controlled the centre of the capital of Western Algeria. There was no attempt to hide the fact that Salan was the real power there.

I arrived in Oran for a brief visit on a comparatively quiet day; seven Moslems and one European had been killed in sporadic attacks and two shops were bombed. The OAS had terrorised all Moslems until they had left the heart of Oran to the Europeans although memories of past battles had emptied the cafés, the large departmental stores and the hairdressers. There was only one food market open on the streets for Europeans – a street closed to traffic and with OAS thugs guarding the entrances. All the schoolchildren I saw were wearing OAS badges. The Moslem suburbs presented a very different picture. European taxi-drivers refused to enter these areas which were mostly empty as Moslems tended to stay indoors, terrified as they were of the OAS. The iron shutters of the shops were permanently pulled down so that to enter one had to bend double. Machine-gun bullets had pock-marked many walls, windows remained smashed and the blackened remains of cars straddled two cross-roads. All the rich Moslems had left the city but there were still twenty thousand Jews living there. They were well armed and they were behind the OAS. It was difficult to decide whether they had been terror-ised into supporting Salan or whether they had taken to arms as the oldest European inhabitants of Oran.

The real battleground, however, was Algiers where hatred and violence were constant companions. Soon after my arrival, within a hundred yards of where I was sitting sipping coffee, gunmen broke into a café and opened fire with sub-machine guns and seriously wounded four people.

A few nights later at the Aletti Hotel three men entered the bar at 2 a.m. One was an elegantly-dressed Parisian wearing the red ribbon of the Légion d'Honneur and the others, who were without collars and ties, were either German or Italian. The two men immediately began fingering their revolvers. After ordering drinks, they announced that they had come to shoot a French captain, who was drinking at the far end of the bar. The captain, they said, had refused an order by Salan to take command of an OAS company. Still maintaining his refusal to become a traitor, the captain bared his chest and shouted, 'Shoot me now!'

By this time, the other occupants of the bar, most of whom were foreign correspondents, were becoming alarmed, but OAS gunmen outside the bar prevented them from leaving. After an hour of drinking, arguments and tears, during which the gunmen unloaded their cartridges and re-loaded them several times, they and their victim left the hotel. The captain was told he had twenty-four hours to consider Salan's order and if he did not report for duty with the OAS he would be 'liquidated without further argument'.

Throughout the entire incident, two machine-guns were mount-ed outside the front door of the hotel to prevent anyone entering or leaving. As the gunmen disappeared into the streets, they fired their weapons indiscriminately. We never learned the fate of the captain. [I am now ashamed that I did not take action.]

In Algiers it was often confusing in any given situation to assess who was supporting whom and why. There was the night when a curfew was imposed on the heavily-populated 'poor white' European quarter of Bab-el-Oued after twenty Moslems had been shot within four hours. The French paras who went to the scene were showered with rotten eggs and tomatoes from European balconies and sometimes a chamber-pot was emptied over them. The provocation was designed apparently to turn the soldiers on any Moslems around since the Europeans never thought for an instant that French soldiers would fire on them. They would have been surprised to know that there were still some liberal-minded Frenchmen in Algiers who felt that 'a whiff of grapeshot' among the Europeans might have done a lot of good.

Bab-el-Oued was always surrounded by troops although Moslems were allowed to enter and leave the area. In the centre of this carefully patrolled *quartier* many public supporters of Salan met at the Café du Consulat. There, the landlord, Jesus (a name common among Europeans of Spanish descent) held a daily court surrounded by men who boasted they were OAS thugs. He was often visited by foreign correspondents, who found themselves on the 'mailing list' of OAS bulletins, which had been printed in Italy.

From their Oran power base, the OAS made a ruthless attempt in late February to take over Algiers itself. They killed forty-two Moslems and wounded many more over a three-day period. They evidently hoped to bring them out on to the streets in wild protest where they would be targets for both the army and OAS marksmen. The Moslems, however, remained under remarkable restraint although on the third morning of these outrages the corpse of a beheaded European was found in a sack in Bab-el-Oued where twenty Moslems had been shot in one afternoon.

Within half an hour of the gruesome discovery, ten Moslems were shot dead by gunmen firing from cars speeding down the main shopping street – rue Michelet. All the victims were sellers of fruit, vegetables and flowers and they were all known as like-able, harmless characters. One of the dead was a veiled Moslem woman, the first to be killed by terrorists in the latest outburst of violence. That afternoon I watched French paratroops move in force in armoured cars into rue Michelet, a rather late development which was emphasised by the failure to clean away two large pools of blood on the pavements.

The appearance of the paras was 'Operation Super Valentine',

which was designed supposedly to protect the civilian population. As many officers and men remained committed to 'Algérie
Française' it was clear that they followed a policy of inertia in
implementing law and order. The troops obeyed orders – just.
Although they patrolled the streets in armoured cars they were
often far from the spot of an act of terrorism or if they did happen
to be close to a bomb attack or a sudden burst of fire they either
looked in the other direction or departed at some speed.

This was symptomatic of the military attitude in Algiers and
Oran. Many officers would have joined Salan without hesitation
if they thought he had a chance of winning the struggle in Algeria
but without that guarantee they stayed in the army to be sure of
their pay and pension. Outside the army there were, however,
many loyalists among the police, the anti-riot squads and, in
particular, the navy.

Covering the Algerian scene was somewhat dangerous and
difficult for all foreign correspondents. They were liable to be
shot at from all sides and unravelling the truth in a complex
political situation was highly frustrating. But I had excellent
contacts among the FLN, who operated from the Casbah, that
walled warren of twisting streets where Moslems lived well away
from OAS gunmen. One morning I left the Aletti to buy some
soap, laundries having ceased to function. I walked down the
street of Bab Azoun, which has arches on either side not unlike
those in the rue de Rivoli in Paris. The street bordered the Casbah
and the atmosphere was uneasy, with some shops open, others
closed. French troops guarded the street corners with fingers on
the triggers of their sub-machine guns.

A car passed. There was a shot and a Moslem shopkeeper
dropped from his doorway, mortally wounded. The police did
not blow their whistles, the troops did not fire at the fleeting
car, which they could have hit easily, but one did try to comfort
an hysterical European woman on the other side of the street.

The dead shopkeeper was a friendly acquaintance who had in
happier times given me small cups of sweet black coffee. By his
silence or his smile and through the position of his shutters (fully
up suggested no tension, half-way up an uncertain atmosphere,
nearly down danger), he indicated to me in a general way every
morning what he thought of the current political scene. Moments
after he was killed there came another fast car, a shot, and another

Moslem shopkeeper was dead.

I did not go into the Casbah that day. I was warned off by a Moslem and that was good advice. It may seem that I have often taken risks but that is not altogether true. There was an afternoon when I invited Tom Pocock of the *Evening Standard* to come for a walk. We approached the dangerous streets between Bab-el-Oued and the Casbah and stopped at a narrow alley that vanished into the Arab quarter. Barbed wire half-blocked the pathway. I said, 'That looks interesting.'

'Don't be mad,' Pocock replied. 'Up there we'd both be killed – and for what?'

I shrugged. 'Very well,' I said. 'Something might well happen to you but I'd just get slops emptied over me.'

We returned to the Aletti. I left Pocock and, of course, returned alone to that street and strode into the Casbah.

When I met Pocock later he wanted to know where I had gone and I told him. He was amazed. So I said, somewhat pointedly, 'You do not know but I go into the Casbah every afternoon. I have good contacts among the FLN. Perhaps one thing that I have achieved in Algeria by my reporting is to give a respectability to the Arab nationalists.'

Certainly the Casbah was sometimes dangerous and frequently the scene of death and destruction. I remember seeing the body of a French soldier, a member of the colonial forces of Zouaves, being brought out after he had been stabbed to death. He was carried to an ambulance as his comrades wept. Then I saw French troops kicking and punching Moslems who had gathered to see what had happened. The troops turned on merchants and overturned market stalls, scattering pots, pans and wares across the street. Many Arabs were beaten up that day and later in the mixed quarter of the Clos Solembia, Moslem gunmen opened fire from a car and killed a French soldier and wounded another.

Admittedly, I never felt entirely safe wandering into the Casbah, not because I feared the Moslems so much as being tailed by the OAS, who most certainly did not like me at all. They had broken into my hotel, torn up all my clothes and underwear and smashed up everything in sight, including my typewriter. They threatened me frequently with telephone calls, saying, 'Get out or we will get you!' Occasionally, typed notes were left warning me to stop writing 'treachery for the Manchester Guardian'.

The strange relationship between the OAS and foreign correspondents reached crisis point early in March when they ordered an Italian reporter to leave Algiers within twenty-four hours or be shot.

'It's the Italians today, tomorrow it will be the turn of the British correspondents, and then the Americans.' That was how it was put to me by an OAS commando, a thug with an open-necked shirt and a pistol in his pocket, as he marched Alberto Giovanni of *La Stampa* from the bar of the Aletti just before dinner on 3 March.

He was helped by another armed thug and they themselves were protected by eight OAS gunmen wearing their uniform of leather coats and blue trousers. Giovanni was taken in a truck to a place where an OAS tribunal was secretly meeting. His escorts told him that he was to be executed. The OAS leaders complained of 'false news about the OAS' in the Italian Press and on the radio. They offered to spare Giovanni's life on condition that all Italian newspapermen and radio workers left Algiers immediately. 'If not, you will be shot at once,' they said.

Giovanni returned to the hotel, frightened and ready to leave the following day. French police were called in but they acted like theatrical props doing absolutely nothing. Giovanni had just lifted the much-needed brandy to his lips when another OAS truck arrived to take him away again.

This time another Italian journalist, Nicolo Caracciola, rushed to a French major, a former parachutist, who was sitting in the bar with a mixed party. Caracciola begged the major to stop the second kidnapping but the officer said it was nothing to do with him and remained unmoved by the situation. Caracciola pleaded again and received the same reply.

'I compliment the French army,' the journalist snapped with acid contempt.

The jibe inflamed the major, who attacked Caracciola and knocked him down on to the stone floor of the hotel's reception hall. Then, in front of my eyes, he kicked the fallen journalist.

Two British journalists, John Wallis of the *Daily Telegraph* and a friend, offered to go with the OAS thugs and Giovanni. They all left in the truck escorted by armed motor cyclists. The British reporters told the OAS that they harmed their cause by using such violence against the press and they returned soon after trying in a diplomatic manner to excuse the kidnappings by saying that the OAS thugs were drunk. That was certainly not my impression.

The next morning eleven Italian journalists left for Rome. Caracciola was the only one who stayed, saying he would not be intimidated by the OAS thugs. He demanded an official letter of apology from the outlawed General Salan or at least one of his staff.

Little good did it do him. That night an OAS commando arrived at the Aletti seeking Caracciola, who immediately went into hiding by closeting himself in the rooms of other journalists while the OAS thugs hustled through the corridors looking for him.

They were followed apparently by men in OAS uniform but who turned out to be police. They ordered all eighty foreign correspondents into the main hall where we were told to raise our hands while our identities were checked. They, too, were after the missing Italian journalist. I was extremely annoyed at this treatment and I told their commander in French, 'Go away at once, monsieur, or I will have to hit you over the head with my shoe, which is all I have.' This was not bravado – I was absolutely furious.

I was then pushed to one side and the French commander said, 'Very well, we will take him.' He grabbed the arm of another British reporter and dragged him towards the front door of the hotel.

Without really thinking, I shouted, 'Come on! Let's all go too!' And we all poured outside, wanting to free our colleague in the hope that those gunmen whoever they were would not open fire on a crowd of international reporters. The hostage was thrown back among us, the trucks were revved up and then we heard the click of safety catches. Someone shouted, 'Down! They're going to shoot!'

We all hit the ground together. But the shots were never fired. The police and the OAS drove off, leaving us to climb to our feet feeling rather self-satisfied, I suppose, that we had saved two colleagues from mysterious officialdom.

However, I was not prepared to leave the situation there. The following night I tracked down a man who was one of the senior OAS organisers. He explained that the previous evening's

incident was the unauthorised work of one drunken OAS commando. He said that the OAS leadership had apologised to the
Italians although the organisation was mainly anti-Italian because
it believed that the Italian industrialist, Signor Enrico Mattei, had
obtained a major concession from the rebel government to exploit
the oil reserves in the Sahara. Mattei had denied the story but the
OAS remained unconvinced.

I returned without incident to the Aletti to concentrate on
the real news. The whole of Algiers seemed at that time to
be packed with troops. I watched them standing idly by as
new OAS posters were being stuck on hoardings. The caption
read: 'Wanted for murder. President de Gaulle and his club of
barbouzes.' Underneath was a picture of General de Gaulle with
photographs of eight barbouzes – an anti-OAS group – giving
their names and aliases, four of whom had a cloth over their
faces indicating that they had already been assassinated.

That weekend knife, gun and bomb attacks resulted in many
more deaths throughout Algeria. And European gunmen continued their raids on banks, business houses and military posts,
picking up millions of francs as well as hauls of guns and
ammunition.

More terrorist outrages accompanied by calculated confusion
marked the first half of March as French and Algerian nationalist emissaries met at Evian on the Swiss border to try to reach
a ceasefire agreement. The OAS intensified its poster campaign
with placards pasted on walls in Algiers and Oran threatening
that any citizen paying taxes would risk assassination and any
tax collector who accepted them could expect the same fate. This
created predictable consternation among the French civil servants
at Rocher Noir, the new administrative centre the French had built
outside Algiers to avoid pressure and terrorism.

There was no doubt that OAS tactics were well conceived
and carried out with great efficiency.

One morning, Algiers was shaken by explosions, mortar and
machine-gun fire along a twenty-mile front from Maison Carrée
to Guyotville, an operation which could not have been carried
out according to a senior French officer I knew without the
acquiescence or even collaboration of certain elements of the
police and army. Nevertheless, the latest attacks were executed
brilliantly with confusion arising from the appearance of OAS

gunmen wearing stolen army uniforms.

Almost all of the attacks were directed against Moslems and their property. About sixty lock-up shops in the centre of Algiers were completely destroyed. The Moslems accepted their losses with pathetic resignation. Many asked the same question: 'What are we to do? Use up what remains of our small capital in rebuilding the business or move out, which is what the OAS want?' In the mixed Moslem and European middle-class outer suburbs, householders told the same story of telephoning the police for help when the explosions rocked their neighbourhoods and all without exception complained that it took the police two hours to reach them. Since so many Moslem middle-class homes were attacked it seemed clear that the OAS were concentrating on clearing them out so that Europeans could take over their property for practically nothing.

In Oran at the same time a gang of OAS commandos dynamited the civil prison in the centre of the city, killing more than forty Moslems and wounding more than two hundred. It was an act of exceptional daring.

An OAS agent hid inside a prison van returning to the jail and, immediately the gates closed behind it, he hopped out, held up the guards, opened the gates and signalled to six vehicles packed with his comrades. They planted a huge dynamite charge and several gas cylinders beside the cells, poured petrol over walls and floors. Then they exploded the dynamite and opened fire with machine-guns on the flaming buildings. They left without haste closing the gates behind them.

The next morning in Algiers an Arab was found hanged in Bab-el-Oued with a card dangling from his neck. It said: 'I killed, but the OAS were watching.'

With this kind of violence threatening the Evian cease-fire talks, the moderate elements in Algiers were hoping for the imposition of martial law but this was, of course, out of the question. The French administration regarded the proposition as dangerous and untenable since it might well persuade many military units to give their full support to Salan and try to instal him as military governor of Algiers. The OAS claimed to have considerable support in that part of the army which was officially loyal to General de Gaulle. It maintained that many officers had offered their services to Salan, who had told them to return to their units and await his orders. There was little doubt in my mind that this boast could be substantiated and that the so-called loyal units were from time to time operating for the OAS. There were signs, too, that the OAS was moving towards abrogating various functions of the State not only by its anti-tax campaign but by over-stamping bank notes with its initials. It announced that an OAS office would be opened in Geneva to maintain contact with the outside world and issue visas for people wishing to visit Algeria.

The OAS was, after all, in virtual control of the entire country through its reign of terror. In the French naval base of Mers-el-Kebir there were savage clashes between Europeans and Moslems after a French mother and her two children were murdered. Arabs armed with knives and hatchets were invading the caretaker's quarters in the local football stadium when they saw the mother with her little boy and girl nearby. They cut her down as she tried to protect her children. Then they smashed the skull of the little boy and chased the girl into a garden where they beat her to death. She was found in a pool of blood, clutching a bunch of geraniums. When the news of these barbarous attacks spread through the town, youths armed with clubs charged through the streets of the Moslem quarter seeking vengeance. They beat one Moslem to death before marines from the naval base intervened and, in the wild scrambles that ensued, the marines shot dead three fleeing Moslems.

The OAS tactics that followed these outrages were unexpected and more subtle than usual. Instead of open violence, they warned the Moslem population that if it did not support a European demonstration against General de Gaulle their jobs and, indeed, their lives would be in danger. And so for the first time in two years the two communities joined in a march through the streets of Mers-el-Kebir carrying the tricolour and shouting 'Algérie Française' and singing the Marsellaise. About two thousand Moslems joined the demonstration. Most of them lived on the hilly slopes near the docks and below the homes of Europeans, an area Moslems had to cross whenever leaving their district.

Finally, the long-awaited political breakthrough came on Sunday, 18 March with the announcement in Evian that a ceasefire agreement had been reached. General de Gaulle broadcast an appeal for support but a pirate broadcast by Salan from Oran blacked out the President's words. Salan called on the French army to mutiny and join the OAS; he denounced the ceasefire as 'a crime against the history of our nation'.

In the Casbah, there were a few cries of 'Yu, Yu', the Moslem form of cheering, when they heard General de Gaulle's first words but once his picture vanished from television screens and his words were drowned by Salan, the shutters were slammed shut and the streets emptied.

I toured the city by car that night. There were only a few troops to be seen but the beat of 'Algérie Française' could be heard from behind the shutters of European apartments.

The OAS had made its preparations well. The crackle of gunfire soon after dawn the next day and three bomb explosions hailed their general strike and the breakdown of all utility services. The OAS had already warned Europeans to keep off the streets so that their commandos would have clear fields of fire against Arabs venturing from their homes. Salan also announced the formation of a political body calling itself the National Council of French Resistance, which claimed to be the moral heir to the Free French Council, which General de Gaulle presided over in London during the war. A document circulated in Algiers on that first day of the ceasefire proclaiming that the council had deposed General de Gaulle because he had ruled France through a coterie in disregard of both the spirit and the law of the French Constitution. The council declared itself faithful to that Constitution, in particular to the provision that the Head of State must protect the integrity of the territory. It also reaffirmed its determination to continue to fight against the Algerian rebels until they were finally defeated. To this end, the council appointed Salan as commander-in-chief of land, air and sea forces. One of the points of the declaration was a passage denouncing Jewish banking firms like Rothschilds and Lazard Frères as being only interested in retaining revenue from the oil fields and being completely indifferent to keeping Algeria French.

The war actually ended with a 'flash' signal from the French commander-in-chief in Algeria, General Charles Ailleret, to every unit to stop military operations. In an order of the day, he told the army that it could be 'proud of the success brought about by its arms'. The order described the insurgents as an 'always courageous adversary'.

In the Casbah, a minute's silence was observed when seventy

thousand Moslems stood with their heads covered in a gesture of respect for those who had lost their lives in the seven-year rebellion. The OAS general strike made it unnecessary for the Moslems to leave their enclave to go to work and the shops, cafés and markets were busier than usual with only one subject on everyone's lips.

I went into the Casbah to find that the dustbins had not been emptied for three days so the streets were ankle deep in refuse. An FLN NCO guided me through the alleys and up a darkened staircase to a room where I met the central committee of the underground FLN. All eight men were well-dressed and proud of the discipline they had maintained among Moslems in the Casbah. But not a single FLN flag was visible anywhere and no one sang the national songs. There were no outward signs of celebration. The committee members said that they were content with the ceasefire but there would be no festivities until *istiqual* – independence – had been achieved. I was given hot bread to eat and other food to take away as the Aletti had ceased to provide food or water or service of any sort.

But the calm of the Casbah was soon shattered. On the afternoon of 20 March, five three-inch OAS mortar shells were lobbed on to a Moslem crowd in the Place du Gouvernement, close to the main entrance to the Casbah. I arrived there soon after the explosions. A lawyer, who was having his shoes cleaned by one of the many shoe-shine boys, gave me this description which was published the next day in the *Guardian*:

'After the shells fell, the wounded and everyone else ran from the spot in panic. This rush of bleeding and wounded people set up a second panic. Some firing took place.

'I don't quite know how it started but a crowd of Moslems who had rushed into a street, the exit of which was blocked, were certainly fired on by a soldier and two Moslems in the crowd were killed.

'In a crowded street nearby, a harka (Moslem soldier in French service) began threatening to shoot when a French major who is in charge of the defences of the Casbah and well-known and liked by the population there snatched the revolver from the harka, smacked his face and ordered him back to barracks. He then shouted to the Moslems, "Obey your own orders and not mine – go home." The major then chose two likely-looking youths

168

from the crowd and said, "Get cracking, get your people off the streets and into their houses." '

Moslems were ordering people back into the Casbah when I reached the spot and those who did not obey were given a sharp cuff on the ear. Four taxis, a private car and several food stalls were destroyed by the mortars and pools of blood amid the wrecked vehicles and a stained bread basket were no less moving sights because they had become common over many months. The mortars which were stolen from the French army had a range of about one thousand yards so they could have been fired from Bab-el-Oued. I walked towards the European quarter and went into a bar for a much-needed brandy. A group of Europeans were drinking the health of Salan and I heard one comment: 'We have shown them we are there and they never know when we shall strike by day or night.'

Until that abominable incident, Algiers had been remarkably quiet. Helicopters had been dropping leaflets, which outlined the ceasefire terms and portrayed a Moslem and a European walking side by side towards a splendid and happy future depicted on the horizon by a house, a motor car and a plough.

I had seen Europeans who had picked up the leaflets beaten over the head by men, who tore them up on the spot. But some Europeans were disappointed that the leaflets did not contain some message of explanation or encouragement from the OAS. Even outside police headquarters this sentiment was openly voiced. The guard on duty boasted to me of his intimate ties with the OAS and made excuses for the failure of Salan to carry out his sensational threat to seize Algiers completely in the event of a ceasefire. Many of the Europeans of Bab-el-Oued were frankly dismayed by what they saw as inaction by the OAS. One woman put it this way: 'The OAS have not yet lit a gigantic fire around the Casbah with all the Moslems inside.'

To counteract this feeling the OAS issued a crop of posters, one parodying that walk into a happy future by marking the sand dunes in the picture with crosses and pillars marking Moslem and Christian graves. One grave was labelled 'M. Dupont' and another 'Mohammed' and the slogan underneath declared: 'They did it for nothing.'

Salan then played his final card with desperate ferocity. This arrogant ex-general, bolstered by European support in Algeria, really believed that he could undermine the power of Paris. He gravely misjudged General de Gaulle, who had been playing a waiting game by establishing the foundation of peace while making preparations to crush the European opposition if it finally refused to accept his formula for the future of Algeria.

On the night of 22 March, the OAS launched a massive attack on government buildings in Algiers and Oran. Bursts of bazooka, mortar and machine-gun fire were concentrated around the Summer Palace, the former residence of the delegate-general which overlooked Algiers.

It was the first phase of Salan's threatened war against the French army. Much of the OAS fire came from Bab-el-Oued and soon after dawn the next day, French Army helicopters were buzzing low over the European quarter dropping flares to pinpoint rebel positions for the besieging forces.

The army was represented by a mixed force: red-bereted paras – once the darling of the local population – commandos, infantry, gendarmerie and mobile police who were supported in the air by ten helicopters and four fighter aircraft. At dawn the forces went into a small section of apartment buildings to search out OAS gunmen while residents threw Molotov cocktails from their windows on to passing armoured cars. At street corners thick oil and broken glass were spread across the roads to hamper troop movements. Scattered fighting continued throughout the day with angry Europeans leaning over balconies and rooftops for a bird's-eye view of the operations. They all disappeared quickly enough when helicopters clattered across the area only a few feet above them.

It was thought initially that French troops would hesitate to fire on their countrymen but undoubtedly their resolve to try to bring some law and order to Salan's calculated chaos was stiffened by General de Gaulle's declaration to his cabinet that day that the armed insurrection had to be pitilessly repressed.

By the end of the ensuing weekend it was pretty clear that his forces were taking control of the situation and they arrested eight hundred Europeans in Bab-el-Oued, from which the OAS had escaped with large quantities of arms. Even so the searching gendarmerie and riot units uncovered big caches of arms, including rocket launchers and heavy machine-guns, as they burst down the front doors of European homes, broke open cupboards and even dug up tiled floors.

The position of the poor whites of the European quarter was pitiable. They were certain to lose their jobs once independence arrived and many feared for their lives. Few had ever visited France and they all had no wish to settle on the mainland. But any sympathy for their ultimate fate vanished quickly once they revealed their true character as colonial rulers. I saw a Roman Catholic bishop trying to make arrangements for the evacuation of the wounded during that bloody weekend. He was jeered and spat upon from the crowded balconies as a lackey of General de Gaulle. He eventually left the scene amid a volley of unrepeatable abuse.

For the first time, however, Salan himself was being vilified in Bab-el-Oued for failing to launch an action in another part of the capital to take the pressure off the European quarter. Many Europeans knew instinctively that their cause was lost although they all agreed that the rebel general must have had more diabolical tricks up his sleeve. The latest OAS documents were particularly interesting since they were no longer calling for an all-out war against the French armed forces. The newest pamphlets, scattered in their thousands, urged French troops: 'If you are ordered to fire, do so wide of the target; if you are searching for arms, close your eyes; if you are told to seal off an area, allow people to pass.'

The authorities had sealed off Bab-el-Oued but the OAS were calling on the Europeans in Algiers to march on the quarter to express support and sympathy. Thousands defied the government order by gathering in a street leading to Bab-el-Oued and marched down it, over-running flimsy barbed wire barriers. A group of soldiers was forced back and their young officer was demanding, almost hysterically, over his walkie-talkie phone orders from his headquarters. Suddenly, there was a shot from a balcony in the rue d'Isly.

The hard-pressed troops opened fire in all directions, believing they were under imminent attack. Other army units joined in, ignoring shouts from their officers to stop shooting. In a few moments, the dead and dying were lying in heaps on the roadway. As the firing spread across the city, I saw groups of young OAS youths making theatrical attempts to storm barbed wire barricades manned by gendarmerie and anti-riot squads. These foolhardy youngsters demanded to be shot on the spot but their melodramatic display and other attempts to inflame the security forces completely failed.

Everyone knew at that time in late March that it was only a matter of weeks before the OAS would be crushed despite their calls 'to fight to the death'. Bab-el-Oued was outwardly cut off by the army although I had no difficulty in getting in almost effortlessly by climbing through broken windows to assess the latest reaction from the beleaguered Europeans.

An OAS general strike added to the misery of Algiers which quickly became a dead city, but so did all the small towns within one hundred miles with large European populations. They were soon shuttered and deserted. The French army blockade of Bab-el-Oued lasted five days and certainly subdued the inhabitants.

Europeans in Algiers at last began to admit that the power of the OAS had been broken by the French security forces. A European café owner expressed the attitude of most whites: 'We are proceeding as though we were millionaires. Who else could afford to have maintained a general strike since Friday? Having made our protest about the treatment of our brothers in Bab-el-Oued and the massacre of Europeans in the rue d'Isly we should like to go back to work. But the OAS refuses to allow this and we Europeans are still far more frightened of the OAS than we are of poverty or hunger.'

Politically, there was progress on the Moslem front. The FLN leaders recognised the governing committee for Algeria inside the Casbah, whose members were in contact with the provisional Algerian government and those areas of the country where the FLN had already taken control of the administration and considered they were responsible for law and order.

In the end, the OAS collapsed with singular speed. Bombs continued to claim lives in the weeks ahead, but the arrest of Salan in Algiers at the end of April marked the last phase of one of the bloodiest eras in French history. Subsequently, I covered the trial of Salan in Paris. He and three other generals were sentenced to life imprisonment but within a decade they had all been pardoned and freed under amnesties proclaimed by General de Gaulle. Salan died in 1984.

After a brief break from the war, I returned to Algeria to report a visit General de Gaulle made to review the terms and prospects for independence and the future prosperity of the country.

He travelled to the small town of Tlemcen in the north-west as part of a provincial tour. While he was visiting the town hall for a pre-lunch apèritif, a hostile crowd of Arabs gathered in the adjoining square, chanting: 'À-bas de Gaulle'.

When he emerged and walked down the town hall steps into the square he was beaming and because he was rather deaf, he obviously did not hear the angry cries. He got into his car and then realised that the reception was hostile. He heard what the Arabs were shouting. General de Gaulle told his bodyguard to open the car door. The officer protested. 'Non, non, non, mon président.'

'Ouvrez la porte!' General de Gaulle ordered. 'Moi, je suis le président!'

The car door was opened. The President got out and strode into the centre of those angry Arabs. Fists were raised. Head and shoulders above the mob, General de Gaulle spoke to the Arabs pushing around him. A phrase of French, a few quiet words in Arabic. I could not hear exactly what he said but it was quite plain that the magic of this remarkable man completely calmed and won over the demonstrators.

After twenty minutes in that hot square, he started to return to his car. The fists that had been shaken against him grabbed his hands. When he bent to enter his car I saw that they were wet with the spittle of Arab kisses.

My companion on that trip, Joseph Alsop of the *New York Times*, was so overcome by the emotion of it all that he sat on the kerb and burst into tears.

11 Donald and Melinda Maclean ...
The Kim Philby 'third man' scoop ...

On 25 May 1951, Donald Maclean and Guy de Moncy Burgess, Foreign Office diplomats, defected to Russia and created the biggest spy scandal Britain had ever known. They were tipped off that the security forces were on their track by H. A. 'Kim' Philby, a top Foreign Office official and traitor, who became known as the 'third man' and who escaped to Russia in a Soviet freighter from Beirut on 23 January 1963. On 11 September 1953, Mrs Melinda Maclean, and her children, Fergus, aged nine, Donald, seven, and two-year-old Melinda, left their Geneva home on a secret journey to re-join Donald Maclean in Moscow. A close associate of the diplomat spies was Sir Anthony Blunt, former Surveyor of the Queen's Pictures, who was stripped of his knighthood in 1979 for spying for Russia. Blunt, who had been a senior member of MI5, Britain's spy-catching organisation, was a director of the Courtauld Institute, an acknowledged expert on Poussin and a highly respected art historian. He died in disgrace in 1983, aged 75. Guy Burgess died in Moscow in 1963. Twenty years later, Donald Maclean died in the Soviet capital. Philby survived until 1988, when he died in his apartment in Moscow. I did not know Burgess or Blunt but I did know Maclean, his wife, and Philby, very well. Today, Melinda is living incognito in the United States.

Geoffrey and I first met Donald and Melinda Maclean in 1948 at a dinner party given by Sir Bernard Burrows and his amusing wife at their house in Bayswater when they were helping them to prepare for diplomatic life in Cairo. Donald Maclean had just been appointed first secretary and head of chancery. We liked them both. Melinda appeared to Geoffrey to be charming but lacking in self-confidence while Donald was posing as a strong, silent man interested in all we had to say about Egyptian politics.

My husband had edited the *Egyptian Gazette* before the war and remained to cover the desert campaigns, the civil war in Greece and as Middle East correspondent of *The Times*. He was now about to return to Cairo as the Middle East correspondent of the *News Chronicle*.

We arranged to meet the Macleans in Cairo after a few weeks. In fact we lived very close and our rear gardens abutted with a gate leading through to the Macleans' property. Geoffrey and I were living in the British Consul-General's house while he was away for six months. We 'chaperoned' his charming daughter, who had just obtained a job. For the first time in my life I was well looked after because I had five servants, which is just about right for me!

Maclean was on top of the world in his new milieu and for him life was marvellous. He found work in the embassy agreeable and he was doing extremely well there. At the age of thirty-six he was perhaps a rather carelessly-dressed figure, often slumping into a deep armchair with one leg flopping over the other, the free foot jerking constantly. He frequently commented on the obtuseness of many of his colleagues with humorous cynicism. He appeared to take a slightly condescending, mocking view of his wife but on the surface their relationship was certainly amicable. They both liked to visit us when there were no compulsory diplomatic parties and talk politics over bridge although Melinda's interest in foreign affairs was decidedly limited.

She was a vivacious personality, shrugging off her husband's occasional disparaging remarks. Since her arrival in Cairo she had acquired a new sense of confidence; it was striking when she entertained the Duke of Edinburgh at her home. He was visiting Cairo briefly and staying at the British Embassy. Officialdom felt that the heavy list of engagements might be given a light-hearted touch and Melinda was asked at short notice to arrange a young people's party for him.

Twelve members of Cairo's younger set were invited to dine with the Duke at the Macleans' abode with Melinda acting as hostess. Other guests arrived later. It was a most successful evening enlivened with rather juvenile games like 'murder'.

In the following weeks, Maclean developed a noticeable aversion to Egypt, particularly the contrast between its awful poverty and the wealth of the arrogant ruling élite. The intense round of social obligations bored him. Britain's policy of non-interference irritated him as he was openly advocating pressure from London to persuade the Egyptian government to institute much-needed reforms. That alone, he declared, could save the country from communism.

That was the only allusion he ever made to communism in the company of Geoffrey and myself. Yet in a most clever, even wily, way he influenced British policy in the Middle East to complement Russia's line of approach. Moscow favoured a pro-Zionist policy and Maclean was certainly a Zionist in those days.

At the end of the summer my husband had to go to Pakistan and during his absence for two or three months it became clear that Maclean had a drink problem. When he was drunk in the evenings after dinner he acquired homosexual tendencies and would chase the servants from one bedroom to another. They complained bitterly to me about his sexual advances and, at first, I found their tales difficult to believe. But, eventually, I caught him actually playing this game and could well understand their pleadings that he should not be allowed upstairs in our house.

Melinda put a brave face on it all. She liked life in Cairo and by this time had plenty of friends of her own. She also fell into a nervous silence when her drunken husband expressed his strong feelings against King Farouk and criticised the British government and its foreign policies. Geoffrey was very sympathetic towards her but much later admitted to me that he felt she had taken him in and knew far, far more than she dared to reveal.

Maclean's drunkenness worsened but his condition was kept from the Ambassador, Sir Ronald Campbell, who was rather fond of him. Heavy drinking, in any case, was not unknown at the embassy. Matters became even more critical when Philip Toynbee, son of Arnold Toynbee, arrived in Cairo as correspondent of the *Observer*. Toynbee, who was then suffering after a traumatic divorce, stayed with the Macleans and Melinda was immediately thrown out of the matrimonial suite and took refuge with the children, Fergus and Donald, on the floor above. The two men roamed the nightclubs carousing and indulging in drunken orgies. Melinda often cried on Geoffrey's shoulder and frequently related to me how the two men behaved, sometimes being brought home from the centre of Cairo roaring drunk.

The crisis came at an official reception at King Farouk's Palace. It was, of course, a formal affair demanding white tie and decorations. But Maclean and Toynbee arrived in scruffy clothes they had been wearing all day. Melinda was not with them.

The grand stairway was lined with ladies-in-waiting – pretty Egyptian girls spaced at every few yards looking charming in their long graceful dresses. Up the stairs came Maclean and Toynbee. They paused to stand in a corner of the stairs where they urinated openly in front of the girls. Then they joined the party where they brazenly teased a secretary from the US Embassy before leaving to continue their drunken binge.

At 4 a.m. they were knocking at the flat of the American secretary. She opened the door wearing a nightdress and when she saw the two men she grabbed a dressing-gown and escaped upstairs to a friend's flat. Maclean and Toynbee burst into her apartment, finished off all the whisky and gin in her sideboard cupboard and then, with a hammer, set about smashing everything in sight: tables, chairs, ornaments, pictures, the bidet and lavatory basin. Then they fell across her bed in a drunken stupor.

Meanwhile, friends of the American secretary had telephoned Melinda, who appealed to Geoffrey for help. The US ambassador was informed and at breakfast-time he contacted Sir Ronald Campbell and told him that the two men were still unconscious in the secretary's apartment. Geoffrey arranged for Maclean and Toynbee to be carried home. The American envoy told his counterpart that if Maclean was not sent back to London at once the matter would be reported to the Egyptian authorities. Apparently, Sir Ronald had been quite oblivious that for some time Maclean had been late for work, smelled of drink and spent most of the day asleep at his desk. It was arranged that Maclean should return to Britain the following day on the grounds that he was on the verge of a nervous breakdown and needed medical treatment.

What Sir Ronald did not know was that there had been an earlier drunken affair, which had been hushed up.

Donald and Melinda with some friends, including Lees Mayall
– whose wife was Mary Ormsby-Gore, sister of Lord Harlech –
sailed up the Nile to a dinner being given for Melinda's sister,
Harriet, who was visiting them. There was plenty of whisky and
gin on board but no food and, owing to a sudden change in the
wind, the boat made but little progress and the journey expected
to last two hours at most, took about six. Donald drank and
drank and attacked Melinda in a frenzy when she attempted to
take the bottle away from him. When they eventually arrived at
their destination a night watchman shouted questions at them
from the shore. Maclean then jumped off the boat and beat him
up. As Lees Mayall moved to protect the night watchman Maclean
literally leapt at him and quite deliberately broke his leg – badly.
Their hosts had given them up and gone to bed so, although the
hullabaloo awoke them, it took a long time to organise transport
to take the injured diplomat to hospital.

This story never came to the ears of the British Ambassador.
However, he acted swiftly after the orgy in the American secretary's apartment. Melinda and Toynbee accompanied Maclean
to Cairo airport to see him off. Toynbee, still half drunk, was
shouting, 'Goodbye, Sir Donald. Thank God I am a journalist
and can get drunk without being recalled.'
By extraordinary chance, Geoffrey was on that airliner that
brought Maclean back to London. Maclean was sober on the
plane and on arrival in London he went to the Foreign Office to
see George Middleton, who was then head of personnel. From
his mother's house in Kensington, Maclean wrote a letter to
Melinda:

'. . . I am tucked away in the womb very comfortably . . .
George Middleton was very understanding and has fixed for
me to see a Dr Wilson tomorrow morning, who is said to be
a leading psychiatrist and who the FO employ as a consultant
when their employees' psyches miss a beat. I still have my lid
off and I am prepared therefore to ask help . . .
'I am grateful to you my sweet for taking all you have
had to put up with without hating me. I am still rather lost,
but cling to the idea that you do want me to be cured and
come back. I am leary of making promises of being a better

husband, since past ones have all been broken; but perhaps if some technician will strengthen my gasket and enlarge my heart I could make a promise which would stick . . .'

But Maclean refused Dr Wilson's advice to enter a clinic and approached a private psychiatrist, who treated him by analysis over six months. It was by no means an intensive course of treatment, but Maclean apparently enjoyed these occasional trips to the psychiatric couch and they did him some good for a time. By the end of the treatment, however, he was turning up for those chats with bottles of whisky in his overcoat pockets.

He was pronounced fit for work when the six months' treatment was completed although he was advised to continue having psychiatric care. This he ignored completely.

Back in Cairo, I was alone with Melinda who had thrown Toynbee out of her house. He seemed very angry about this even though her mother, Mrs Dunbar, and other members of the family were coming to stay with her. It appeared to many of us that at that moment the Maclean marriage was at an end.

With Geoffrey away, I saw a good deal of Melinda who was relieved when her mother paid all the bills and took over responsibility for the house. She encouraged Melinda to buy clothes and continue to live a social life. However, by the beginning of July it was clear that Maclean was not returning to Cairo as some embassy officials had suggested earlier. So Melinda packed her belongings and took the children with Mrs Dunbar to spend the summer in Spain. Maclean joined her there and begged her to take him back, promising that he would give up alcohol and 'young boys'. That summer of 1950 she became pregnant.

Maclean returned to London and began drinking heavily again. His appearance was described by relatives as 'frightening'. Early in September, Melinda received a desperately sad letter from him; she doubted that she could ever take him back, but she flew immediately to London, leaving the children with her mother. In London she talked not only with her husband but with his mother and the psychiatrist. They convinced her that alone he would be completely lost. With some misgivings, she agreed to resume married life.

She persuaded him to live in the country and they moved to Beaconshaw, a rather large and isolated house at Tatsfield near

Chartwell, in Kent. She told me that the first two or three months there were among the happiest of her life. But by the following spring Donald had reverted to his old drunken habits. He often vanished for several days at a time. One of his acquaintances was Guy Burgess, who was also known to be a heavy drinker and a homosexual, who had been sent back from Washington, where he was second secretary at the British Embassy, in disgrace.

Burgess was violently anti-American and he was under suspicion by the British security forces. He was planning to avoid dismissal from the diplomatic service by resigning in the hope of being taken on as a diplomatic correspondent for the *Daily Telegraph*. This never materialised and he remained at the Foreign Office. There was no evidence that his meetings with Maclean were more than casual. They were not close friends although at Cambridge they had been members of the same left-wing groups.

In May 1951, when Melinda's sister, Harriet, was staying at Beaconshaw she noticed how deeply worried Maclean appeared to be. Quite by surprise one day, he suggested openly that he was a communist. He railed bitterly against his life and his job, mocked himself as a sheep among hordes of other sheep going off to London every day with a black hat and briefcase. He claimed that he was sick of it all and longed to 'cut adrift'. But in those days he did not talk so wildly to his wife. When I later visited the house I noticed that most of the books in Donald's study were about Russia. The subjects ranged over classical Russian novels and histories to the works of Marx and the revolutionaries. There were books on Soviet architecture, music, literature, the theatre and the ballet. There was one entitled *How Beautiful It Is To Live On A Collective Farm*. They were all dated in his late 'teens and early twenties and they had all been well read.

With Maclean's birthday on 25 May in view, Melinda baked a special cake and planned a quiet dinner with him at home. But the previous day, he told her that a friend of his would be dining with them on his birthday evening. The man's name, Roger Styles, meant nothing to Melinda and she was annoyed that her plans had been upset. Maclean arrived home for his thirty-eighth anniversary at the usual time before his guest arrived.

He told Melinda, 'After dinner Roger and I have to go out on business. I shall take a few things in case we have to spend the night away.' She protested and, very upset, she followed him into their bedroom where he was packing his pyjamas and shaving gear into his briefcase. She begged him not to go. Did he not realise how much she had wanted the evening with him to themselves? How could he now talk of departing with an unknown friend and leaving her alone? Did he not understand that with her relatives arriving the next day for the weekend there were numerous household chores such as making up more beds that she could not manage on her own? Maclean replied that he had to go – and Melinda stormed out of the bedroom.

Their voices awakened Fergus. He got out of bed and went into his parent's bedroom. 'Why are you going away, Daddy?' he asked. 'Can I stand at the window and watch you go?'

Donald answered, 'You get back into your bed, you little scamp. I'm not going far; I shall be back soon.'

Guy Burgess arrived in a car he had hired in his own name and was introduced to Melinda as Roger Styles. She thought he was charming. Dinner was a perfectly normal meal with the trio talking amicably and giving no signs of the mental turmoil that enveloped each one of them. After dinner, Maclean announced that he and their guest had to go out on business. Melinda asked politely whether the business could not be put off until morning, but Maclean regretted that it could not and so off into the night went the two diplomats. Melinda read for a while and then, as there was no sign of her husband's return, she went to bed, exhausted.

At that moment Burgess and Maclean were heading for Southampton to board the cross-Channel steamer, the *Falaise*, to St Malo and on across Europe to Russia.

Geoffrey and I were in Paris when Maclean disappeared with Burgess on 25 May 1951, and the story broke in the *Daily Express* on 7 June. Shortly afterwards, Geoffrey received a call from Lord Layton, Chairman of the *News Chronicle*. He told Geoffrey to make every effort to find Maclean, whom he suspected was on a drunken binge. He reminded my husband that Maclean's father was a distinguished Liberal and, even more important than the story, he wanted to get Maclean back to his family without further scandal.

I went off on a false trail to Normandy where a good friend of the Macleans, Lady Smart, had a house. Melinda thought that her husband and Burgess might have gone there to dry out in private. But, of course, no one in the village had seen him because they were, in fact, staying at a little hotel near the Gare du Nord in Paris. For the first few days after the Burgess and Maclean story flashed around the world, Melinda certainly appeared to believe that her husband was on another wild orgy despite strong speculation that he was heading for Moscow with Burgess. Then she received a telegram from him which caused her deep distress. It was incorrectly addressed and badly spelt. It said: AM QUITE WELL NOW. As far as Melinda knew he had never been ill.

Although Maclean and Burgess were officially 'fired' from the Foreign Office, Melinda had no acute financial worries as her mother once more assumed responsibility for the household.

Melinda's attitude towards Donald appeared to change almost from one day to the next and this was later confirmed by an extremely affectionate letter she wrote to him before going into hospital to have her third baby – a daughter – two weeks after he disappeared. Shortly after this, he sent her £2000 through Mrs Dunbar's bank and this shook her. Melinda felt that with his overdraft and debts in London this must mean he now had access to large sums of money as he had not had sufficient time to earn any wherever he was. She pretended to accept the view of some of his friends that he had gone off with a wealthy woman.

Every day she complained bitterly about the treatment she was receiving from the press, who, she claimed, 'persecuted' her children. The two sensitive little boys had indeed suffered from the badgering of reporters. A few days after Maclean's disappearance, Mrs Dunbar saw Fergus crawling among the bushes flanking the garden. She asked him what he was doing and he replied, 'I am going to shoot the reporters who are making Mummy unhappy.'

Although the attitude of the villagers was sympathetic to Melinda, the local children were extremely cruel to her sons. They followed them home from school, chanting, 'Your father's in prison.' Led by girls, who were far worse, they once even stoned Fergus and Donald. For years the children had nightmares and awoke screaming. One night when Mrs Dunbar tried to comfort Fergus, he cried, 'Oh! You don't know what it's like to be a child.'

To avoid the attentions of the press, Melinda moved with her mother to an obscure hotel in Paris where we saw a good deal

1   The author, 1932

5   Just back from Vietnam, 1966

6 Ian Brodie on the author's right, Michael Hornsby (far left);
   near Danang, Vietnam, 1970

7 Suez Canal, Egypt, 1970

8 Donald and Melinda
   Maclean dining in Cairo

9 Kim Philby with Melinda,
   USSR

10 Lossiemouth, 1966

11 The author with Chou En Lai
(left), before a banquet in
the Great Hall of the People,
1972

12 Taking soup at a street kitchen, Peking, 1974

13 Talking to Edward Heath, Peking, 1988

14   On leaving the *Daily Telegraph*; Bill (Lord) Deedes, then editor, on the author's right, 1981

15   The Old Rectory, Thistleton, Rutland

of her and, later, when she took a house in Normandy we spent several weekends with her. We agreed that it would be sensible for her to move to Switzerland and in September she and her children arrived in Geneva.

I went to Tatsfield with Mrs Dunbar to see if there was any furniture to be put into store. I drove Mrs Dunbar to London where she stayed at the Russell Hotel. I took another room there and arranged for all calls to her to be put through to me.

When I returned to Paris and talked with Melinda by telephone about the house and furniture, it was quite clear that she had by then given up any hope of her husband's return. Under the influence of her kind and generous mother, she began to take active steps to regain her American passport and to divorce him. I went to see her at her flat in the rue des Alpes in Geneva in October and she seemed relaxed and content. Her boys were happy and attending the International School. Generally, life was apparently going well for her although there were times when I telephoned her from Paris when she sounded lonely and depressed.

But suddenly during the evening of 16 September 1953 there was renewed drama. Geoffrey and I were just beginning dinner with friends when the telephone rang. It was Mrs Dunbar, speaking from Geneva, and begging my husband to go there by the next plane. 'Melinda', she said, 'took the children away for the weekend on Friday (11 September) to stay with an old friend at Territet and she has not returned although she had planned to be back on Sunday evening.' She said that she had informed the British Consulate and they had said they would notify London 'through the normal channels'. She had then rushed to the post office to telephone the Foreign Office and Mr William Skarden, the MI5 investigator, who had already questioned her at length about Maclean. He promised to be in Geneva within a few hours.

Geoffrey grabbed his typewriter and, with a few words of apology to our somewhat irritated guests, flew immediately to Geneva.

In the *News Chronicle*, he quoted Mrs Dunbar as saying:

From 6 p.m. on Sunday I sat at the window and waited for Melinda and the boys. Since Donald's disappearance, we have all lived in a state of great anxiety and if ever Melinda was going

183

to be later than she expected she would invariably telephone me. In fact, we all telephone each other madly whenever apart. When she neither returned nor telephoned on Sunday evening, I was frantic but thought perhaps there was too much traffic on the roads and she had decided to postpone her return until Monday morning. On Monday, I went to the British Consulate. They told me my report of her absence would go through ordinary channels. But as I knew this was an urgent matter I telephoned straight to the Foreign Office in London to the chief security officer – and got immediate action. Why had I not told the Swiss police up till then? Well, I didn't know any of the top men and thought it would be useless to try to explain to a subordinate, who might never have heard of the Maclean story.

Mrs Dunbar, heartbroken and exhausted, then flew to Paris. We met her almost every day and gradually built up from her re-collections of what had happened. Just before her disappearance, Melinda had admitted privately that she believed her husband was in Moscow. Earlier in the year while her mother was in the US, she was contacted by a Soviet agent who begged her to join Donald Maclean in Russia.

It seems that when Mrs Dunbar returned to Geneva, Melinda had appeared miserable and utterly uninterested in the clothes, presents or even news brought by her mother from New York. Melinda's moods changed from one day to the next; she was, however, generally apathetic and strangely anxious for her mother to go away again. She was obviously troubled but her mother could not persuade her to talk about her worries. Mrs Dunbar, in fact, thought her daughter was anxious about the sale of the house in Tatsfield.

When Melinda vanished, Mrs Dunbar thought that she had taken only a few clothes with her. But five weeks later when her mother returned to the Geneva flat there were few clothes inside the wardrobe, apart from a mink coat and some evening dresses. Subsequently, Mrs Dunbar discovered that while she was in the US, her daughter had had her photograph and those of the children taken under a false name and bought copies of the exact size demanded by the Soviet Consulate for visas.

More evidence was uncovered about her mysterious departure

from Geneva. On the Friday when she had left her apartment she put her black Chevrolet car in a garage in Lausanne saying she would be back after one week. She used her mother's name. In the car, she left a triptyque, the customs registration of all journeys in and out of Switzerland. It showed that in one year she had made sixteen journeys over the Swiss frontiers: three of them in one day across the border into Italy.

Among the picnic crumbs and toys left behind in the car was a child's book: *Little Lost Lamb*. Inside the cover it was stamped: 'Property of Norwalk, Conn. Schools, Washington School'. Mrs Dunbar had never seen it before. It was far too old for the baby and yet too young for the boys. Then why was it there, left so prominently on the front seat of the car? The preface said:

When the little black lamb scrambled up the mountainside by himself, he didn't think he would get lost. He was only having fun exploring.

But when it was time to go home, there was no little black lamb among all the other sheep . . .

Then came a cry which the shepherd knew meant danger for all little lambs away from their mothers.

Was that Melinda's farewell message? Was she a 'little lost lamb' venturing into a dangerous wilderness but still frantically trying to tell her mother that she was safe?

Melinda had certainly not gone to Territet. She and her children had boarded a train to Zürich where they transferred to the Arlberg express to Schwarzach Saint-Veit in Austria. There they were met by a Soviet agent and, after a meal, left by car on the final stage of their journey – to Moscow.

Although Melinda complained about the telegram she received from Donald after her disappearance, those she sent to her mother followed the same pattern and mentioned a pet name known only to the inner circle of the family to demonstrate that they were genuine. But the spelling and comments indicated that the author was neither Donald nor Melinda Maclean. In fact, the first one received by Mrs Dunbar had indeed been handed in at Territet, but the text said: TERRIBLY SORRY DELAY IN CONTACTING YOU UNFORESEEN CIRCIONSTANCES HAVE ARISON AM STAYING HERE LONGER PLEASE ADVISE SCHOOLBOYS RETURNING ABOUT

A WEEKS TIME ALL EXTREMELY WELL PINK ROSE IN MARVEL-
LOUS FORM LOVE FROM ALL MELINDA. 'Pink Rose' was baby
Melinda.

Mrs Dunbar said the telegram was 'phoney' and, later, after
seeing the original, declared: 'The handwriting is not my daughter's.'

At the end of October, Mrs Dunbar received a letter from
her daughter. It was undated and had no address. But it was
postmarked Cairo 24 October – six weeks after Melinda had
vanished. The letter was brief and pathetic; the handwriting was
definitely Melinda's.

It began, 'Darling Mummy' and said that 'we are quite alright
and well'. She hoped 'with all my heart' that her mother would
understand how deeply she felt the 'sorrow and worry' her departure would cause her. It said that they all missed Mrs Dunbar
and would always think of her, and asked her to believe that 'in
my heart I could not have done otherwise than I have done'. It
sent 'our love' to Mrs Dunbar and Melinda's sisters and ended,
'Goodbye, but not forever. Melinda.'

Geoffrey always felt that the letter did not ring true; it was
perhaps an authorised version of an earlier draft. In writing to
her mother, Melinda would normally have used the children's
names and would have said something particular about them
and not just the almost anonymous 'we are quite alright'.

Mrs Dunbar gave up her Geneva flat and she stayed with us
in Paris for a time. When she finally departed, she left behind
Melinda's fur coat and bathroom scales, commenting: 'When
Melinda comes out of Russia she will need the scales because
she used them every day.'

Melinda's fur coat, rather tattered, and the scales remain
to this day in my London flat.

Melinda's life with Maclean in Moscow was even more disastrous than in Washington or Cairo, as we know from the family.
She was never at ease and constantly terrified that anything she
did or wrote or said would offend his masters in the Kremlin.
After a few years of deep unhappiness in Moscow, Melinda,
who had enjoyed the occasional short-lived *affaire* in London
and even Cairo, fell into the arms of Kim Philby, the Foreign
Office diplomat and 'third man', who had tipped off Burgess and
Maclean to flee from Britain to Russia.

By then Philby was a senior officer in the KGB with considerable influence in Moscow. It was reported that he and Melinda married but in fact they merely lived together and subsequently he threw her out for another woman. Poor Melinda had no alternative but to return to Donald Maclean: what a dreadful loss of face that must have been.

After her husband's death in 1983, she returned to the US, but she has not seen any of her former friends. Neither has she spoken to reporters. The last phase of her life in Moscow remains obscure. But however much she may have known about her husband's activities as a Soviet agent and however much she may have assisted him in the West, it is easy to understand that a woman with her background would wish to leave the bleak, grey communist world of Moscow to return to the US.

Kim Philby was a vaguely familiar figure to me in the late Thirties. In the years following the defection of the two British diplomats, I was quite certain in my own mind that Philby was the 'third man' despite denials and evasions by the British government.

I first met him at a grand ball at, I think, Londonderry House – in any case, one of the few remaining 'great' houses in Park Lane, London – on 9 October 1937.

As the music of the foxtrot ceased at around midnight, my husband, Vandeleur Robinson, kissed me on both cheeks and said, 'Happy birthday, darling.' A good-looking young man who I knew by sight in white tie and well-cut tails was standing near-by. He approached us and he kissed my cheek and said, 'Happy birthday, twin.' I then recognised him as Kim Philby, a young man-about-town, who was often seen at parties and receptions. His father was the distinguished Arabist, St John Philby, who wielded enormous power in Saudi Arabia.

Whenever we met in London after that first encounter, he always greeted me with the words, 'Hello, twin'. Many years later, in fact after I had given his wrong date of birth when he disappeared, I discovered that he was not born on 10 October: his ploy was a confidence trick to enable him to make useful friends quickly. I did not see him during the war except early in 1940 when I was in Paris. Philby was then a war correspondent and as a good communist – and he was certainly that – he always went to the Ritz bar, the favourite meeting place of British war correspondents in France at the time of the 'phoney war'.

He was already a heavy drinker but he did not appear to get drunk as quickly as some other correspondents. He spoke with a definite right-wing bias about the Spanish civil war and the political scene in France. Before the war he belonged to an extreme right-wing pro-German organisation, the Anglo-German Fellowship. No one then had any idea of his real political interest.

It was not until after Burgess and Maclean vanished behind the Iron Curtain that I met Philby again. The meeting-place was Beirut. By that time Mr Harold Macmillan, then Foreign Secretary, had stated in the House of Commons that Philby was not the 'third man' who had tipped off Burgess and Maclean. Philby had, however, left the 'foreign service' and was working as a correspondent for the *Observer* and *The Economist* in the Middle East, a position I had held before moving to Paris in 1951. At first, Philby tried hard, of course, to establish friends among his colleagues in the foreign press corps and make contacts with local officials and diplomats. Although he was generally liked, he quite clearly drank too much and his enemies suggested that at the age of forty-six he looked like a 'tired adventurer' who had become middle-aged too soon. He lived at irregular intervals with his famous father – who by then had quarrelled with the Saudi royal family – in the hills behind Beirut, which was at that time an enchanting city, coming down every day to collect his mail before lunch from the Normandy Hotel. He always went into the bar around noon to read his letters and chat with friends and contacts.

Philby travelled widely and appeared to please his editors in London although they were informed that he was causing something of a scandal by having an affair with Eleanor Brewer, then wife of the popular correspondent of the *New York Times*, Sam Brewer. But criticism was blunted when he talked of marrying her, discussing romantic plans to buy a house in the hills where she would paint and he would write far away from the fleshpots of Beirut. Life, he said, would be 'one long dream'.

Although they married and appeared to be extremely happy they first lived in a flat in the city. It soon became evident that Philby still had a serious drinking problem.

A friend who entertained them to a buffet supper told me

how as the last guests were leaving he noticed Philby and his wife lying apparently dead drunk in a corner of the room. Realising it would be difficult, if not impossible, to get them to their feet he covered them with blankets and put cushions under their heads. Shortly after dawn, Philby's host was awakened by a succession of loud thumps. He got up and went downstairs to find Philby still drunk, consuming all the left-overs from the glasses of the previous night's party and stretched out on the floor playing bowls with stone cannon balls once used in the Crusades and which were treasured collectors' pieces.

It was extremely interesting that even when drunk Philby never said anything indiscreet. He was often very rude to friends, but, unlike Donald Maclean, he did not express sympathy for the down-trodden or the Communist Party. Neither did he chase young boys after an over-indulgent dinner. In his case it would have been girls. This was almost as important in Beirut as it was in London, Istanbul and Washington because although he can have had but little to report, Philby was still working as a freelance for British intelligence and full-time for his KGB masters. He admitted this later in a rare press interview in Moscow given in 1988.

One of the mysteries of the Philby case history was why the Russians trusted him so completely. While Burgess and Maclean were mere Soviet agents, Philby boasted after he subsequently arrived in Moscow of being 'an officer' in the KGB before the war. He must have done something really special, possibly in Spain, such as risking his life more than once to convince them of his utter devotion and reliability. I have tried unsuccessfully to discover what this was.

Few members of the British intelligence service were convinced by Macmillan's statement exonerating Philby from any connections with Burgess and Maclean and, undoubtedly, throughout his stay in Beirut he was under surveillance.

The US Central Intelligence Agency were perhaps even more anxious to know what he was up to and, indeed, they played an active role in obtaining information about his clandestine operations from one or more of the high-ranking Russians who had defected to the US. A senior Soviet defector, Anatoli M. Golitsin, a major in the First Chief Directorate of the KGB, gave Washington all they needed to know about Philby. A senior Intelligence officer was sent from London to Beirut to confront Philby with the facts in the hope that he would make a full confession and return to England.

Philby made a written confession and signed it but I was unaware of this until recent years. Why was he not arrested and brought back to Britain? Or, alternatively, why was he not seized and forced back to stand trial for treason? It would have been possible but, presumably, for reasons of state he was permitted to operate freely in Beirut. After his confession he was still being invited to the house of the British Chargé d'affaires with Miles Copeland, the CIA representative! But somewhere in Whitehall that written statement admitting to being the 'third man', as I had always accepted in my mind, has been filed away. Philby later said he was helped to escape by British Intelligence to avoid an embarrassing trial.

Just before Philby disappeared on the night of 23 January 1963, the ruthless Iraqi dictator, Ben Kassim Krim, was assassinated in Baghdad. Television cameras caught the murder as it happened and I was told by the *Guardian* to go to the Iraqi capital to cover the story. The first reaction to any coup anywhere is to close the airport. I did, in fact, have a visa but with the airport closed all I could do was to get to Beirut and wait until Baghdad airport re-opened.

So while I was hanging about I telephoned Philby. He was not at home. Eleanor answered, saying, 'Kim is with the tribes in Saudi Arabia.' This sounded strange to me because by this time he could not live without his whisky and he was certainly not going to find much alcohol among the Saudi tribes.

I then met Miles Copeland, whose official title was first secretary at the US Embassy. He had quite another story to tell about Philby. Copeland said Philby had been expected at a dinner the previous evening given by Glen Balfour Paul, the British Chargé d'affaires. Philby, however, did not turn up. Eleanor attempted to explain his absence. 'Kim has just gone to the cable office to file a story to the Economist and will be along any moment.' The guests waited until 9.30 p.m. for him before the Balfour Pauls decided to have their meal. Copeland took Eleanor back to her flat later. Philby was not there either.

The story of his disappearance seemed to me to be of more

interest than the events in Iraq. Melinda had told me of 'the tremendous intimacy between Donald and Kim'. That is one of the reasons why I was certain that Philby was the 'third man' and after he had vanished my suspicions were reinforced a hundredfold.

Glen Balfour Paul had nothing to say about his missing guest. The Lebanese police and frontier forces assured me that Philby had not left the country legally. No one in authority professed to know anything about his whereabouts: the lips of officialdom were sealed tightly. But Copeland stuck to his story.

So I bought a copy of a fortnightly sheet of *Le Journal du Levant*, which listed ships entering and leaving Beirut.

On the night of Wednesday, 23 January 1963, when Philby should have been at dinner with the British Chargé d'affaires, a Soviet ship left Beirut for Odessa. The Lebanese police swore that Philby was not aboard but, under harsh questioning from me, they admitted that a drunken Russian sailor had been found on the quay after the ship had left. His landing card was missing and it was this document that permitted visiting seamen to leave their ships for a night out in Beirut. I discovered that all seamen on board the Soviet vessel – and there were few Soviet ships visiting Beirut in those days – had been accounted for before she left for Odessa, thus it seemed obvious that Philby had taken the place of the drunken sailor. (As Philby admitted that he was in Russia four days later but never explained how he got there, I am confident that this was his route.)

I immediately filed a story to the *Guardian* reporting that Philby, the 'third man' who had tipped off Burgess and Maclean, had disappeared. At that very moment Baghdad airport was re-opened and I rushed to the airport to take the first plane there. Sitting beside me in the airliner was Eric Downton of the *Daily Telegraph*, who told me amid congratulations that I had won 'The Journalist of the Year' award and the Hannen Swaffer Prize for my coverage of the Algerian war.

During the next few days of excitement in Baghdad, I was amazed not to hear any reports on the BBC about Philby's disappearance. Why was my story in the *Guardian* not being followed up? The answer was simple: it had been spiked. Three weeks passed before I returned to Beirut. I then telephoned the

Guardian editor, Alastair Hetherington, and demanded to know why my Philby story had not been published.

'Be your age, Clare,' Hetherington retorted. 'Macmillan has said that Philby is not the "third man" and your story would involve us in millions of pounds worth of libel.'

And so I was left sitting on this sensational story for months. It was not until April when I was back in the *Guardian* office in London that the deputy editor confessed one evening, 'There's no news today – nothing to put in the paper.'

'What about my Philby story?' I suggested. 'He is still missing.'

'Well, check it out again.'

I telephoned all my contacts in Beirut. No one had any news of Philby; there was still no trace of him. I re-wrote my earlier cable and the story made a full column on an inside page with a picture of Philby.

Cautiously written, since there was no way of confirming the suspected escape aboard that Soviet ship, the story was unquestionably a scoop. It said:

On a warm Spring evening in Beirut three months ago, the correspondent of the 'Observer' and the 'Economist', H.A. Philby, disappeared, and since then nothing has been heard of him.

But statements made by his wife, Eleanor, to the Lebanese police and letters and telegrams that have been received in his name – though not from him – suggest that he did not fall accidently over a cliff into the Mediterranean. Kim Philby left his wife in a taxi on the way to a dinner party, promising that he would join her 'in a few moments'. That is Mrs Philby's account of his disappearance.

Philby spoke Arabic and he was well known throughout the Arab world as the son of the famous writer and explorer, Harry St John Bridge Philby, who had been an intimate friend and personal adviser to the late King Ibn Saud. But it would be difficult for him, a good-looking Englishman, to disappear in an Arab country.

He lived with his third wife – who was formerly the wife of Sam Pope Brewer of the New York Times – in a large flat in Beirut. She reported the fact that he was missing to the British Consul and the Lebanese police. However, after

she received a telegram in his name from Cairo she informed
the authorities that there was no further cause for anxiety and,
indeed, appeared angered by the local Press which published an
account of his disappearance and a statement by the Lebanese
police saying that he had not left the country 'through any of
the normal frontier posts'.

Later, the Egyptian authorities issued a statement to say
he had not entered the United Arab Republic and that the
telegrams were not signed in his handwriting. Mrs Philby
said that Philby was on an assignment and appeared not to
be worried by the mystery. Indeed, she implied that if people
stopped bothering about him she was sure he would return.
Mrs Philby, too, was reluctant to talk about him even to her
friends.

There is some evidence to suggest that the letters which
she claimed to have received in Cairo were typed on an old
machine he had left in his Beirut flat. Mrs Philby is also said to
admit that he took a small suitcase away with him. Did Philby
write the letters before he left?

The telegrams were strangely similar to those sent by Donald
Maclean to his wife when he left for the Soviet Union in 1951.
Philby knew Maclean and had been a great friend of Guy
Burgess. He was accused at the time of their disappearance
of being the 'third man' responsible for having warned them
that they were about to be questioned by the Foreign Office
security authorities.

The MP who had made the accusation offered an apology
in the House and Mr Macmillan, then Foreign Secretary, stated
positively that 'no evidence had been found that he (Mr Philby)
was responsible'.

There are reports, too, that he was a friend of Blake, the
spy, who was ordered to return when at Shemlam, the Middle
East Centre for Arab Studies near Beirut.

It seems unlikely that a luxury-loving man of 51 would
want to go to Moscow and there is nothing to suggest that he
would be of any use to the Russians when he arrived there. It
is over twelve years since he left the Foreign service or had the
opportunity of reading secret or official documents.

Philby might be on some secret mission for the Saudi-
Arabian government or he might have felt suddenly tired of

the gay life of Beirut and rushed off to live with one of the tribes. But three months is a long time for a man to hide himself from wife and employer.

The story astonished Fleet Street and every newspaper put teams of reporters on to it. MI5 men, whom I met when Mrs Dunbar was being questioned by them about Maclean, contacted me and without actually saying so in so many words let me know that they were aware that Philby was in Russia. Shortly after this the British government admitted that Philby was believed to have fled to Russia following accusations in *Newsweek*, the American magazine, that he was the 'third man'. Again, the Burgess-Maclean affair was given another full airing.

I received many congratulations for my scoop however belated it may have been. It was certainly the starting point that led to the government's admission that Philby had been a spy. Trilby Ewer, at 78 still then diplomatic correspondent of the *Daily Herald*, told me: 'For the first time in history the Daily Express is leading today with what the Guardian said yesterday.'

The Philby–Burgess–Maclean operation was part of a much bigger circle and I believed that there was another top communist agent still lurking in Whitehall academic circles with links with that notorious trio. The fourth man was, of course, Blunt and I am now fairly certain that the fifth man is dead. This Soviet agent was far more highly placed than Maclean, who was an inner agent. Burgess, for instance, was known as an outer agent and of no great significance. Philby, as he has admitted, was a KGB officer in 1938–39 and as such was not under any particular pressure from Moscow as the other two must have been. Philby did not do so badly. He lived in a comfortable dacha on the outskirts of Moscow with a flat in the city and access to luxury food, drink and other facilities normally only available to senior members of the Communist Party. He lived with his fifth wife, a Russian. He must have had some wry thoughts when he considered that he was finally exposed by Lord Rothschild. I believe it was information provided by Lord Rothschild – a brave, highly-intelligent man – that finally put the finger on Philby.

At the height of the Philby scandal, people suggested that I should write a book about the 'third man'. My husband was most discouraging. 'I have written one – The Missing Macleans,' he said. 'We don't want to become known solely as writers on communist spies in high places.'

12 Defence Correspondent for the *Guardian* . . .Washington . . . Aden . . . India and Pakistan . . .

When the editor of the *Guardian* invited me to consider the post of defence correspondent in 1963, I naturally consulted Geoffrey and he rightly said, 'Of course you must accept it.'

Initially, the move from the Middle East to Paris had been difficult for me as the *Observer* and *The Economist* already had offices and good, efficient staff correspondents in France. Further, the French number two in the *News Chronicle* office in Paris was not amused when I helped out. However, thanks to Darsie Gillie I soon found a niche in the *Manchester Guardian* – as it then was.

At our Paris flat not only did we have a quiet study but the luxury of a guest room and also one for an *au pair* girl. We had various girls take up this post. We allowed them to live rent free so long as they made our early morning tea and fetched the morning papers from the concièrge's lodge. All had jobs, generally as secretaries. When one left us a friend in the British Embassy suggested we took on a French girl who was working as an accountant in the embassy 'Commissary'. She wanted to improve her English and we wanted to improve our French; thus Janine Poirier, aged twenty-one, entered our lives. She gradually took over the housekeeping. Geoffrey had uncomplainingly looked after the flat when I was away but, after Janine arrived, she did almost everything. We also had a woman to clean and to wash clothes.

We had many friends to stay at that time especially Peter

Norton who was frequently in Paris buying pictures and meeting her friend, Roland Penrose, who was working for the British Council and writing a biography of Picasso. Roland's wife made no secret of her former close relationship with the great painter.

Indeed, we had a full social life in those days for when Nato was in Paris and OECD more influential than it now is, I think senior French officials as well as foreign diplomats entertained senior foreign correspondents far more than they do now. Whenever I was away, Geoffrey was invited to Shape to play bridge with the American officers there. Le Cercle de l'Union Interalliée – our club next door to the British Embassy in the centre of Paris – was not only good for entertaining but for swimming too.

When I was away from Paris I missed Geoffrey not only as a husband and companion but also as a colleague with whom I could discuss politics and work in general. Although I was always extremely happy to get back I sometimes wonder, in retrospect, whether we should have been quite so happy had we been together all the time. When I was covering Algeria for the *Guardian* I was often away for two to four months at a time. Geoffrey would come down to Nice to meet me when I returned and we would have a few days in Tourrettes-sur-Loup where we owned a 'cabanon' and a wild hillside. I had bought this for the proverbial 'song' in 1951 because it had a good and powerful fresh water spring and the 'savage' property had not been cultivated for some years. Initially, the 'cabanon' had been built to enable the farmers growing grapes, and the violets for which Tourrettes was then famous, to 'sleep' near their crops in order to prevent theft. I bought it because of the dung beetles and rare birds that interested Geoffrey so much. At the end of our visits he generally took dragonfly larvae or insects back to breed in Paris.

After becoming defence correspondent for the *Guardian* I took a small flat in Bloomsbury which was near to the office in Gray's Inn Road. In those days the return fare to Paris was only £10 if one departed before 8.00 a.m. and returned after 8.00 p.m., so Geoffrey came over once or twice a month; and with Nato in Paris I was frequently working there, we also telephoned most days. When I did not go to Paris for the weekend I generally went to stay with the Nortons who had a pleasant house near Newbury in Berkshire.

After living in the flat in the rue du 4 Septembre for some years, the owner wanted to dispose of it so we delightedly bought the place. We had, too, the extremely modest cottage at least three hundred metres from the nearest house in the Valley of the Grand Morin – an hour's journey at most from door to door. There was no electricity or main water supply but an excellent well that provided water for hot showers and dish-washing. The French telegraphic authorities had had to set up no less than twelve telephone posts to bring the line to us. Within a few miles were good restaurants and we often entertained Parisian friends down there and had such people as our old friend Lord Justice Donovan to stay.

I kept a 't. and t.' – toothbrush and typewriter – in all our shacks and flats together with paper, a dictionary, underwear and some old clothes. In London and Paris I kept long dresses and, at least, one fairly smart outfit. In fact, I really divided my modest wardrobe between London and Paris.

My job for the *Guardian* took me to the capitals of the world to cover developments in Western defence and size up trouble spots at their source. Nato affairs occupied much of my time since those were the days of far-reaching plans to improve the military bastions in Europe, the Middle East and the Far East. Many of the major proposals of that period were still-born, like the oddly-conceived multi-lateral force, which envisaged seamen of many nations manning the British Polaris submarines with their sixteen nuclear missiles. It came to nothing mainly because the language problem finally proved to be insuperable as one might well have expected. There was the TSR-2 warplane on which millions of pounds were wasted and the revolutionary F-111, the fighter bomber with the swing wings invented by the late Barnes Wallis, that amazing British aircraft designer, whose idea was rejected by the British government only to be copied by the US and transformed into a formidable fighting machine. Barnes Wallis was the genius who gave Britain the immensely strong Wellington bomber in the 1939–45 war and the 'bouncing bomb' that destroyed key German dams in the Ruhr. All these projects plus troubles in Aden, Malaysia, Borneo, India and Pakistan catapulted politicians and diplomats into ceaseless journeyings and discussions in Washington, Ottawa, Paris, London, Aden,

Tehran, Athens, Ankara, Singapore and many other capitals.

I covered their conferences but my first major task as defence correspondent was to report the Nato foreign ministers talks in Ottawa in May, 1963. Some progress was made on the integration of trans-Atlantic forces despite the indifference of President de Gaulle towards Nato and his determination to establish his own *force de frappe*.

The conference, however, gave me the ideal opportunity to fly on to the US to brief myself on the latest American thinking on the Soviet threat and how to meet it. I talked with Robert McNamara, the secretary of defence, General Curtis LeMay, the US Air Force chief of staff, Air Marshal Roy Slemon, deputy commander of the North American Defence Command at his headquarters in Colorado Springs, and the dynamic General Thomas Power, who commanded the Strategic Air Command from its base in Omaha, Nebraska. I found the American brass-hats still over-concerned with conventional warfare and anxious about the dollar-deficit, which was due to the cost of maintaining troops in Europe. I was assured, however, that there was no intention to withdraw US troops from Europe and, indeed, that vital promise still holds good.

In Colorado Springs, Air Marshal Slemon admitted that while the US possessed the only international command operational in space 'we have no defence against attack by weapons fired from platforms orbiting in outer space or against Soviet inter-continental ballistic missiles.' Nearly a quarter of a century later, his words assume a contemporary pertinence in the light of President Reagan's Strategic Defence Initiative or 'Star Wars' project, which is designed to destroy enemy missiles in space before they appear over US territory. This may be an exercise in wishful thinking for even 1 per cent of missiles breaking through the defensive screen could represent, in my opinion, totally unacceptable damage. Yet as a device to pad the pockets of manufacturers not only of arms, SDI is a gigantic money-spinner.

Thus in 1963 Washington realised that the main struggle in the future would be for control of outer space. In his underground command post near Omaha, General Power favoured an aircraft that could enter and leave space where a command platform would be permanently manned to control operations hundreds of miles above earth. His immediate demand, however, was for more bombers and missiles, nuclear as well as conventional, with improved communications as the most vital element in his armoury.

At that time there were two telephones on his desk. A yellow one linked the general to the White House and the Pentagon and over the other, a red telephone, he controlled his eighty SAC bases throughout the world as well as the 'looking glass', the airborne command post, which was always aloft with a general aboard ready to direct operations in the event of a sudden missile attack on ground headquarters. Every day, General Power deployed more than two thousand bombers and re-fuelling tankers, of which half were then on 'ground alert'. This meant that crews slept and ate in flying clothes within a few yards of their aircraft in order to be airborne in from three to six minutes.

I remember that I was deeply impressed by the efficiency of this gigantic nuclear force although rather stunned by the down-to-earth chat about outer space and the predictions that are slowly coming true. And I could not help feeling that there was incongruity in the first words General Power uttered to me: 'Peace is our mission.' I wondered all the same whether he was the kind of commander who could press the nuclear button, but after talking to him I felt convinced that it just could not happen.

Britain had more immediate problems to tackle. By the end of 1963, President Ahmed Sukarno, the despot then known as 'the Hitler of Indonesia' was stirring up trouble in Borneo through communist infiltrators and indulging in a military confrontation with the British colony of Sarawak. British troops, who had crushed the communists during the 1950s' insurgency in Malaya, faced a guerrilla war that many local commanders expected to last for twenty-five years. In fact, it petered out in 1965 when the Indonesian army crushed a communist coup attempt to unseat Sukarno, who had been president since independence in 1949. Thousands of communists were slaughtered and Sukarno remained in office but only as a figurehead for the army who took control of the country.

Sarawak itself had for more than one hundred years been ruled by the Brooke family, who were known as the White Rajahs, after the Sultan of Brunei had granted governmental powers to Sir James Brooke in 1841. From 1888 Sarawak was a British protected state finally being ceded to the United Kingdom by the Rajah on 1 July 1946. Brunei shared the northern region of Borneo with Sabah and Sarawak and it was the former British dependency inhabited by Malay people that did not join the federation of Malaysia in 1963. It was not until 1983 that it became a fully sovereign and independent state.

However, in the early 1960s, Sukarno planned to take over those tiny nations bordering his territory in Borneo with Brunei as the main target because of its oil deposits. His operations were not only focused on those vulnerable countries. He sent hundreds of communist agents into Singapore and other Malaysian cities to stir up opposition against the federal government in addition to massing troops on the Borneo borders and sending warplanes on reconnaissance flights over Malaysian territory.

When I arrived in Singapore in November, 1963, the Malaysian government announced plans for conscription to meet the growing communist campaign of subversion. The government expressed its deep displeasure with the supply of US arms to Indonesia, which had only just obtained warplanes from Russia. It was also disclosed that Indonesian agents had reached Singapore to train and direct terrorists while some twenty-five thousand communist supporters were operating in Sarawak and Sabah. Border raids by Indonesian troops and 'supporters' were intensifying. In this land of almost impenetrable jungle where rivers formed the main arteries of communication, a new type of war was developing and I decided to take a close look at it.

I flew first to Tawau in Sabah close to the Borneo border and then crossed the country to Sarawak where the military authorities allowed me to visit Jungle Fort in the Fifth Divisional Area.

There I met Sergeant Harry Rankin, 1st Battalion, Royal Leicesters, who instructed me in the jungle lore his unit had acquired when it occupied the fort commanding one of the main mountain passes from Indonesia into Sarawak. 'When all goes silent in the night as the frogs cease croaking, there is danger from someone moving,' he said.

Sergeant Rankin pointed to the trench where I would have to take cover 'if the whistle blew'. I was to jump through a hole in the first floor of this rather ramshackle bamboo fort and not climb down the crude wooden ladder. There would not be time in an emergency.

In this stifling, steaming jungle heat, Gurkhas had created the fort on a small hill in the style of the local long houses built on bamboo stilts and, alas, with corrugated iron roofs. Just before I arrived these structures were thatched with leaves and bamboo. The rooms were divided by bamboo screens with a terrace running along one side.

Around the fort at seven or eight points were Bren and heavy machine-guns in well sandbagged positions. On the camp perimeter sharpened bamboo sticks were embedded in the ground behind the outer circle of barbed wire, mines and booby traps. Beyond was a landing area for RAF helicopters, which always operated in pairs over the jungle so that if one crashed the other would know its position.

For a time I 'camped' with the Leicestershire Regiment and learnt much from them about dealing with leeches and buying odd souvenirs from the few local tribesmen, who tapped wild rubber trees and who were or professed to be friendly. In the Company there was only one black soldier, 'Bert', who seemed to get along well with everybody. One day when I was alone with the sergeant-major I brought the subject around to 'Bert' and said how splendid it was that there were no racial hang-ups and that everyone got along so well together. The sergeant-major turned on me in fury. 'If you are suggesting Bert is black you can go back to Kuching on the next helicopter, which will be here in two hours. Bert is as good a Leicester boy as you are a Leicester girl.'

I was with the Leicesters when President Kennedy was assassinated and to illustrate how bad communications were in the jungle, a group of soldiers thought Sukarno had been killed when they heard the Malaysian radio reporting the assassination of President Kennedy in Dallas. On this assumption they brought out the last remaining bottle of whisky to celebrate Sukarno's demise and their speedy return to Britain. How disappointed they were when I told them I had heard the BBC reporting Macmillan's tribute to the murdered American president.

This was a war zone of little action. It was more a confrontation although I did see American-built Hercules transporters flying supplies twice or three times a week to terrorists encamped just over the border in Indonesia.

The British troops under Major-General Walter C. Walker, operated efficiently in an integrated task force known to us as 'Britcomber' despite the appalling lack of communications. There were only a few second-class roads around the Sarawak capital of Kuching and, with a 970-mile frontier to control, troops could only be supplied with food and arms by river or helicopters. With vast mangrove swamps at sea-level and jungle covering mountains that rose to nine thousand feet, the terrain made the Malayan jungle, Major-General Walker said, 'look like a piece of cake'.

It took a party of Gurkhas trained in the Malaysian emergency an entire day to cut their way through one thousand yards. For the British troops the so-called Indonesian war was one they could not win but, more important, they could not afford to lose either.

It spluttered on for another two years and early in July, 1965, I returned to be fortunate enough to go on jungle patrols for several weeks with the crack British Special Air Services unit.

From a jungle post deep in the Central Brigade area of Sarawak, I went off into the thick jungle with a platoon heading for the Indonesian border. It was extremely hard going and I learnt the value of years of jungle warfare in the Far East, which finally had lightened the load the soldier had been expected to carry on forays into enemy territory.

Rucksacks had been discarded because they were too heavy. Cooking stoves were no longer part of essential equipment since a trained guerrilla could smell cooking or a brew-up half a mile away. We were each given five days' ration of dates, sweets, biscuits, dried fish and tinned jams which slotted into our belts, a water-bottle, and a light groundsheet which could also be used as a hammock. The officer led the way with a map and compass, one member of the patrol carried a radio set and the rest shouldered the weapons and ammunition.

I had been granted permission to make this trip on condition that I should not file immediately to the *Guardian*. In single file we followed already established tracks, sometimes weaving off to cut new paths through the fronds, sometimes brushing the wild orchids hanging from overhead branches away from our faces.

At the time I did not know that we had crossed the border

into Kalimantan (Indonesia). We slept on hammocks and, perhaps because of the heat, appeared to require but little food. I was well covered with anti-leech ointment and did not get seriously bitten. During the nights there were usually one or two false alarms and alerts as strange noises convinced the troops that we were being approached by 'an enemy patrol'. Nothing happened until we reached a small hill in the jungle where some miles inside Kalimantan the SAS had set up a small camp with a well-screened watchtower. They were polite to me but obviously amazed that I had been given permission to make that particular journey. After a few hours of talking, eating and drinking water, we took a boat and drifted down a river.

We passed a few human settlements on the river banks and were watched with deep curiosity by friendly, scantily-clad natives who appeared to do nothing but sit on the water's edge eating fruit. In fact, they were hunters and they grew a little rice. The knives they carried supported their claims to have been headhunters until a few years earlier.

I discovered that the British jungle tactics were taken straight out of Mao's experiences of waging guerrilla war. Whenever the enemy was anticipated we melted into the jungle, hiding underneath the thick foliage, hardly breathing. We never spent two nights in the same area and after darkness fell we kept well away from native settlements.

For me this was one of many kaleidoscopic experiences in the 1960s, which were extremely hectic. In between spells in London and Paris I made several trips to the Middle East, including Aden where tribesmen were waging a war against Britain's Crown colony that eventually led to the withdrawal of the British forces and the creation in 1967 of the Marxist People's Democratic republic of Yemen.

The turmoil of the 1960s in this region of searing deserts and mountain ranges arose after the Federation of South Arabia came into existence in 1963. It was the brainchild of the British High Commissioner, Sir Kennedy Travaskis, who had been trying since 1954 to amalgamate the sheikdoms, emirates and sultanates along the coast of the Gulf of Aden under the administration of the former Crown Colony and protectorate. Thirteen royal enclaves joined and although little effort had been made by Britain to develop the regions the various monarchs received substantial help in cash or kind on the understanding they would keep their tribes in order and be loyal to Britain. But there were many loose ends to the constitution so far as the Arabs were concerned and the neighbouring Yemen Republic, supported or encouraged by Egypt, began a campaign to stir up anti-British feelings among resentful tribesmen.

It was a tinderbox that quickly flamed into a national rebellion against the British-controlled federation. The British authorities declared a state of emergency in 1963 and the battle was on with British troops under fire in Aden and in the wild, daunting interior.

I had visited Aden several times in the 1950s as a correspondent covering British bases from Europe to Hong Kong. Indeed, I recall writing a series for the *Guardian* on how important Suez, Aden, Singapore and Hong Kong were to Britain. Aden had then appeared as a pleasant place, if a trifle warm, dominated by the trading firm of Besse, which endowed St Antony's, Oxford.

When I arrived in Aden in May, 1964, the whole question of security was under review along with plans to give the federation independence. The intelligent Arab view was that with large-scale development programmes spread over five or ten years the hands of President Nasser of Egypt and the local extremists would be weakened.

The tribes on both sides of the federal border with the Yemen Republic had been fighting each other since the days of the Queen of Sheba but they had not been inspired by foreign powers. Now they were armed with modern weapons and trained in subversion and propaganda. The British forces had faced a delicate situation in which they had to maintain order and control the tribes without inciting them to sustained action against British authority, an almost impossible task. They often dropped leaflets warning civilians of impending air strikes against rebel elements so that families could leave the target area.

For the RAF these raids and reconnaissance flights demanded the best from their pilots, as I experienced on a trip I made in a Hunter jet with Wing Commander John Jenner, who threw the fighter around the mountains like an expert juggler. His mission was a general low-flying reconnaissance over the Radfan area with these objectives: to observe the territory on either side of the Aden-Dhala road; to fly well inside the federal borders to observe traffic – camel caravans and tribesmen using wadis leading to the Yemeni headquarters of the 'liberation army'; to inspect damage inflicted on watchtowers and strongpoints by Hunter rockets earlier in the day; to try to identify rebel positions for the East Anglian Regiment operating in Wadi Taym.

Our flight took one hour and twenty minutes and it all seemed so easy flying at somewhere between three and four hundred miles an hour at low altitude over the Aden-Dhala road. Smoothly and calmly, we zigzagged over the track, rolling from one side to the other to identify a truck or see whether a shadow on a rock was a camel or something else. We talked through our oxygen masks as we rose suddenly to avoid a high peak or dived to investigate the activities of figures in the desert.

Indeed, flying through narrow wadis and banking suddenly as the scenery changed was, it seemed to me, far safer than travelling on the M1 on a bank holiday Monday. Jenner's experience, like that of other pilots, came from the sheer daily task of flying over this dramatic terrain because maps of the area were few and those that existed were often inaccurate. As we swooshed between the hills, we spotted the targets of the Hunters' raid a few hours before and I could see quite clearly that they were all hit with absolute accuracy.

We landed with the help of a parachute to save the brakes on the hot runway. In the de-briefing room we were informed that rebels had fired on our aircraft, but I had certainly not noticed it.

The following day Hunters were shooting up rebel strongpoints in the area I had flown over. British troops had withdrawn from a fortress town south of the Wadi Taym to enable the warplanes to attack the rebel camps nearby. The Third Parachute Regiment had been in action there in a trackless area where they literally had to manhandle their Land Rovers out of the sand. Centurion tanks were also in action for the first time since the Korean war, firing 105mm shells into the western flank of rebel-held territory in the Radfan mountains.

Operating in the desert and mountains was slow and tedious and the difficulties facing British troops were outlined to me one evening by a rebel tribesman, who had slipped into Aden. Partly through an interpreter, he explained that tribesmen were greatly worried that the British were building roads and tracks in the desert and had promised that land communications would be improved even more once peace was restored. He was obviously much dismayed by the prospect. 'Roads enable infidels and wheeled traffic – a most unnatural work of the devil – to penetrate our tribal mountains.' Then he added, 'What will happen to those tribes who have lived for centuries by transporting goods across the mountain passes? What will happen to the camel drivers, breeders, muzzle-makers? They will all be redundant and then all that is left for them to do is to become rebels.' This situation had already occurred, he claimed. The Aden-Dhala road had been constructed and it was his view that it represented the strongest grievance the Radfan tribesmen had against Aden. The tribes who so hated wheeled vehicles felt aircraft were respectable because 'after all, the Prophet himself had flown on a magic carpet'.

I experienced a somewhat similar viewpoint on a trip through Afghanistan in the early 1970s. I was driving alone in a hired car at between 90 and 100 miles an hour along a splendid four-track Soviet-built road without a car or bicycle in sight when I suddenly saw camels moving across the road ahead. Naturally, I slowed down . . . to discover a whole tribe on the move. They should have passed under the road through large, narrow arches. Among the camels I saw one man in a jeep with a radio. He said that he was head of the tribe and had returned home from America two or three years earlier to take over when his elders all died suddenly and unexpectedly. He boasted that all the tribe, except himself and his young son, were illiterate. Why should they read? It only enabled the authorities in Kabul to send forms to be filled in and that was an excuse to raise taxes. When I protested about their inability to read newspapers, the young man, who spoke with a strong American accent, said they could obtain any information they needed from the radio. His father, he said, had told him to kill any tax collector who came near as that discouraged others from following.

I imagine that the invention of the wheel must have produced the same kind of reaction. But I knew, too, that even the Egyptians, who were engaged in a war in the neighbouring Yemen against royalists, had complained that in the mountains the people lived as though they were on another planet. They certainly had hardly heard of newspapers though they listened to radios, nor were they aware of a postal system even though their leaders could write. Their Moslem religion was mixed up in a great deal of paganism and witchcraft.

It was in this strange ambience that British troops were conducting operations, often having to blast their way through hostile territory to create tracks and paths. They had to be supplied with food, water and even trucks by air in the more remote regions.

I was lucky enough to be given permission to accompany a regiment in a mopping foray in the Wadi Taym area. It was comparatively uneventful as we made no direct contact with the Arab rebels but in terms of the normal day-to-day military operation it provided a most valuable insight into the difficulties faced by British soldiers.

All the villages in the wadi had been deserted. The women had obviously driven all the goats and camels into the valleys well away from the British force and the men had vanished into the mountains south of battalion headquarters where the hard-core resistance was believed to have its base.

While I was eating sausage and beans with 'compo' tea – unexpectedly good in such circumstances – a patrol returned to report that they had been fired on from a nearby hill. A minor incident but indication certainly that we were not entirely alone.

As darkness stretched across the mountains, Lieutenant Colonel Jack Dye organised 'Operation Newmarket' for the next day. The targets were three large stone fortresses strung in a line across the Wadi Marabine which ran into Wadi Taym. They were protected by six-feet deep communication trenches. Although a way nicknamed 'Pall Mall' was blasted by sappers into the wadi it still remained only a track for the foot sloggers; lorries and Saladin armoured cars found the going too tough. To overcome this problem six Land Rovers and light-weight Ferret armoured cars had been helicoptered into the British camp a few days before my arrival.

Lt Col Dye briefed his officers and periodically 105mm guns fired into the distant hills to deter any rebels trying to slip back into the deserted villages to pick up possessions left behind in the hurry to escape from the approaching British column. The atmosphere smacked of 'Beau Geste' despite the sophisticated equipment employed.

So at 5 a.m. 'Operation Newmarket' began. Water-bottles were filled. Orders to the troops were issued. Within an hour, two Ferrets set off over the bumpy wadi and Lt Col Dye flew off in a helicopter to spy out the hills. He was soon back in reassuring, enthusiastic mood and we all moved off.

We advanced slowly over country covered with small bushes and boulders. At 8 a.m. we reached the steep bank of a minor wadi. The commander called up an air strike and within minutes four Hunters were rocketing and machine-gunning two towers – probably observation posts – on a mountain about two thousand feet above us. The towers disappeared in a cloud of dust.

Pickets were sent ahead to protect the main party as we headed for the fortresses. Occasionally, we stopped for a sip of water as the sun climbed high into the sky. There was no shade and the heat of the stony ground pierced the thin soles of my rather worn desert boots. Infantry entered the small deserted village. They burned the stores of red nuts, the staple diet of the men of the mountains.

I set off with three Land Rovers, one towing a light Mobat gun, to cross the wadi. The Mobat, incidentally, was a see-saw shaped weapon that superseded the heavy wartime 17-pounder. In 1948 it was decided to produce a 120mm gun to replace existing anti-tank weapons and the first – the Wombat – was almost as heavy as the gun it was supposed to replace. Out of this slightly embarrassing development came the lighter model – the Mobat – but it was still slow going trying to trundle it across the desert. It took us two hours to drive across the wadi and at one point the troops had to use explosives to destroy hillocks barring our path.

Then we started to make good progress finally arriving at the three fortresses, which took a heavy battering from our Mobat gun and others dotted around the escarpment. The infantry went in to find the fortresses and the trenches empty. But they captured a big cache of ·303 ammunition, old French rifles and food and water.

The fortresses were interesting. It was obvious that they were not built by local tribesmen, who produced wonderful work in stone but never used concrete. Nor did they dig elaborate trenches.

I returned to Aden wishing that there had been some contact with those wily mountain tribesmen. There were, of course, many savage battles as the British penetrated the Radfan range, suffering dead and wounded. The struggle went on in a low key until 1966.

The Radfan campaign had been ideal for foreign correspondents who could either spend a few nights in colourful discomfort in the desert and go out with dawn patrols or, as some preferred, take a helicopter up to the so-called combat area, see what was going on and return to the delights of the Crescent Hotel in Aden that same day. Communications were excellent and cheap and the people one had to deal with very helpful.

Suez and Harold Wilson's 1966 election victory had, of course, turned British policy in the Middle East on its head. The people of Aden were told quite suddenly that there would be no British base there after 1967. The traditional rulers as well as the middle classes of the city were stunned by this dramatic change of policy. The British had already been severely criticised for their pro-Israeli and anti-Nasser line at Suez when according to the local papers 'even the United States had not backed the Israeli action'.

The South Arabian army, which had gradually evolved, as well as many of the inhabitants of Aden were divided between those supporting the National Liberation Front – the NLF – which was a Marxist organisation linked with Egypt, and the Front for the Liberation of the Occupied South Yemen – FLOSY – which enjoyed loose connections with Saudi Arabia. The traditional leaders, sultans, sheiks and emirs were not unnaturally concerned about their future as they had been led to believe Whitehall would support a new and independent state within the Commonwealth and maintain a military base in Aden. An appeal was made to the United Nations which sent a delegation composed of officials from Afghanistan, Venezuela and Mali, who accepted the anti-British propaganda they were given in Cairo on the journey to Aden.

The 1967 Six-Day war between Israel and Egypt had further inflamed the anti-British factions in Aden. A mutiny of the South

Arabian army was barely controlled by the courage and skill of Lt Col Dye and the less tactful but brave Colonel Colin Mitchell or 'Mad Mitch'. There was bloody rioting in the Crater district. Major-General Philip Tower, who was in command, played a cool hand as the expatriates were gradually evacuated to British aircraft carriers and British and other European businesses were sold or handed over to their local assistants. Well-furnished flats once occupied by Europeans were looted. And before the last British High Commissioner, Sir Humphrey Trevelyan, left the colony all the traditional Arab leaders had been evacuated – mostly to Saudi Arabia.

Their kingdoms were initially overrun by the NLF rebels, who in turn faced a rebellion called by the rival political group, FLOSY, which was responsible for the anti-British rioting and out of this mini-maelstrom came the People's Democratic Republic of Yemen.

War lured me to other battlegrounds in the East. In September, 1965, I was sitting on the hood of a Pakistani Sabre jet, which had been shot down in one of the many clashes between India and Pakistan over the disputed mountain region of Jammu and Kashmir. Pakistan had launched an offensive near Jammu in the northern-most region of the Indian sub-continent. It was a short war lasting only three weeks and it did literally nothing to solve the question of who ruled Kashmir.

Border skirmishes flared up frequently and in 1965 they grew into a full-blooded attack by Pakistan across the cease-fire line. The *Guardian* ordered me to New Delhi where the government was trying to capture some kudos from a situation which was not going well for them. The capital was packed with foreign correspondents, all eager to get to the front line but they had not reckoned with Indian bureaucracy. The Minister of Information, Mrs Indira Gandhi, refused to allow any reporter to go near the area of fighting.

I knew that it was vital to see her and I had the advantage of having known her well in Paris when she was the Indian representative at the United Nations Educational, Scientific and Cultural Organisation headquarters (Unesco). It was no easy task. Her lackeys were adamant that there would be no press passes to the front. I was equally bloody-minded as I was sure that they were not passing my messages on to the Minister. This proved to be correct at a press conference she called. When she arrived she noticed me and immediately smiled and waved. After the briefing ended I was shown into her office. The attitude of her staff changed abruptly. After an hour and a half with her, Mrs Gandhi gave me permission to go to Kashmir. Before leaving I felt I had to make some effort on behalf of two good friends.

'Would it be possible, Minister,' I asked, 'for me to take two servants along?'

'Two servants? Who are they?'

'One is a Mr Creighton Burns and the other Mr Thomas Pocock.' She agreed that I could take two 'servants' and Burns and Pocock were delighted with the outcome of my little masquerade.

Whether Mrs Gandhi realised that Burns was a reporter with the *Melbourne Age* and Pocock, with whom I had enjoyed many forays into wars, was in Delhi for the London *Evening Standard*, I did not then know. But she asked no further questions. Years later when I interviewed her as Prime Minister I gathered that she had indeed known.

We drove to Kashmir where I met Major Puri, who had been with the 4th Indian Division in the 8th Army and whom I had known in the Libyan desert. We greeted each other as old friends and, naturally, he arranged for Burns, Pocock and myself to be driven by jeep to the charming town of Akhnur where the Pakistanis were trying to capture a strategic bridge.

The town and the bridge were being shelled and big V-shaped clouds of smoke and dust rose from craters into the hot air creating a haze over the ruined streets. Our driver put his foot down and we bumped and rocked through the town amid the crash of high explosives. I remember that as we emerged from the target zone into the scrubland beyond that I turned to my companions, exclaiming, 'Now *this* is what makes life worth living!'

I do not recall their reply but I am quite sure that they heartily agreed. This does not mean that I am brave but that some forms of danger in the open are stimulating and exciting. I am not frightened by gunfire though I look quickly for protection and a safe retreat. But I am terrified of being stuck in a lift and feel nervous and apprehensive every time I enter an old and creaky one. (Once I was stuck in the lift in the Beijing Hotel in the Chinese capital. Fortunately it possessed a telephone but the only answer I could obtain from the operator was, 'Wait a moment, please.' After a quarter of an hour this became very tiresome.)

We reached what the Indians called the front line in the small town of Jaurian where the war had taken on a long-range dimension.

'One of our patrols is under heavy machine-gun fire and calling for artillery.' A signals sergeant holding a field telephone shouted the message to a major only five yards from me in the open at battalion headquarters as mortars crashed around us.

After the major had given an order to fire to the commander of a 25-pounder battery some miles away, we walked a few yards under cover of broad-leafed trees to gaze upon three thousand yards of no-man's-land, which separated us from the Pakistani positions on the low foothills in the misty distance. The terrain was green with trees here and there, but the ground was iron hard and excellent for tanks.

Indian officers told me that they had two or three patrols, armed with old Lee Enfield rifles and Sten guns, out day and night and so managed to dominate the domain between them and the enemy. While we talked the 25-pounders opened up and ten rounds swished over our heads.

I discussed the situation with Indian soldiers – Jawans – in the integrated unit comprised of troops from all over the country that occupied the indeterminate front line. Their morale was fairly good and those who had experienced war in the Western Desert were more relaxed and happier than the younger soldiers who had never heard the sound of small arms fire.

A Gurkha, looking as though he had just come out of a shop in Bond Street, in strong contrast to myself and the dusty soldiers around me, said, 'This is not a real war: it's a stop-go war.' He feared that there would be a cease-fire before the Indian Army had been able to reoccupy the area from which they had withdrawn before the first Pakistani attack.

Many officers expressed the belief that they were fighting a political war but, unhappily, it was a real one for about sixty thousand refugees who had left the front line and Akhnur just to the rear. This was the key sector and the main military and political objective of the Pakistani government in the entire sixty-mile-long front. By cutting or capturing communications here they could have severed Kashmir from India.

The Indian army, however, had all main roads and bridges covered by anti-aircraft guns for some miles behind the front line. It was then the fourth largest in the world and equipped with British weapons from the Second World War.

The Indians had counter-attacked further south against the Pakistani town of Lahore, which had tended to draw off Pakistani armour, and followed that up with an offensive directed at the communications centre of Sialkot, about thirty miles from Jaurian. Sialkot was Pakistan's main depot for fuel and ammunition and the meeting place of air, road and rail links, a town in fact from which any attack on Jammu and Kashmir had to be mounted.

There were constant Pakistani air raids and I witnessed eight in the two nights spent at the front. There were attacks on airfields which were carried out with considerable precision if only because India possessed only limited radar. During the day, the Pakistani F-104 supersonic fighters carried out reconnaissance flights without hindrance.

For a border war of limited proportions and duration, considerable damage and casualties were inflicted on both sides, each committing two armoured divisions and two infantry divisions to battle. According to officials in New Delhi nearly four thousand Pakistanis and one thousand Indians had been killed with India losing thirty-two warplanes to sixty-four Pakistani aircraft. The imbalance was obvious as propaganda always tends to be but it was clear, nevertheless, that there was heavy loss of life on both sides. In the middle of it all, China made threatening noises in support of its ally, Pakistan, but while the diplomatic temperature rose Peking evidently decided that she had no role to play in the conflict.

Another cease-fire was agreed and calm returned to the line dividing Indians and Pakistanis in Kashmir, leaving a bitter aftertaste in New Delhi over what the government believed to be the failure of Britain to support them.

That had been the third conflict between Indian and Pakistan since Britain gave them independence in 1947 amid bloody Moslem-Hindu strife. And another was not very far off.

It was fortunate that the British High Commissioner, John Freeman, formerly editor of the *New Statesman*, was well liked and deeply respected by most individual members of the Indian government and senior officials, all of whom praised his intelligent, dignified behaviour throughout the crisis in Anglo-Indian relations. But India was left to face inevitable inflation, a severe loss in foreign exchange earnings, increased defence spending and cut-backs in development plans. Pakistan experienced similar hardships.

In 1971 relations between the two countries deteriorated again after a Pakistani army crack-down in March against Bengali separatists in East Pakistan, which had very much become the poor relation of West Pakistan. Partition had deprived East Pakistan of Calcutta, its main port, which was part of West Bengal until it joined India. This was an economic blow at the heart of East Pakistan since its main export was jute and all the jute-processing mills were in or around Calcutta. Although new jute mills were built in East Pakistan, Bengali resentment grew, accusing the government in Islamabad of using earnings from their jute exports to build up industries in West Pakistan. East Pakistan, the Bengalis claimed, was no more than a colony.

In 1970 for the first time free elections were held and they coincided with Bengal's worst disaster for many years – a catastrophic cyclone that claimed half a million lives. The Bengalis charged Islamabad with withholding aid and voted overwhelmingly for Sheikh Mujibur Rahman's party, the Awami League. He immediately demanded autonomy from West Pakistan except for foreign policy and defence.

The Pakistani president, General Yahya Khan, and his prime minister, Zulfikar Ali Bhutto, who was destined to become president later in 1971, rejected Rahman's proposal.

The general then ordered a campaign of repression by his army in East Pakistan where guerrillas known as the Mukti Fouj were supported, trained and armed by India. The Pakistan army killed hundreds of Bengalis and virtual civil war soon broke out. Nearly nine million refugees fled across the border into India. Rahman was arrested and taken to West Pakistan to face a treason trial.

I spent some weeks in Calcutta making trips along the border with East Pakistan visiting refugee camps and attempting to find out what was happening. On several of my trips I shared a car with a Catholic priest named Father Kennedy, who was an American of Irish descent. Sometimes he stayed at a mission but, naturally, he chose a place where he could say Mass before he began the day. He was writing a report on the refugee situation for a Catholic charity.

Although devout, Father Kennedy did not always look like a priest, which was indeed the case when we were both arrested by Pakistani troops in a fairly remote part of the border about two hundred miles north-east of Calcutta. We were accused of crossing the frontier illegally. Our driver had taken us through a village to a single track railway line that he could not cross by car. We got out and walked over the well-used track. As there was no one around and no signs that the railway line was the legal boundary between India and Pakistan we crossed over and walked on a few yards only to be picked up by a handful of Pakistani soldiers, who marched us off to three English-speaking officers. We had left our briefcases containing our passports in the car.

The Pakistanis said we were under arrest and they would telephone to Islamabad to inquire what they should do with us. As Father Kennedy was wearing shorts and an open-necked white shirt, they refused to believe that he was a priest and they all too obviously thought journalists were dangerous anyway. After two hours' detention they gave us lunch. I then visited a somewhat remote toilet and, realising that I was not being closely watched, I slipped off and re-crossed the line back into India.

Father Kennedy not unnaturally thought that I had deserted him. From our car I picked up our passports and some documents proving that Father Kennedy was certainly a priest. I told the driver what had happened and gave him enough money to telephone London to alert the *Guardian* if we failed to return. I returned to the Pakistani camp and handed over the passports. They still refused to release us until they had heard from army headquarters in Islamabad. Then just before sunset we were freed and allowed to re-cross the railway line into India.

Early in November I arrived in East Pakistan and witnessed the final stages of the war out of which the nation of Bangladesh was born. It was a very bloody affair to be followed in the first days of the new break-away state by Bengali lynch mobs pursuing Pakistani soldiers and the local quislings, who supported them, through the streets of the capital of Dacca and other cities. Revenge is never sweet and in Bangladesh it was ugly and horrifying.

To obtain an objective picture of this confusing mélange of slaughter I travelled to the remotest corners of East Pakistan and was often interrupting my coverage by having to fly from Dacca to Islamabad via Sri Lanka – about two thousand five hundred miles. On occasions it was quite hair-raising as trying to find the front line in the Ganges delta encumbered by so much disorder and tumult did have its dangers.

On one trip I was accompanied by Arnaud de Borchgrave, now editor of the *Washington Times* then a senior correspondent on *Newsweek*. We were lucky to find schools and medical missions along the rivers which were pleased to put us up for the night for a contribution to their funds. The missions also collected a good deal of political and economic information.

By the time I made my second trip, this time with Robert Shaplen of the *New Yorker* the security situation had deteriorated. Two days after leaving Dacca we heard that a Catholic priest had been murdered nearby. We spent two extremely uncomfortable nights in our boat with our boatman, before being directed to a landing stage and a few yards further on to a small mission where we were offered accommodation and supper.

Although it was early in the evening we were both glad to be shown to a huge room with two single beds – one at each end. It was immediately behind the altar. Covered with mosquito nets we both slept. But because my bed was near to the door I was frequently awakened by the arrival of groups of people at the mission. Eventually, there was a crowd of about thirty Bengalis talking and sometimes shouting behind the door. Although they spoke Bengali there must have been some language problem among them because every now and then something was said in English.

Listening intently in the darkness, I gathered that this mission was the one where the priest had been slain in the bed now occupied by Bob Shaplen. Occasionally, someone said quite loudly and clearly, 'Dead men tell no tales!' I thought of waking my colleague but decided that a visit to the toilet might give me a better idea of what was going on. So I opened the door and walked out among this strange gathering. Their hostile eyes followed me. The atmosphere was extremely alarming and I returned to bed but not to sleep.

Shortly after dawn I woke Bob and told him what had happened during the night and that we had to get away fast. He got up quickly and we crept out of the mission. We traipsed for hours along the banks of the Ganges before we found a boat with a Bengali willing to take us out of that highly dangerous area.

Back in Dacca I was fortunate to enjoy excellent relations with the senior Pakistani officers, including the second-in-command, Major-General Farman Ali, who had attended the British Staff College. This enabled me to tour Dacca after the nightly curfew was imposed and also, of course, provided me with up-to-the-minute information on the war front – at least, from their point of view.

The Pakistan High Command also allowed me to make many trips into the interior. Early in December, I headed north for Jessore and Rangpur after India had entered the war in retaliation for a surprise air raid by Pakistani bombers on Indian airfields. It was the start of a lightning thirteen-day campaign by India's forces.

The garrison town of Jessore was under heavy Indian shelling when I arrived there but seven miles away the Pakistan army repulsed an Indian attack on the village of Burinda. There had been some doubt whether the Indians were involved in that area or whether they were helping the East Pakistan rebels. However, I spoke through a neutral interpreter to an Indian sergeant who was seriously wounded in the fighting. He was only able to croak but told me that he did not know where he was but he had not expected any opposition to the Indian offensive.

In Jessore and up in Rangpur, the Pakistani army acknowledged the Indian successes in taking a string of towns and villages in their advance across the border.

It was obvious that the Indian forces were intent on quick

victory. Dacca airport was raided five times in one day by Pakistani Sabre jets, which burst through a sky dotted with exploding anti-aircraft shells to rocket the airstrip. From the top of the Intercontinental Hotel I had a grandstand view with other correspondents of the air-raids. Indian jet fighters took off to intercept the raiders and dogfights developed above us. It was all pretty noisy and exciting but, in fact, little damage was caused in the city.

Right up to this moment there had been no declaration of war but a total curfew and blackout had been imposed by the martial law authorities. During the curfew the Intercontinental Hotel ran out of beer and whisky and there was but little service. However, I had a car and soon discovered that the streets were totally deserted and that it was easy to drive across town. The Indian Air Force had by then badly damaged the Pakistan Army headquarters but a platoon of soldiers were still on duty at the entrance. I decided to go in and see if anyone was around and managed to bluff my way through the guards.

In the building about a hundred yards away I scrambled up, with some difficulty, where the stairs had been. Some offices were destroyed by a bomb and there was no one on duty. I admit that I looked into the tidy cupboards of various senior officers, hoping to discover some whisky but none was visible. Desks were generally clear but looked as though the officers had expected to return. Maj-Gen. Farman Ali's blotter was clean and his 'in' and 'out' trays empty. In one office I found three pages of orders – in English – that had come from Islamabad before the headquarters had been bombed but after the total and indefinite curfew had been imposed. According to the orders, the president and chief of armed forces in the West had told the army in East Pakistan to continue the fight against the Indian invaders in a totally unrealistic manner. Either the headquarters in Dacca had not reported the true situation to Islamabad or army headquarters in Islamabad were living in an unreal world. In fact, the forces in East Pakistan had 'given up' and the headquarters staff was hiding out in their well-guarded living quarters, although they had not formally surrendered. All the aircraft at Dacca airport had been damaged.

My visit to the deserted military headquarters before the Indians arrived on the spot had one advantage. The Mukti

Fouj, who gradually assumed control before the Indian Army appeared, made loud accusations against various Pakistani officers and claimed that there was a list of Bengalis, who were due to be shot at dawn, on the blotter of General Farman Ali.

Indeed, after Pakistan accepted Mrs Gandhi's cease-fire offer on 8 December, they demanded the general's head. However, I was able to tell the Mukti Fouj leaders that while a Pakistani guard was on duty at the Pakistani army headquarters certainly neither Indians nor Mukti Fouj supporters had entered that building and that there was no execution list on General Farman Ali's desk. It all became rather hairy but with the Indian army officers taking control and my explanation the general escaped a nasty fate. For the Mukti Fouj were already killing and torturing Pakistani officers and bureaucrats in public, producing some of the worst scenes I have ever witnessed.

The Red Cross and the guerrilla leaders tried to pacify the blood-thirsty rank-and-file with little success. General J.F.R. Jacob, the Indian chief of staff in the Eastern Region, called the Mukti Fouj officials to a conference and told them: 'I want this transfer of power to go bloodlessly and without incident.'

'We will try our best,' they answered.

'Don't try,' barked the general. 'Just do it! If not, I'll start shooting you fellows!'

Nevertheless, the surrender of the Pakistani Army was followed by gunfights and wild disorder in the streets of Dacca. The cheers of the crowd celebrating the birth of Bangladesh turned to screams with the sound of machine-gun fire as mobs of guerrillas cornered *razakars* – collaborators. Some Pakistani police captured by the Indians were released with a fifty-yard start over the mob pursuing them. Some of the older men could not run fast enough to escape the howling avengers.

Lorryloads of armed guerrillas roared into the city to join the lynching parties. One *razakar* trapped on the top floor of a building next to the Intercontinental Hotel leapt to his death with his machine-gun blazing away at his hunters as he fell to the street below. Three others were shot down at the gates of the British High Commission. I saw one dragged from a doorway by guerrillas who beat him to death on the pavement. Many other *razakars* were bound and blindfolded to be led off into the back streets amid crowds shouting for their blood.

The rebels broke into Dacca prison and freed their compatriots along with criminals. And in the middle of all this mayhem a Swedish Red Cross official spent five hours in a ditch sheltering children who had been caught up in the street fighting.

The blood-letting continued for nearly four weeks. Not even the announcement that Sheikh Mujibur Rahman had been freed from West Pakistan helped to ease the atmosphere of unbridled hatred for the former rulers. He attempted to quieten his supporters by requesting the International Commission of Jurists to investigate how the Pakistan Army 'killed my people, violated our women, burnt our homes and looted our property'. Re-establishing law and order was his main task and that achieved he faced the grim prospect of re-settling nearly thirty million people – forty per cent of the population – at a cost of £1,100 million. Staging camps had to be built for the ten million refugees who had fled to India.

Rahman himself appeared to have little idea of how to conduct himself. Despite an enormous armed bodyguard, I managed to enter his crowded villa to conduct a promised interview with him. The downstairs rooms were crowded with people wanting favours while orderlies were sitting on the stairs. After waiting some four hours without even a glass of water, I was taken to his bedroom where his wife was already in bed with a small child. I talked with him in a corner by the window as he was interrupted every other minute by urgent telephone calls from provincial towns. It was not a very productive interview.

I then flew to Rawalpindi for an exclusive interview with President Bhutto, who was destined to end his life on the gallows in 1979 after General Zia's coup. Bhutto made it clear that there would be no relaxation in Pakistani-Indian relations.

A former lecturer at Southampton University, Bhutto was inclined to speak thoughtlessly in public. But in private, with a glass of weak whisky and soda in his hands, he gave the impression of being shrewd and intelligent. Certainly, he did not deserve the tremendous indignities, pain and humiliations that preceded his execution.

In his office, Bhutto accused India of constant and serious breaches of the Kashmir cease-fire and he declared that martial law would continue in Pakistan while Indian military and political designs on Pakistan remained as they were. India, he said, was still trying to stir up trouble in the provinces of Sind and Baluchistan.

When Rahman returned to his capital on 10 January 1972, to rule a nation of seventy million Bengalis, most of them were destitute. The future offered an overwhelmingly daunting canvas. The communications system was ruined. Demolished bridges prevented any road or rail traffic except over temporary structures built by the Indian Army. So the only possible method of transport was by water yet thousands of boats and ferries were damaged or missing. To complete this unhappy picture most of the landing stages were wrecked.

The economic situation was chronic. Many mills were unable to reopen as the raw jute could not be moved from the country-side to the factories. Other plant was idle because cotton and raw materials from West Pakistan or abroad were impossible to import because there was no foreign exchange. The tea gardens, which had been run by British tea planters, were hampered by an acute lack of currency to pay wages and repair the factories. Ironically, the first nine planters attempting to return were stuck in Calcutta unable to obtain visas for Bangladesh. So they abandoned their plan completely, leaving thousands of workers, many of them returned refugees, sitting idle in the plantations.

Rahman's popularity and charisma, which stemmed from his proclaimed love of his people, was undermined by this worsening situation. Within two months the price of rice doubled in Dacca. In some areas the cost of cooking oil, eggs, fish, chickens and paraffin had trebled over the previous year. And owing to lack of transport there were many areas where food was extremely scarce. The country peasants really believed that independence would bring good living such as Pakistani officers enjoyed.

The main problem was that there was no spending power because millions of people were unemployed. With little work available in the dry season, more than two hundred thousand men from the countryside arrived in Dacca hoping to find jobs there. They camped in bamboo huts in the city's main squares and public gardens and on the outskirts they created new slums. Rahman's popularity slumped.

Massive foreign aid channelled through the United Nations helped to keep him in power for two more years. By that time

Rahman had become appalled by the extent of corruption in his own government. He was equally depressed at his own failure to restore living standards to a reasonable level. So he set up a one-party state with himself as president. His days were numbered and in August, 1975, he was overthrown and killed in an army coup. His family were also slaughtered.

13 Vietnam . . .

The Vietnamese was polite and courteous. He had asked for
me at the reception desk in the Caravelle Hotel in Saigon. He
was given my room number and when I answered the tap on
my door he suggested that I might like to discuss a business
matter.

Once inside my room, he offered to change money at high
black market rates. I expressed firm lack of interest. Then came
the reason for his call. 'Never mind,' he said. 'We expect to see
you at Mass in the cathedral tomorrow.'

'Why?'

He did not answer directly. But had I known certain Algerian
FLN leaders? An oblique question but it was the kind of clandestine, roundabout contact usually made by communist agents
when every word implied something else. The man was either
Viet Cong or North Vietnamese.

I have reaped more rewards from Algeria than winning the
Journalist of the Year award. It must have been through that
that the FLN and, later, the Algerian government, knew my
long and difficult name. One of their senior ambassadors once
told me: 'We knew we could trust you because if you said you
would not mention the name of a man or a place you kept your
word.' During the troubles in Sri Lanka in the early 1960s, a man
approached me in my hotel and demanded that I should go for
a long walk with him. So I did but I was contemplating a swim

until he mentioned the name of two or three Algerians. During the walk he gave me an excellent briefing on the Tamil uprising. I think of him as the man who said officials in Sri Lanka 'mistook an appetite for hunger'.

I arrived promptly the next day – 1 May 1968 – for Mass at the cathedral that was reminiscent of any to be found in the French provinces. It was immediately after the Vietcong Tet offensive had brought death and destruction in all the major cities in South Vietnam and shaken American morale with a direct attack on the US embassy in Saigon and given significant impetus to the anti-war crusade in America. The Vietcong were only just defeated in that operation with heavy loss of life but North Vietnamese reinforcements poured south to continue that appalling war.

Now something else was on. The Vietcong and North Vietnamese agents were everywhere in Saigon. They would have had no difficulty in shadowing me; they knew from my reporting that I appreciated the inevitability of the American withdrawal from Vietnam.

I joined the churchgoers entering the cathedral in the centre of the city. Was it all a hoax? I did not have to wait many minutes for the answer. A man came to sit beside me and, after kneeling for a short prayer, said, 'Miss Hollingworth?'

'Yes,' I murmured.

He thrust some documents into my hand. I moved into the light of a flickering candle. One glance was enough. The credentials carried the stamps of the Vietcong and North Vietnam. They were impeccable. After a few more prayers, the man nudged me and suggested quietly that we should move.

I followed him into the darkness near the empty Lady Chapel as priests and choir walked in procession to their places in the main body of the cathedral. The congregation stood and joined the choir in a hymn. The candles cast dancing points of light on the stone walls but in our shadowy corner we were just two other worshippers with bowed heads. Our whispers had nothing to do with prayers.

'What have you to tell me?' I asked in barely audible tones.

'Listen carefully. Peace talks between Hanoi and Washington will open very soon. We expect them to last for at least a year.'

'Where will they be held?'

'That has to be decided. But the talks will – must – produce agreement on terms to end all American bombing of North Vietnam.'

'And what will Hanoi offer in return?'

'Hanoi would withdraw one or even two of its divisions from the south. After that it would not be difficult to arrange a general ceasefire.'

'After that?'

'Then, but only then, can the real peace talks begin. There is no alternative to a coalition government in Saigon. We would agree to a South Vietnamese prime minister on condition that we have at least two or three key cabinet portfolios. And free elections must be held.'

'And you believe that the Americans will cooperate?'

He hesitated. I could almost sense the smile in the darkness. 'We are sure that the Americans are willing if not anxious to withdraw one or two divisions immediately the talks begin. The American people and most American troops want nothing more than to go home.'

My informant put one question to me that I could not answer then nor can I now. Why had the Americans not recalled all their officers on leave in Bangkok and elsewhere and refused to allow the South Vietnamese troops to leave their posts during Tet? 'We were extremely worried,' he said, 'because we knew that the Americans had by accident obtained some highly secret orders to the Vietcong to attack Saigon, Hue, Da Nang and other major cities during the lunar New Year holidays.'

Certainly, in the past there had been an unofficial but well observed ceasefire between the two sides during the festive period. But the Americans not only had the plans for attack but also tapes of orders, appeals and political speeches to be broadcast when the communists took over the radio station in Saigon. I learnt later that recalling officers and ordering the South Vietnamese troops to be on the alert and not celebrate Tet would have caused such problems no one was willing to give the necessary order. It was hard to believe.

My informant interrupted my thoughts. 'Now you must go. Leave me here.'

What a scoop! I left the cathedral, blinking in the sunlight and walked back to the Caravelle Hotel. Whatever the ifs and buts here was a major development and one that proved to be the beginning of the end of the American involvement in the Vietnam war. The next day my exclusive story was front page news in the *Daily Telegraph*, which I had joined just over a year earlier.

My informant was absolutely right in his prediction about the peace talks, which opened in Paris within a month. They were the last of a long, involved process but the contact between Washington and Hanoi had been established publicly in Paris, and secretly elsewhere the two sides negotiated an agreement that ostensibly led to communist victory in the south and American withdrawal with some essence of honour. But as in the years before, the war continued to be fought with savage ferocity on the ground and in the air while the politicians tried to frame ceasefires and plans to end the fighting and restore peace to a nation so long shattered by conflict that the people could no longer remember what it was like to live without the thunder of guns and bombs.

The many visits I made to South Vietnam for the *Daily Telegraph* confirmed my convictions born during my first trip in 1965 for the *Guardian* that this was a war the Americans could never win.

Not only were American commanders and troops inept at jungle warfare but the Pentagon itself failed to appreciate and understand that the overwhelming factor against US involvement was one of geography right from the moment in 1961 when the first American 'advisers' stepped on to Vietnamese soil. Even assuming that the US could have invaded North Vietnam, she would have been committed to a permanent army of occupation policy constantly harassed by guerrilla action but, over and above this awesome prospect, China would then never have permitted an American presence on her southern border.

All arguments along these lines were brushed aside by the Pentagon generals, who apparently believed that their crash-bang tactics of massive air raids, defoliation and terror campaigns against villages suspected of secreting Vietcong fighters would finally cow the communist army – north and south – into defeat.

Rather like the British during the blitz, the Vietnamese people in the north and the guerrillas in the south became increasingly defiant and, in the final stages, the North Vietnamese forces routed the American army and the Saigon government of the day. The last American troops left Vietnam on 29 March 1973 and three days later American prisoners of war were released in Hanoi. The ceasefire that enabled the US withdrawal to take place broke down and the war went on with the North Vietnamese and the Vietcong increasing their onslaught in the south until they marched into Saigon on 30 April 1975 hardly firing a shot.

The prospect of a coalition government raised during that whispered chat in Saigon cathedral had never been part of the communist format. Vietnam was reunified but under total communist control. All anti-communist elements were crushed and a new type of refugee appeared – 'the boat people' – civilians terrified of the northern army, who streamed out of the south in every conceivable kind of boat. Many were drowned in the ensuing months and years as their small craft foundered in storms in the South China Sea and hundreds were killed, wounded and raped by pirates operating from bases in Thailand. But thousands were picked up by passing ships of friendly nations and in the end managed to reach sanctuary after weeks of perilous voyages to Malaysia and beyond.

My experiences in Vietnam ranged from bombings to helicopter missions against groups of communist guerrillas encamped beside canals; dropping supplies and visiting Americans under siege in Khe Sanh, and other fortresses on the demilitarised zone, and many other outposts; accompanying American and South Vietnamese troops on forays into the jungles and watching them fight it out in the suburbs of Saigon. When the Vietcong were trying to take over Cho Lon, an outlying Chinese district of Saigon, a European military attaché took me into the middle of it. We moved from one bullet-pocked building to another and there was little danger to worry about because he had been a first-class house-to-house fighter in the 1939–45 war.

My first few hours in Saigon on 1 April 1965 were unforgettable (although it was not my first visit to Vietnam). I was in an airliner flying through thick cloud over South Vietnam. On the approach to the airport, we came out of the cloud-belt and, at the same time, the sun broke through transforming the waterways below into eye-dazzling strips of silver. A line of bomb craters across a paddy field revealed the deep red earth like spots of dried blood

on a bandage. Fields and plantations smouldered from unnatural
fire.

We landed on what was then to me the largest and most
active airfield I had ever seen. Hundreds of aircraft were parked
wing-tip to wing-tip on huge aprons, some for the US army and
others for the navy. There were bombers, fighters, transport aircraft, helicopters large and small – and they were all wide open to
sabotage. 'There's nowhere else to put them,' an American officer
explained when he pointed out the queue of planes awaiting take-
off after six Sky Raiders taxied slowly by, the brass of their bombs
gleaming beneath each wing. 'We made 1,700 sorties last month
from this airfield,' the officer added, waving his hand towards
the extension being built to the runway and the new dispersal
aprons near the former French-built hangars.

Saigon evoked memories of Beirut, Algiers and Tunis – those
warm-weather cities planned by Parisians, who also planted trees.
Many houses were surrounded by barbed wire, a few roads were
blocked to traffic, but there was little or none of the tension there
was in Jerusalem after the King David Hotel was blown up. Nearly
all the street cafés had moved indoors, hotel bars were transferred
from the ground floors to the rooftops to guard against the odd
grenade being tossed in among the drinkers, and there were barricades around the cathedral and post office to stop vehicles with
explosives getting too close to the walls.

I found accommodation in a reasonable hotel, The Majestic.
The porter who carried my luggage to my bedroom was followed
by an elderly, small, one-toothed man.

'Do you want Vietnam or Vietcong money?' he asked in
French. I produced a pound note but he said he was interested
only in dollars, for which he would pay one-third above the official rate. (The Vietnamese, when the economy had reached 'rock
bottom' early in 1988, still only thought in US dollars never yen,
sterling or francs.)

He explained that when the Americans departed, Vietnamese money would have no value and although he could not
express any view when they would go – go they would. Did
he think the Americans would fare better than the French?
How could that be possible? The march of communist revolutionary parties could not be stopped in Vietnam. Prophetic
words.

I declined his offer and took a taxi instead to the United States Information Service building (in 1988 this had become the Rex Hotel), although the driver did not want to go too near. We passed a column of marching men not in uniform whom I discovered were being trained by the Americans as officers for the Vietnamese army. One thousand had completed their thirty-eight days training a few weeks before and three thousand more would be putting on their uniforms within a month.

Street vendors pressed sugar cane, mangoes and paw-paw into my hands as I rushed around trying to accredit myself to the Vietnamese army. I finally tracked down the accreditation card on a clerk's desk just as his clock struck noon. 'Come back at three after you have had lunch and a siesta,' the clerk said.

Within a quarter of an hour, the crowded streets were empty, stalls, shops and offices closed. There was little I could do but follow the local custom and begin my three-hour lunch break.

Naturally enough, the American military viewpoint was eternally optimistic in those days. The political situation, so often rent by coup attempts, had stabilised; there was then some evidence of success in the policy of pacifying villages in the delta; there was a lull in the fighting – explained by the impending rainy season and the need of the Vietcong to regroup before the land became a vast swamp. However, American officers agreed, albeit reluctantly, that even back in 1963 the Vietcong had established a skeleton administration throughout the country, a fact underlined in official announcements referring to the capture of a village headman or provincial governor. The French planters, who stayed on after the communist victory at Dien Bien Phu in 1954, generally paid tolls to the Vietcong to use the roads to the towns.

The US administration machine, military or political, remained its usual free-and-easy self, always helpful to reporters and willing to discuss operations. So it was a simple matter to obtain permission to go on a helicopter mission into enemy territory.

I joined the pilot and his crew of two gunners with two other helicopters for a trip into Vietcong domain to open up an enemy-controlled canal. We whirred off from the major airbase at Can Tho, about one hundred miles from Saigon, zipping just above the trees. On the way, an order came over the radio diverting us to evacuate two wounded casualties. As we approached the landing spot in a paddy field, the pilot told his gunners at the machine-guns that poked through the open doors in the fuselage, 'It's most dangerous when the Vietcong don't open fire.'

He explained that until recent days the guerrillas had never been able to resist taking pot shots at helicopters. Only rarely had a helicopter been shot down, or so I was then told, but in engaging them from the ground, the guerrillas gave away their positions and brought American warplanes down, strafing, bombing and burning the surrounding area.

A minute later we landed, somewhat tensely, in the paddy field beside a half-dry canal. I was encouraged by the sight of hand grenades and smoke bombs in our aircraft if we needed to make a fast get-away. A few seconds after touch-down, twenty to thirty villainous men emerged from the high undergrowth and despite their appearance they were 'friendly'.

The men, wearing basic Vietnamese army uniforms to which they added coloured scarves and headdresses, quickly carried and pushed a wounded American and a Vietnamese soldier into the back of the helicopter. Our pilot took off without delay, flying low and fast. About eight hundred Vietcong were reported to be in this area and I could not help noticing the taut fingers around our machine-gun triggers. We returned to base while the two helicopters accompanying us earlier carried on with the main operation.

I had seen a similar combined operation begin two days before when two Vietnamese battalions were flown by US helicopters from the Can Tho airbase to a forward zone to rout the Vietcong from an important canal. Unfortunately, it was doomed from the start as too many people knew about it.

A river attack group included two US assault landing craft, to which Bofors guns had been fitted forward and machine-guns to the port and starboard sides, and two armed river patrol vessels, which were manned by locally recruited crews and troops with

American naval advisers, who manfully attempted to keep in the background. A group of nearby sampans loaded with supplies waited for the canal to be cleared of Vietcong forces.

When I arrived on the scene, the operation was already three hours behind schedule. The Vietcong had doubtless been moving troops into the canal during the previous night. They had already gained control of a considerable part of the two thousand five hundred miles of waterways in the Mekong delta.

Soon after the US-directed vessels entered the canal they ran into heavy machine-gun fire. A US adviser was killed and one of the attacking boats was sunk by a mine. The troops on land fared no better as they came under accurate mortar fire which rendered movement difficult. US air support, which accompanied almost every Vietnamese operation, was intensified. Twelve B-57 bombers, a fleet of helicopter gunships and a crack Ranger battalion were ordered into the battle and, as government troops withdrew, the air attack went in blasting everything in sight.

After it was all over, the Saigon government claimed that two hundred and seventy six Vietcong were killed and thirty three captured along with a cache of new Chinese, Czechoslovakian and East German guns. Six Americans had been killed and three US helicopters shot down. This was described as a successful operation although the canal remained in Vietcong hands and the sampans never left their moorings.

At that time in the Spring of 1965, there were eight thousand US Marines in Vietnam, five thousand of them guarding the large US base at Da Nang, the port four hundred miles north of Saigon. It was less than a year after the Gulf of Tonkin 'incident', in which two American destroyers opened fire believing they were under attack from North Vietnamese warships during a tropical storm, which had caused their electronic equipment 'to go crazy!' In fact, there had been no attack although two days previously the Americans had sunk two North Vietnamese patrol boats while on a mission to test radar installations along the communist coast.

In Washington, President Johnson reacted to the Gulf of Tonkin incident by ordering the bombing of North Vietnam and signalling the start of direct US involvement in the war, which was to cost the lives of fifty eight thousand Americans and around two million Vietnamese.

For the Vietnamese people war had been almost a way of life for centuries. The French had established colonial rule in 1887 but back in the mists of time the Vietnamese had been defending their land against attacks by the Chinese in the north. They were accustomed to an interminable background of violent death and destruction, a ready-made trap awaiting the US in swamp and jungle.

In retrospect, the Americans walked into an appalling situation because they simply failed to understand the vast problem – militarily, politically, economically – that was destined to lead them into a grotesque situation: the defeat of the western super-power by a Third World nation.

When Mr McNamara, the US Secretary of Defence, announced in April, 1965, that the war was to be intensified it was patently accepted in Saigon that the battle for the hearts and minds of the Vietnamese people would be superseded by deadly war fought to retain control of the air and sea bases as well as the towns held by government forces. The guerrilla movement controlled 40 per cent of the country and it was making headway.

American advisers were, however, reluctant to face the fact that even during the dry season when conditions were ideal for their type of air warfare they had been slowly losing ground to the Vietcong. But the main question was where the government would find up to one hundred and twenty thousand Vietnamese to train and arm for anti-guerrilla warfare. Mr McNamara announced a conscription plan to do just that without mentioning it to the government in Saigon.

At the political level, Dr Phan Huy Quat, the prime minister, was another puppet dangling on strings operated by the Washington Treasury. He genuinely wanted Third World recognition for his country and, to his credit, he was not responsible for the corrupt, inadequate and inefficient civil service. The custom of rounding up men between the ages of eighteen and thirty-five and, without checking their papers (if any), transporting them to an army training camp miles from the city began long before he became prime minister. It was indeed an army of resentment that was being recruited. That the men entered the army in an angry and rancorous mood, particularly as they had not been allowed to inform their wives or employers of their enforced call-up, accounted in part for the flat refusal of many South Vietnamese units to make contact with the enemy.

I challenged a senior police officer about these press-gang tactics and he retorted, 'The Americans insist that the Vietnamese army be kept up to strength. How else can we do it?' The police, too, were hamstrung in knowing just who could be conscripted. It was imperative that they did not recruit middle-class men because their relations would soon protest to the Saigon government, who would order their immediate release.

No doubt Mr McNamara was unaware of these trip wires but assuming that the Pentagon had evolved an overall defence strategy for Vietnam and, indeed, the whole of South East Asia, they had built up the military arm without any determined attempt to co-ordinate it with the internal and external policy, which depended almost exclusively on the Saigon government. Nor was there any apparent effort to co-ordinate American moves in the economic field. No one knew, for instance, what proportion of American aid found its way into Vietcong hands. Certainly, American medical supplies and equipment, including food and clothes, were in general use by the Vietcong inside South Vietnam.

But whatever policy governed 'aid' the Vietnamese merchants continued to amass great fortunes, which they kept in Hong Kong banks. Many were poised to escape to France or Singapore if the situation worsened. For no one believed in an American victory because the expensive campaign to win the sympathy of the people had failed completely and the American had replaced the Frenchman as the hated 'imperialist' even with those Vietnamese who were benefiting financially from the war.

The South Vietnamese were well aware that there were at that time two million three hundred thousand of their own people who were refugees. Most were confined to the coastal plain after being driven from their homes by bombs and napalm directed entirely without discrimination against scattered and elusive bands of Vietcong rebels in their midst. Their dissatisfaction with the treatment they had received was heightened by the reckless American bombing over the forests and against people without any concern or knowledge of their allegiances. There was one particularly ironic development from the American bombing of North Vietnam. Many elderly men and women travelled from the north seeking death in a more comfortable environment in

South Vietnam. They found respite and comfort in the refugee centres and camps run by the Catholic Church which did a splendid job looking after and educating hundreds of orphans from the north. Many non-Catholics gave their services to the sisters, including my friend Pamela, Lady Egremont, who spent much of the nights nursing the dying and her days teaching the children.

In spite of all the American operations there was military stale-mate with the Vietcong controlling all key areas but unable to dislodge the Americans and the Saigon forces from the principal towns. By maintaining a formidable array of sophisticated and powerful weapons, the Americans had dug themselves in – often literally – in an effort to secure their firm hold on Saigon and the six main airbases.

The Americans had earlier sought the advice of the British military expert, Sir Robert Thompson, whose plans and projects for dealing with communist rebels and infiltrators had been so successful in Malaya. Sir Robert went to Vietnam and gave wise counsel, which was either exaggerated in execution or ignored. Basically, he claimed that it was essential to operate from a 'clean' base that had not been infiltrated by 'moles' or, in the villages, by Vietcong agents. This was impossible in Saigon for we now know that many of the trusted clerks in both the South Vietnamese government and American military headquarters were active Vietcong supporters in spite of their impeccable French bourgeois background.

In the countryside, Sir Robert urged the establishment of 'safe' or 'clean' villages to be inhabited only by farmers, who were supporters of the South Vietnamese government. The Americans were willing to give adequate funds to make the villages prosperous as well as safe. This should have prevented the flow of rice and other foodstuffs to the rebels but things went badly wrong.

From the 'safe' village the pacification should have spread slowly like oil over the countryside. To be absolutely certain that the farmers were isolated, the Americans built what were called 'strategic hamlets' and moved the villagers into these new, ugly dwellings by force. They were allowed out to work in the fields during the day but at night the gates were closed and guarded by soldiers of the ARVN – the South Vietnamese army. Despite the extra funds channelled into the 'strategic hamlets', they were loathed by the peasants, some of whom joined the Vietcong to get away from them!

Another problem arose from the wish of Americans of all ranks to claim that they had 'pacified' – placed under the control of the ARVN – large tracks of territory to demonstrate how successfully the project was developing. These assertions were pressed not only in GHQ in Saigon but also in Washington. Thus, instead of taking Thompson's advice to move ahead slowly with pacification they proceeded far too quickly.

I saw an example myself in the delta south of My Tho where I accompanied Harry Walston (now Lord Walston) on a tour of 'safe' villages. We drove from My Tho airport along a well-kept main road before turning off to the village where we saw the school, drank coconut milk and watched the prosperous villagers fishing. It was all too perfect. I smelt a rat and left my almost empty handbag behind deliberately as an excuse for returning later. We drove back to My Tho and when Harry Walston and his staff had departed I hired a car and returned to the village. There the road was blocked and guarded by a French-speaking Vietcong officer, who was unimpressed by my reason for visiting the village. He had no intention of letting me continue my journey. He explained that the village was open during the day to the government so that peasants could market their fish and fruit. At any other time, it represented Vietcong territory.

He invited me to spend a week with the Vietcong if I agreed to stay. But with an office in London, a husband in Paris and hotels booked in My Tho and Saigon it seemed that my disappearance would cause more trouble than even that excellent story was worth. I talked for some time with this officer, whose main interest appeared to concern his old haunts in Paris. What was on he asked at the cinemas in the Avenue de l'Opera? Finally, after consulting a superior officer, he said he had permission to let me go. I was not even aware that he had been detaining me! I was fortunate as many people who met the Vietcong in 'isolated conditions' were taken prisoner.

It was evident that the Americans had made little preparation for the kind of limited war in South Vietnam. Senior American officers in Saigon complained that the Pentagon had been so pre-occupied with nuclear strategy since the end of the Korean war that they had given but scant attention and thought to guerrilla or subversive war of the kind, for instance, that the British fought in Malaya. They certainly had no tactics to compete with the latest refinements of Mao Zedong techniques, which the Vietcong had developed and adapted during the long years of fighting since the end of the Second World War.

The Vietcong could deploy quite easily considerable effort at little cost to themselves while the Americans were forced to expend resources on a vast scale. The rebels enjoyed the sympathy of a large majority of the Vietnamese or local tribesmen in the areas where they operated. They had a superb intelligence network and it was impossible for a foreigner to distinguish between a Vietcong rebel and a Vietnamese government soldier because they were the same people who dressed, talked and behaved in an identical manner. The terrorist could and frequently did walk safely in the streets of Saigon.

The Americans had produced nothing to attract the rebel population to their side. President Johnson's offer of millions of dollars for aid and development was dismissed by Vietcong radio as *'pour les oiseaux'*. Nor did the Americans have any clearly defined objective other than to save the country from communism and even this was a difficult enough task with each of the services following a slightly different policy.

The Americans and the Vietnamese government troops had no really effective intelligence service. From time to time a paid agent would provide some worthwhile information or a captured rebel would be 'persuaded' to disclose the position of a communist unit. It was a matter of luck rather than of management.

In an effort to discover where and in what numbers the rebels and supplies were crossing the frontier from Laos into South Vietnam in the isolated and forested areas of the Central Highlands, the Americans set up a number of Special Forces' posts. It was planned that those excellent American soldiers would also be able to recruit and train the local warlike tribes as soldiers and then use them to help patrol the area. The experiment was not a success. Some of the posts had to be withdrawn because of the difficulty of maintaining supplies to remote forests. In one case, five American aircraft were lost in a series of drops. And while the tribesmen were willing to accept the equivalent of the 'Queen's shilling' to enlist they quickly slipped away with a few weeks' pay, their rifle and uniform.

Attempts to spot guerrilla movements from the air were useless. Only long-range patrols – such as the British employed in Borneo – could keep a close watch on the Ho Chi Minh trail, that route of easy infiltration that ran down the border with Laos from the north of Vietnam. On the Cambodian frontier in the Mekong delta, the rebels made great use of the seven thousand miles of navigable waterways and, apart from the two or three months at the end of the dry season, they had good cover in the ricefields. They mined the rivers and the roads and, occasionally, resorted to comparatively easy forays to leave bombs in the towns and cities or lob mortars on to airfields.

In this hide-and-seek war, the Americans began to develop the helicopter as an attack aircraft equipped with machine-guns and rockets. I always felt that the helicopter produced a totally false sense of security because the engine roar drowned the noise of small arms fire and I always sat on my bullet-proof waistcoat folded double whenever I went on operations. It was only on return to base that one realised by the bullet holes in the fuselage that contact had been made with the unseen enemy.

General Westmoreland and his successors were convinced that one of the main aims of the North Vietnamese was to extend their territory to include Hue, if not Da Nang, in the south. This accounted for the periodic concentration of operations in that area and the massive manoeuvres there during and after the Tet offensive when the communists did take over Hue.

The Americans remained baffled by the complexity of the war they were fighting and failed to appreciate the importance of security since communist agents frequently penetrated the inner sanctum of US headquarters. And the Americans never tackled the issue of corruption. I remember once bribing seven officials to obtain an exit visa (to which I was fully entitled), and, on another occasion, an official at the airport told me my name was on the black-list of people not allowed to leave the country but as it was in pencil he would rub it out for U.S. $100. Whether I was on the list, I shall never know. Maybe one reason why the Americans did not worry too much about corruption was because they were less subjected to it than those of us who needed visas and special permits.

But suddenly for me the war and the American build-up, which sent two hundred thousand troops to Vietnam by the end of the year, was temporarily over.

In Saigon, I received a letter from my husband, who complained of having pains in his arms similar to those he had experienced before having a heart attack some years earlier. He said he was going to London in the near future to see his doctor and have a check-up. Sensing danger, I requested my editor for permission to take immediate leave 'for personal reasons' for the only time in my life. Alastair Hetherington gave his authority and, within a day, I was on my way to London, arriving there at the same time as Geoffrey.

He had a minor heart attack within hours of arrival but cheerfully entered the King Edward VII Hospital for Officers after buying books to read in bed. He persuaded people to smuggle cigarettes into him, and he was recovering after ten days of treatment, but he had another massive heart attack and died a few hours later. My friends were wonderfully supportive and the editor sent me off to Algeria immediately following the funeral – one of the kindest things he ever did. Life has never been quite the same since.

I returned to Vietnam for the *Daily Telegraph* in the spring of 1968, which was arguably the turning point in the war with American morale sagging, the North Vietnamese forces under their brilliant commander, General Vo Nguyen Giap, tightening their control in the south, and President Nguyen Van Thieu in Saigon finally beginning to realise that the only way out for him would be political rather than military. The increasing use of herbicides and weedkillers by the Americans to defoliate the jungles was a clear sign of the desperation they felt in their failure to track down the enemy's lairs.

Although the US commanders boasted of the successful uses of defoliation as a means of rounding up enemy infiltrators, they were forced to admit that at that time there were more than ninety thousand North Vietnamese troops and thirty five thousand Vietcong in South Vietnam – a record figure which neither weedkiller nor artillery was able to curb.

The official statement on defoliation claimed that the deadly spray from low-flying planes posed no harm to either human or animal life. This was patently untrue. Two years before I wandered along a jungle track near Da Nang where there were hundreds of rare and exotic birds and butterflies. Wild orchids were hanging from the trees and dragon-flies hovered over stagnant pools. In 1968 along that trail there were a few gaunt, burned tree trunks standing above the brown, soggy evil-smelling mass of dead vegetation. Maybe some birds escaped but they certainly lost their feeding grounds.

After four months in the rainy season green shoots did appear and a few – very few – trees survived but there was no doubt that the defoliation operations would have serious adverse effects on plants, animals and people in South Vietnam for many years. Indeed, vast areas of forest, jungle, grassland, mango swamp and even paddy-fields had been reduced to desert by the aerial application of '2-4-D' and to a lesser degree cacodylic acid, which contained arsenic.

The US military command was pleased with the results but they were – understandably – shy about producing vital statistics. However, during the first nine months of 1967 the USAF sprayed more than nine hundred and sixty five acres with defoliants or leaf stripping and crop-killing chemicals. The US Defence Department increased its expenditure on this form of warfare from about £5 million in 1965 to £30 million in 1968.

There were many problems frustrating the Americans in this tropical environment. An elusive enemy highly skilled in jungle warfare, communications always under attack whether on the ground or in the air, growing infiltration from the North despite massive bombing operations, but above all, the worsening morale among the lower ranks.

When I flew in with supplies to a hilltop landing zone overlooking Highway 9 between Khe Sanh, the beleagured US outpost, and the Laotian border, I discovered that the troops' main interest was concerned with the date when they would return home. They had all heard about the peace talks due to open between Washington and Hanoi. One GI said he hoped that this would result in returning to the US by the autumn rather than Christmas. Another young soldier was even more downright. 'Charlie (the

Vietcong) can have the whole country so far as I'm concerned. Remember, the Number One hit here is "We Wanna Go Home".'

The American soldier was well fed, well paid and splendidly equipped. But his heart was not in the war. Even among junior officers there was little interest in tactics or the course of the war. Although most of them wanted nothing more than to get out of South Vietnam, in my opinion the period of a soldier's effective service at just over eight months was too short. The GI spent at least the first two months learning his job – getting acclimatised – six months in operations, and then two months in 'disengagement' when his efficiency flagged rapidly. There were, of course, in every unit – especially the Marines – a group of hawkish officers, who were ready to bomb more villages, burn more forests and napalm more mountains. They were openly bitter at Britain's absence from the fighting.

Yet already in early 1968, the Pentagon was preparing to de-escalate the war. The new US commander-in-chief, General Creighton Abrams, who succeeded General Westmoreland, was under orders to train the South Vietnamese army into a confident fighting force capable of holding their positions against the enemy. A tall order considering the lack of real leadership, corruption in every branch of the State and too many generals with ambitions to become military dictators. Even General Westmoreland admitted on the last day of his command that a military victory for the South in the classical sense was not possible. 'This is due to the fact that our national policy is not to extend the scope of the war,' he said.

He scornfully belittled the fighting ability of the North Vietnamese, an opinion he shared with few people. When he arrived in January 1964, there were only sixteen thousand American troops in South Vietnam. When he left after building up a 'killing machine' there were five hundred and twenty five thousand Americans serving there. He believed that if he caused annual casualties exceeding the number of young men who came of age each year in the North – about a quarter of a million – he would destroy the morale of the enemy forces. Further, the bombing of the North was aimed not only at hindering the movement of men and materials to the South but weakening the spirits of the civilians in Hanoi and Haiphong, the important North Vietnamese port. Instead, the bombing produced a 'Battle of

Britain' resistance and General Westmoreland admitted himself that in April 1968, the monthly average of communist soldiers taking to the Ho Chi Minh trail had risen from seven thousand to twenty four thousand.

In hard figures, Hanoi and the political arm of the Vietcong – the National Liberation Front – administered more than eighteen hundred of the two thousand five hundred villages and more than half the eleven thousand six hundred and fifty hamlets. Saigon was responsible for less than eight million of the total population of seventeen million and of that eight million just more than half were troops and civil servants.

Although much more blood would be shed over the approaching years, the writing was clearly spelt out on the wall even as early as 1968. As I travelled from one US base to another that year with the words of the communist agent I met in Saigon cathedral fresh in my mind the more I realised that I was witnessing the beginning of the end of this sad American saga.

This became suddenly even more apparent to me while I was sitting on the doorstep of the Association Press office in the Press Centre of Da Nang on 31 March 1968. Over the radio came the voice of President Lyndon Johnson announcing that he would not seek re-election. His statement was taken as a clear sign that he intended to devote all his energies to achieving a successful conclusion to the war in Vietnam.

Three years later the withdrawal symptoms had taken firm root. There was no transport available at Da Nang except upon the pillion seats of motor-cycles, whose unemployed owners traded as local 'taxis'. Civilian morale was at a low ebb as unemployment increased. Even the Marines agreed that the sooner they left the city the better. And the Press Centre, a comfortable enclosed former French motel on the outskirts of the town where we all lived, had been closed.

In 1968 the Press Centre was a hectic hub of communications with war correspondents coming and going all the time. There was plenty of transport and a mass of operations to follow by air or on land. Unhappily, the bathing beach was by then too polluted to use and, sadly, the nearby museum had been denuded of its more easily transportable objects, which were to find their way to antique shops in New York and London.

There were monstrous reports in circulation of corruption.

They were neither confirmed nor denied. 'Loyal' Vietnamese and even ARVN officers were said to have acquired vast stores of arms from American dumps and sold them for gigantic sums to the Vietcong, who, in fact, admitted that they had bought weapons from Marine arsenals in Da Nang. They were certainly close enough: they had one underground base within a mile of the end of the Da Nang runway.

In the annals of American history, however, the name of Khe Sanh will glow with the memory of courage and fortitude. It occupied a vital spot in the extreme north-west of South Vietnam just south of the demilitarised zone where some hundred odd American Marines were under siege for twenty-three months believing that they were holding down large enemy forces. This was largely true although the combat base failed in its original objective to prevent infiltration from the north, which had risen so dramatically.

My first glimpse of Khe Sanh was from a giant C130 US transport aircraft on a supply dropping mission from the Saigon air base at Tan Son Nhut. As we approached Khe Sanh, the words came over the intercom to the pilot: 'There is no Forward Air Control available at the moment – please orbit for five minutes.'

We were the second plane of the US Tactical Airlift due to drop supplies of ammunition to the beseiged troops. No aircraft was allowed to descend below 3,500-feet – the maximum effective range of small arms fire – unless accompanied by a Forward Air Control plane as an escort.

We were all wearing anti-flak jackets. The captain rehearsed the split-second timing of the drop, which depended on radar and a computer. When we came out of the cloud, a fighter plane flashed by. The area around Khe Sanh – about the size of St James's Park – looked like a First World War landscape. There were hundreds of shell holes and burned tree stumps through which trenches twisted and turned.

The runway and the camp emplacements looked undamaged but showed no sign of life as we roared down to five hundred feet. As the navigator gave the signal, the rear doors of the aircraft opened, the pilot put the aircraft into a climb and within five seconds the fourteen platforms carrying ammunition slipped out.

The large parachutes opened immediately and the pilot banked steeply to get out of the area of the neighbouring mountain peaks harbouring North Vietnamese mortar positions.

Everyone gave a sigh of relief. There had been some very light and distant small arms fire but the crew were disappointed to find no marks of it when we landed at Da Nang to pick up the second load of the day.

The dropping operations were directed from an 'ops' room at Tan Son Nhut in Saigon, a slightly larger version of the one at the British Ministry of Defence. The duty officer at Da Nang informed our pilots that the drop had been successful with all supplies landing eight to ten seconds after release within seventy-four yards of the 'bull's-eye'. We were ordered to refuel at Da Nang and take on another load of ammunition. But on this second mission we were not so lucky.

The sun had 'burnt up' many of the clouds and the North Vietnamese were mortaring the dropping zone. We hung around over the sea, which in the pilot's words, was the only safe place in Vietnam. Although six fighters went into the Khe Sanh area to 'hose down' the guerrillas, the mortar bombs continued to fall.

Our control tower finally told the captain to call it a day and return to Da Nang with the hot cargo. When we eventually reached the air base the tired crew were 'debriefed' after fourteen hours of operations. Certainly, the American technical efficiency was then most impressive. The commanding officer was completely confident that whatever happened Khe Sanh would continue to be supplied. With some pride he recalled that 60 per cent of the French parachute drops at Dien Bien Phu, the French enclave that fell to General Giap in 1954, went straight into enemy hands. American drops had achieved a 98.5 per cent success rate. But what the RAF would have called 'a piece of cake' was considered almost dangerous by the better-equipped and equally well-trained USAF. I felt somewhat disquieted that in war so great a margin of safety was required.

During one trip to Da Nang, I flew in an American warplane on a bombing mission. There was some fire from the ground but I did not see or hear it hit the aircraft. We were supposed to make a second raid to blast a Vietnam camp from a mountain top. But on the return journey, the pilot said over the intercom, 'The United States should be proud and grateful for all you have done today.' What, I queried, had they done? He then told me of the 'great bravery' of all in his plane which was, of course, rubbish as we had not known we were in any danger. On our return to Da Nang, he refused to go on the second mission on the grounds of 'the terrible sufferings' of the crew during the trip, which I had just experienced.

A month later, I flew into Khe Sanh with men of the Air Cavalry. They were relieving three companies of Marines, who had been there since January. We landed by helicopter on the base, which resembled a gigantic rubbish dump with a much-damaged runway across the centre. There were huge piles of empty tins and stacks of supplies that had been damaged when they were dropped from the air. It was hardly possible to walk without falling over half-hidden rusty barbed wire. The grassless soil was red, the trees scorched and blasted amid the shell-holes. There were damaged buildings everywhere. The troops lived in ill-constructed bunkers as I did.

During those months of siege the troops were under constant fire and subjected to frequent attacks on the perimeter. Yet few of them seemed frightened, which was strange as I frequently met extremely scared soldiers in Vietnam. But the bunkers – named after 'Fifth Avenue', the 'Hilton' and even 'Buckingham Palace' – produced a quiet, secure background with plenty of books, magazines and pictures of Marilyn Monroe. There was nothing much to do but man the signals room, await orders and the next attack or the arrival of fresh supplies. Everyone walked everywhere since there was hardly one jeep left undamaged and working.

When I arrived, F-100 fighters were attacking trenches and dug-outs about two hundred yards from the edge of the camp. North Vietnamese soldiers were caught in the attack on their positions, which later I was able to inspect.

The trench system was brilliantly constructed to within easy rifle range of Khe Sanh camp. Every twenty yards or so there was an obvious officer's bunker, in which Chinese maps, ammunition and grenades had been left. All the American positions up to a week before were accurately marked on a map I saw. There were rat and snake traps, much-enlarged versions of the mouse traps of my childhood. But instead of cheese being used as bait large pieces of meat were put into the traps to lure the big rats and snakes. They were all made in America. The Vietnamese officers were also stacked with US ration packs and cartons of fruit juice from California, which no doubt compensated for the strong smell of corpses in no-man's-land, which were then being collected for burial.

News of race riots in the US made no apparent impact on the American troops in Khe Sanh. During a minor alert, I jumped into a bunker where one white and one coloured soldier were listening to a radio broadcast describing race riots and looting in Washington. 'They seem to be crazy back on Stateside,' the black soldier said to me in apologetic tones. There was no flag to lower nor ceremonies to observe in Khe Sanh for Dr Martin Luther King – but there was interest in the radio announcement that bathing beaches were to be closed in Da Nang.

I was helicoptered out of Khe Sanh to the safety of Saigon but one month later I went off again on operations that took me to Dong Ha, six miles from the demilitarised zone between North and South Vietnam and the end of the ten thousand mile naval supply line from America. The last one hundred and fifty miles from Da Nang were the most hazardous. Weapons equipment, rations and even folding furniture arrived from Da Nang in landing craft operating along the canals and rivers from Cua Viet five miles away. The shallow waterways were a battleground for daily skirmishes between the Americans and North Vietnamese. Not only were sandbanks a natural hazard for the US relief convoys but they also faced underwater mines and bamboo fences built by the communists.

This trip was part of 'Operation Pegasus', which was launched to break through the North Vietnamese lines and lift the six months siege of Khe Sanh. The withdrawal from the base was carried out in June with the minimum of publicity to avoid jarring the American people, who had been told frequently that their troops were dying to secure this 'crucial anchor'. General Giap himself had visited the communist forces around the base and had narrowly escaped death in a massive American air strike. 'Operation Pegasus' began when squadrons of Chinook helicopters, escorted by Cobra helicopter gunships capable of firing forty five thousand rounds a minute, landed at Calu, the nearest roadhead to Khe Sanh since monsoon rains destroyed most of the highway during the previous September. Khe Sanh could not be supplied by lorry convoys before fifteen bridges destroyed by the North Vietnamese had been rebuilt.

I went in with the Chinooks, which were packed with troops, vehicles and 150mm howitzers and boxes of ammunition, ingeniously slung under the aircraft. Helicopter gunships prowled across the surrounding hills trying to draw fire from the unseen enemy.

Within five minutes of touch-down, the big guns were in firing position and bulldozers landed from the air moved off to start repairing damaged roads. By nightfall at this advance battle headquarters a few miles from Khe Sanh, a runway capable of taking transport planes was almost completed and scores of helicopter pads established. The spearhead of twenty thousand American troops, ignoring shell and mortar fire, had pressed forward to within a mile of the beleaguered US garrison.

Thirteen thousand South Vietnamese troops were also brought into this massive operation against ten thousand North Vietnamese under General Giap. Five hundred American helicopters ferried troops and weapons to Calu and at least twenty were on constant night and day flights against an enemy, unseen and elusive, who continued to shell and mortar our positions with remarkable accuracy. During a night attack on Calu, while I was there, a direct hit on a storage dump destroyed thousands of tons of fuel.

In essence 'Operation Pegasus' was largely a search and destroy affair and with the Laotian border a few miles away General Giap's men were able to disappear into that sanctuary and re-emerge without great difficulty.

Back in Da Nang Lieutenant-General Cushman, commander of the US Marine Corps, claimed that one thousand enemy troops were killed in the first ten days of 'Operation Pegasus'. General Giap had been forced to withdraw about nine thousand of his men but there was no American explanation why so many of the enemy had been allowed to escape by denying them the use of the valley through which Highway 9 ran from Khe Sanh to the frontier of Laos. The First American Air Cavalry Division operated by setting up a series of mutually dependent artillery positions and landing zones. Had they attempted, however, to seal off the frontier, the enemy area between the US advance base known as Stud and the scene of operations would have been largely uncovered by artillery and could have become dangerous for helicopters in flight. Other American troops such as the Airborne Brigade could have been deployed for this type of action both in the Lang Vei area and, even more important, in the Ashau Valley, which was the main supply route for enemy units infiltrating into South Vietnam from the north through Laos.

Khe Sanh was finally evacuated by the Marines on 6 July after sustained attacks by North Vietnamese troops. Major-General Raymond Davis, commander of the 3rd Marine Division, admitted, 'The base has become a yoke around my neck.' His men left behind them a three thousand feet steelmat airstrip and five aircraft bays protected by ten feet high steel walls. The rest was dynamited and bulldozed to the ground.

After a quick visit to Hue, I went into the Ashau Valley where ten thousand American troops and one thousand South Vietnamese were trying to close the infiltration route. The Americans were hoping for a face-to-face battle with General Giap's forces but he was too clever to get caught in a head-on confrontation with a superior conventional force. 'D' Day was 19 April but a week before massive air raids – more than ninety in one day – on the valley alerted General Giap to what was coming and he evacuated all his men with the exception of a harrying group of anti-aircraft gunners and machine gun units. In the first few days of the US attack they lost thirty helicopters through bad weather and ground fire.

Meanwhile, back in the once-beautiful but now battered city of Hue there were justified fears of an imminent attack from North Vietnamese troops, who were taking up positions in the surrounding area. Many of them had been pulled out of the Ashau Valley and they appeared to have escaped two days of air raids by American B-52 bombers. As a precaution inside the city the provincial governor and mayor, Colonel Le Thaun, announced that forty thousand civilians would be armed.

During the Tet offensive two months before, Hue was the scene of some of the worst fighting in the war with the Imperial Palace being captured by the North Vietnamese and held by them for twenty five weeks. When I reached the city it was not easy for the Americans to operate there because of the damage they created in capturing the palace from the communists. In many of the gardens of destroyed homes there were freshly dug graves. I spoke to more than ten families who had lost their homes through what they claimed was random or wild fire power by American Marines. The population was openly resentful of anyone speaking English.

Equally the people of this frightened city were enraged by the atrocities committed by the communists during their brief spell of power. Mass graves of slaughtered civilians were uncovered after the North Vietnamese had made their escape. The population was also disgusted at the extent of bribery and corruption in the municipal life of their city and they put the blame squarely on the American and Saigon administrators.

I returned to Saigon more than ever convinced that the communists had the upper hand in the war and that even in the capital of South Vietnam the North Vietnamese were appearing in the suburbs with the intention of forcing civilians into the centre of the city.

The tactics had all the signs of an attempt to take over Saigon if the Paris talks broke down. Harassing operations from four points of the compass in recent weeks had followed this general rule.

This was well illustrated in the fighting I saw in Phu Lam on the western outskirts in which two North Vietnamese companies attacked an American radar station. Civilian traffic was stopped on Highway 4, the main road to the delta, as the fighting zone was sealed off by two South Vietnamese army units moving in to counter-attack.

Lieutenant-Colonel Dao Ba Phuoc warned me as we reached the area that the North Vietnamese frequently occupied houses next to South Vietnamese troops. There were small blocks of flats, in which the communists were on one floor and the South Vietnamese on another.

Many residents of the small villas in the area had remained in their homes in the hope of preventing looting. We went in just behind the troops, who took up positions on roofs and set up rough barricades in the streets.

They were only too ready to warn us where the communist guns were. We climbed to the top of the highest building where three soldiers had been wounded earlier by rockets, which the communists were still firing from a nearby house. Crawling around the roof, it was easy to obtain a view of the curiously mixed district as the Cobra helicopter gunships dived on a large garage, which was the main communist position five hundred yards from the US radar station.

The noise was ear-splitting as fighter planes joined in, rocketing the target and setting off fires everywhere. I could see the communists in their greyish uniforms quite clearly through field-glasses as they fired on troops in the street below every time the South Vietnamese tried to advance.

A South Vietnamese captain complained that he had had repeated orders to advance but it was quite impossible. Two of his men had been killed and other troops refused to enter into the open. When I suggested that he should lead them he was quite horrified and radioed for more air support.

The planes roared in again. More fires. Continuous rattle of crossfire. Explosions galore. It went on for hours and by early afternoon neither side had made any progresss. By then I decided it was time for me to withdraw and file my copy. I did so without difficulty but I was rather surprised to discover that half a mile away life was relatively normal. Air strikes were not unusual in Saigon.

In the days that followed that scene of noisy, bloody battle was repeated in Cho Lon, the Chinese quarter of Saigon, where North Vietnamese suicide squads caused havoc, panic and flattened half a square mile in the centre of the suburb. It seemed quite possible that the communists could have taken the city whenever they wished but they were content to play a waiting game while their political leaders waged their particular war aimed at winning the battle of the conference table in Paris.

In July, I flew to Honolulu to cover the talks between President Johnson and President Thieu of South Vietnam which produced the agreement that the South Vietnamese would gradually assume responsibility for their own defence, which was the first definite step towards the American withdrawal by 1973. They began pulling out within twelve months.

The Americans promised continued supplies of arms and talked of a bombing halt that was subsequently ordered. But the killing in

South Vietnam went on for another seven cruel years. I returned on many occasions to review the situation, often accompanying American and South Vietnamese units on their forays into the jungle and each time the story was much the same horrifying game of hide-and-seek that produced mounting casualties on all sides.

But it was not until 28 January 1973 that the first ceasefire took place at midnight, marked by the sound of church bells in Saigon where the traffic stopped and soldiers stood to attention and saluted.

The final curtain was falling across the bloody stage of the Vietnam war. The ceasefire burst occasionally into conflict as southern and northern factions tried to consolidate their positions, the Americans prepared for their final withdrawal and the US prisoners of war began to leave for home. President Thieu held on to power despite all the political manoeuvring around him and the inevitable end that was clear to all with eyes to see.

For me the war ended early in February 1973 when after prolonged negotiations with the Peking government I was accepted by them as the *Daily Telegraph* staff correspondent in China. Two brief visits to Peking had finally paid off. Perhaps the most interesting phase of my professional life lay ahead.

14   China ... Mao and after ...

'China? There lies a sleeping giant. Let him sleep! For when he wakes he will move the world.'   Napoleon (1769–1821)

I arrived in Peking in early February, 1973, as the first *Daily Telegraph* resident staff correspondent in China. It was apparent then that the process of awakening to the realities of the outside world was moving fast. China had been a nuclear power for nine years and industry was just beginning to expand in a clumsy manner. But although the Cultural Revolution was then said to have ended at the Ninth Party Congress in 1969, the radical leaders – later known as the Gang of Four – were extremely powerful and, indeed, as a result of their activities it was later decreed that the Cultural Revolution did not terminate until after the death of Chairman Mao Zedong (Tse-tung) in September, 1976. However, Richard Nixon had made his astounding visit to Peking in 1972 – the first by any American president – and Prime Minister Zhou Enlai, who had preserved the nuclear installations from the Red Guards, was just managing to keep the upper-hand in the administration and the Party. His was not an easy task.

I had already visited China twice via Hong Kong from Saigon and I have returned several times a year since I left in the summer of 1976 after three and a half years in the capital as a foreign correspondent.

At that time, perhaps because there were so few resident foreigners, correspondents were invited to all the official banquets for visiting heads of state. This gave one the unique opportunity to see and sometimes meet Zhou and other members of the Politbureau, including Mao's wife, Madame Jiang Qing, who led the Gang of Four rebels.

During the 10th Party Congress in August 1973, which was to organise the succession to Chairman Mao, we foreigners then living in Peking were aware that 'something' was happening in the Great Hall of the People. Scores, if not hundreds of buses took serious-looking delegates through the specially constructed security barriers. After a week of intense but suppressed excitement a firework display signalled the end of the Congress. At the same time a short official announcement over Peking radio stated that Chairman Mao had presided over the Congress which was remarkable for its 'unity, victory and vigour'. The really sensational item of news was that the youthful Wang Hongwen had been elected as the vice-chairman of the Party. Madame Jiang Qing became a member of the Politbureau together with Yao Wenyuan, while Zhang Chunqiao was elected to the Standing Committee. Thus the Gang of Four were placed well in line for the succession.

The nation saw them all on television together with Chairman Mao and Premier Zhou Enlai but they had no glimpse of Deng Xiaoping; although he had recently been rehabilitated and was sitting on the second row of the raised platform behind the leaders that carried the two hundred odd members of the Central Committee. This information, and the fact that he was next to Madame Zhou Enlai, emerged only later when documents and pictures were released.

A few months after I arrived as a resident, a banquet was given in honour of Prince Sihanouk of Cambodia. Mr Ma Yuzhen, who was one of our official contacts in the Foreign Ministry, helpfully remarked that Deng Xiaoping, the former Secretary-General of the Party, who had been in disgrace and working on an agricultural commune and in a factory during the Cultural Revolution, would re-appear that evening. Poor Sihanouk. Few of the three hundred-odd guests paid any attention to him; all eyes were concentrated on the little man with the powerful personality, who arrived with Zhou for the pre-banquet reception. After this Deng played an active role as number two to

Zhou until his second disgrace at the hands of the Gang of Four shortly after Zhou's death in January, 1976.

The entire diplomatic corps expected Deng to succeed Zhou as, indeed, had been planned. But Madame Jiang, who by then controlled the Chairman's 'chop' – seal – loathed Deng. Thus Hua Guofeng, who was generally thought to be slightly sympathetic to the Gang of Four, was promoted to be vice-chairman of the Party after Deng's official disgrace following the demonstrations in Tiananmen Square in April, 1976. Deng was quite wrongly accused of organising the movement disguised as one to pay tribute to the late Premier Zhou Enlai.

The first half of the 1970s was a period of considerable change in China's history. I had the rare opportunity of watching events unfold while studying the effects on the life-style of the Chinese in the city and in the countryside.

Dr Henry Kissinger, who had arranged the Nixon visit through trips – public and secret – to the Chinese capital, was in Peking shortly after I arrived. As Nixon's special envoy, he continued talks on the possibility of establishing diplomatic relations between China and the US.

Fresh from Saigon, I was particularly interested to discover that in discussions about the continuing Paris talks on the future of Vietnam, the American contingent in Peking had informed the Chinese government that they were willing to allow the Thieu government in South Vietnam 'to disappear after a decent interval'.

Although Kissinger's talks were predominantly with Zhou, he was hoping to meet Mao himself for direct conversations on these momentous happenings. Mao granted Kissinger his wish with an invitation at 11 p.m. one night to his eight-roomed bungalow in the well-guarded red-walled Forbidden City. Usually only heads of state were summoned to Mao's book-lined study with its shabby, straight-backed chairs and worn carpet. In one corner stood Mao's iron bedstead and its austere coverings.

For this extraordinary occasion, Mao had brought in a photographer for a rare picture of himself with Nixon's special adviser. In Chinese eyes the gesture was so generous that it was taken for granted that diplomatic relations with the US were only

a matter of time and so this proved to be – in January,
1979.

In fact, the United States Liaison Office, which Kissinger
arranged would be established within months, was an embassy
in all but name. The staff had diplomatic status and the head of
the mission was one of the best diplomats the United States has
ever produced – David Bruce. He had by then served as a highly
successful ambassador in Paris, Bonn and London and the Chinese were so flattered that he was chosen that they allowed him
to retain the title of 'Ambassador Bruce'. His wife, Evangeline,
had lived in Peking as a small child when her father had been
ambassador there and the Chinese liked that, too. There were
some initial problems, not only about Taiwan but the employ-
ment of Marines in uniform guarding the indoor offices, but they
were quickly ironed out by Ambassador Bruce and his high-level
staff.

Later, American businessmen went to Peking in an effort to
obtain contracts together with British, Australian and Canadian
entrepreneurs and salesmen but their numbers were restricted by
the problems and the time it took to obtain visas. An interesting
market awaited them for Chinese industry had been seriously neglected since Soviet technicians withdrew in 1960. State
planning in China then concentrated on developing agriculture
to feed the vast population while the military pressed for the
development of nuclear weapons to deter any major attack from
across the border.

The first British trade exhibition in communist China opened
in Peking in the spring of 1973 to promote the sale of aircraft,
communications equipment, machine tools, petro-chemical plant
and other basic gear needed for an industrial revival.

That first exhibition was great fun. The atmosphere was heady
with the prospects of big business within a communist state. It was
enlivened, too, by a visit of the London Philharmonic Orchestra
which provided an enthusiastic audience with their first concert
of western music since 1964. The programme, I recall, was
devised quite cleverly. The orchestra began by playing the
Chinese national anthem, the 'Volunteers' March', much better
than many local military bands, which, of course, captivated the
fifteen hundred Chinese in the auditorium. Elgar, Brahms' violin

concerto and Beethoven's seventh symphony were followed by renderings of 'The East Is Red' and 'The Happy Women Fighters' from the revolutionary ballet, 'The Red Detachment of Women'. This taste of western culture entranced the Chinese. Even soldiers sitting with their baggy caps on were very impressed, too, with the smart white ties and tails of the British musicians. 'Is that British national dress?' one asked.

The Chinese decision to welcome the foreigner at last coincided in 1973 with a sudden warm spring that almost overnight decorated the eight avenues of trees lining the fifteen-mile long Changan Avenue – the main thoroughfare through the city – with fluffy emerald green leaves, a spectacular sight beside the pre-revolutionary red walls and roofs of the Forbidden City. Unhappily, the leaves would soon be discoloured by the grit and dust blowing in from the Gobi desert, the curse of the Chinese capital. Hundreds of thousands of trees had been painstakingly planted and watered in the suburbs to try to keep down the dust and millions more were planned.

The sudden early warmth was welcomed in the city that has a temperature range of between -6°F in winter to 108°F in summer. The hordes of cyclists abandoned the ugly cotton masks they wore to keep out the cold and dust and also removed a few layers of padded Mao jackets, which en masse made them look like an army of zombies.

The cyclists added to the frustrations of travelling in Peking, which also had other irritations for the foreigner. The underground, which was used only by about sixty thousand people daily, was banned to foreign visitors who were never told why they could not use it. I gathered it was due to 'secret' plans for the mass evacuation of the population in case of a nuclear attack. My first attempt was prevented by a polite official who turned me back before I even reached the ticket office.

Transport was a special problem as there were only three hundred taxis – all more than twenty years old – in a city of seven million people. So after the trolley buses terminated around mid-evening the taxi became extremely rare.

To make life somewhat more attractive for the foreigner, a new international club was built to replace the charming old building that had been taken over by the Peking Revolutionary Committee, the municipality. The new club boasted a billiard room, a tennis court, a ping-pong table, a library and a restaurant. But there was no bar and all the books from the old library were, strangely enough, locked up leaving only *The Thoughts of Mao* available for perusal.

I cannot now recall ever being lonely in China. I enjoy a meal alone with a book. There were generally people staying in the Minzu Hotel, where I lived for the first six months, ranging from the film star, Shirley Maclaine, to visiting foreign communists, who were only too anxious to have a drink or eat with anyone who actually lived in China. After dinner alone I used to go to my room and sit on a hard chair with a straight back and think how lucky I was to be in China! Sometimes I had meals with 'foreign friends' – foreigners who had devoted their lives to China and Communism – who were working for the Chinese Government.

There were so few British subjects around we were all allowed in summer to use the swimming pool in the British Embassy which was an enormous boost to morale and we were also allowed to use 'The Bell' – a combination of pub and reading-room built out of the old stables. There was an honour system and after taking a beer from the refrigerator one signed the book. Alas the place was ruined by students who dossed down for the night there and even stole bottles of liquor. But in my time it was an excellent place for an evening drink with friends where one could also read the latest newspaper from London and the monitored version of the BBC World Service. Naturally, I listened to the BBC twice a day but sometimes it was useful to see the text of the news.

Food, in fact, made up for most of the vexatious shortcomings in Peking life for most foreigners. Restaurants were excellent with splendid settings; such as establishments which were once the residences of warlords. Prices were high at about £6–£7 a head for a dinner including Peking duck, Maotai, the Chinese hard liquor, hot rice wine and beer. But I also managed to eat like an empress for 25p in a down-town cafe in Peking where foreigners were not expected to go, and had the same experience in a dockers' canteen in Shanghai.

By the late 1970s the message from the government that the round-eyed foreigner with the long nose, usually considered to be rather smelly, was 'okay' got down to grass roots. Thus, the major barrier to communication with the naturally cordial populace was the language, which, of course, was pretty formidable. But few Chinese, if any, would discuss anything more serious than the weather or, in summer, the flowers in their gardens. Politics were generally out.

At official level, life was made unnecessarily difficult. Meetings took place at banquets in the Great Hall of the People; never in offices or homes. A pre-arranged appointment had to be made to enter any government or newspaper office and even in the Foreign Ministry Chinese diplomats left their desks – they still do – to greet foreign callers in large, sombre reception rooms.

Nevertheless, the government made great efforts in its own way to make contacts easier and, at the same time, to educate their own élite in world affairs. A Chinese-language bulletin of world news was circulated to officialdom in the principal cities and the *People's Daily*, while not reporting anything that might reflect on Peking's allies, certainly made no secret of the troubles besetting other world leaders.

Every foreign visitor to Peking agreed on one thing: it was the cleanest city in the world in every sense. Buildings were spotless and the wide avenues flanked by vast Soviet-styled government buildings and the narrow streets of old Peking were devoid of litter. All Chinese smoked but not a single cigarette butt was to be seen anywhere. Food was not packaged so residents took their own paper bags and wrappings to the shop counter and disposed of the paper at home.

This was all very pleasing to the foreign eye. Indeed, since Nixon's visit twelve months earlier all the large anti-foreign slogans had been taken down from the streets, shops and hotels and replaced at crossroads by posters thirty feet high and ninety feet long calling on the workers of the world to unite and the Chinese in particular to work harder. Some anti-Japanese posters remained in the suburbs and provinces.

These hoardings in bright red and white offered pleasant contrast and relief to the drab grey buildings and the dark green and blue uniforms of the military and civilian population whose gender was indicated only by their hairstyle – the men's were cut shorter.

However, I did have one particular grouse in those early days. There were no telephone directories in Peking or any other city in China. Embassies provided a list of useful numbers, which helped, but it took me some time to compile my own list of contacts.

After my first year in Peking I was often asked what was the most curious aspect of life in China. My reply was always the same. 'Well, there is no inflation and the cost of living is almost exactly what it was ten years ago or more.'

For a quarter of mankind the price of basic foods such as rice, fish, chicken, pork, beans, tea, fruits and vegetables had hardly varied during the twenty-five years that had elapsed since Mao 'liberated' China in 1949. In spite of chronic inflation during the first half of the twentieth century, the Chinese government claimed with some reason that the yuan was more stable than the dollar. Naturally enough, salaries had not been raised – there was no reason to increase pay when there was no inflation.

Income tax did not exist and a married couple with two children had enough money for local travel, buying the few books available and visiting the cinema or revolutionary ballet. The average wage for industrial workers was 60 to 70 yuan a month – or about £20 (at the then rate of exchange).

The cost of living, however, for the resident foreigner was another matter. One evening as I was quietly drinking a glass of beer in my large over-furnished office, a delegation arrived from the Revolutionary Committee that ran the hotel, to say that all rates would be increased immediately by 35 per cent.

The 'foreign guests' – the Chinese description of overseas visitors – had no choice but to pay up since it was impossible to move to another hotel or cheaper accommodation. All foreigners – there were 2,000 living in Peking at the time – paid 300 yuan a month to the government for interpreters although the interpreter received only 60 or 70 yuan of the wage. Neither ambassador nor any other foreigner could choose or dismiss the Chinese working for them although sometimes permission was given to change them.

The total job security tended to increase the natural sloth-fulness of the urban Chinese, who had the right to an hour's nap, winter and summer, after their lunch. Foreign employers had to provide a room and a bed for the *xicexi* – siesta – of their employees.

Many workers took advantage of exhortations to study the works of Mao to sit around doing nothing and frequently the desire to criticise Confucius or some disgraced minister was just an excuse to avoid hard work. But the peasants, who formed more than 80 per cent of the nation, were still tough and generally worked hard even during the periods of extreme heat and cold.

During the day it was the middle-aged and the young who were out in the streets in the residential areas since every able-bodied person then just had to have a job. The most needed people were mothers-in-law who, after retirement at the age of fifty-five, were usually delighted to care for children as well as shop, clean and cook. Married couples were fortunate to have a room to themselves for privacy was regarded as a luxury. This helped to control the population, which was then increasing by thirty million a year.

Men were given every incentive not to marry before they were twenty-eight, for women twenty-six was considered the earliest age for marriage – and before then it was difficult for a couple to find a corner for a cuddle. Pre-marital sex was a far worse sin than adultery and to have more than two children was a disgrace. Abortions were easy, the pill was free and divorce difficult – all pre-runners to the policy today that says that couples should have only one child. (This has now been relaxed in some districts.) An unhappy thought – China could be a nation where children have no brothers or sisters. Drug addicts were unknown, alcoholism hardly existed and VD almost eliminated. Only twice did I see a Chinese slightly the worse for drink. I found the discipline of the Street Committees, which kept a 'Big Brother' eye on residents, remarkable for the people did just as they were told with pretended pleasure.

There were no dogs, cats and few birds in Peking – creatures that eat and soil the city without contributing to the welfare of the citizen. Yet in this apparently classless nation there were certainly two classes on the railways – soft seats for officialdom, hard ones for the masses.

In 1973 the Chinese were quietly beavering away at improving their relations with the US for good reason, for it was part of their insurance policy against the Soviet threat in the north, although Mao had always prophesied that if the Russians dared to cross the border they would be 'drowned by people'.

The threat was real in both conventional and, Mao believed, in nuclear terms. In his 1973 New Year's message, Mao had encouraged his people to 'dig tunnels deeper, store grain everywhere and accept no hegemony' – the term applied to the Soviet menace. A warren of tunnels – mostly shallow and some extremely claustrophic – was built beneath Peking as shelter against a sudden nuclear attack.

The crisis between the two communist powers had reached its peak in 1959 when Moscow refused to supply Peking with the nuclear know-how they had promised. The Russians were then frightened that China would use nuclear weapons against Taiwan.

Russia had installed new intercontinental nuclear missiles to the north of the border which were capable of hitting targets anywhere in China. Forty-eight divisions, ten thousand tanks and a quarter of Russia's warplanes were deployed with a majority of units ready for immediate battle.

Secretly, the Chinese leaders harboured a long-term fear they never fully disclosed to the people – that the Soviet Union was planning to encircle China. India, already in Chinese eyes a close ally, the Soviet invasion of Afghanistan and political ferment in Pakistan all provided Peking with evidence of Moscow's sinister intentions.

The Chinese government really feared – I thought wrongly – a pre-emptive Soviet nuclear strike against its own nuclear installations at Lop Nor in Xinjiang or missile sites in north-east China. So the civil defence shelters were dug, some sections of the People's Liberation Army (PLA) re-equipped with more rifles and anti-aircraft artillery and volunteer militia encouraged to greater effort in training and vigilance.

On a visit to Shanghai in April, 1974, I encountered a typical militia volunteer, nineteen-year-old Kang Suwen. I met her at a works canteen, where she had a room, just as she was leaving for a spell of duty with an army unit some fifty-five miles away on the outskirts of the port.

Standing before a tiny, misty mirror, Kang tried on her new green army cap, which matched the green Mao jacket and trousers for which, the day before, she had exchanged the blue civilian clothes they so closely resembled. When Kang turned towards the coloured picture of Chairman Mao Zedong, she murmured, 'Give me strength "to take the correct line" and "to go against the tide".' These communist slogans were as soothing to Kang as a prayer is to a nun, whom she did, in fact, look like. She had decided to devote her life to the service of the Communist Party.

A PLA platoon commander had seen Kang giving up her free time to dig underground shelters with the masses. For when anyone was looking the Chinese people always demonstrated by their frenetic activity just how fully they shared their leaders' conviction that they were seriously threatened by an air raid from the Soviet Union.

While Kang and her co-diggers believed in the efficacy of their shelters, Chinese military experts were well aware that the narrow subterranean corridors were far too shallow and could quickly become mass graves. They also knew that China's second-strike capability would not be operational immediately. In the background, however, a second generation of ICBMs using solid fuel was soon to be developed which would enable Chinese missiles to be launched before they could be destroyed on their sites by Soviet warheads.

For conventional warfare, the Peking leaders had started elaborate and long-term preparations on what were considered to be the obvious 'invasion routes' for the Red army of Russia. So the educated youths – men and women – from the over-crowded cities of Peking, Shanghai and Tientsin were settled after the Cultural Revolution along the Sino-Soviet border and the frontier with Mongolia, which cut through the Gobi desert.

These pioneers, who set up agricultural communes supported by light industries, supplied the manpower for a frontier militia of about three to four-and-a-half million men and women. They formed the vital trip wire. The new settlers faced tough living conditions and began their new lives by working hard to build communal shelters, which were improved and extended every year. They were well fed, not only on wheat and the vegetables and pigs on their farms but also on local game which they trapped. Every few months, government lorries arrived with films. There were television sets in many communes and almost every work team was issued with a radio.

Units of the militia combined with the regular army to form guerrilla cells, in which young women played a leading role. China appreciated the necessity of counter-insurgency after analysing the failure of the Americans in Vietnam.

Only a few of the troops were married but as in the People's Liberation Army and the Chinese bureaucracy, married people separated from their partners were allowed two weeks together every year. There were comparatively few women in the PLA with children, who had to be left with relatives. The Chinese always found living in barracks easier than Europeans because even in the cities married couples, other than cadres, took one meal a day in the canteen at work and used their communal kitchen – shared with two or three other families – in the evening.

The Chinese armed forces took their pick of the youth in the country because, although conscription was then still in force, comparatively few people were required to serve out of the millions reaching eighteen each year. There was great competition to enter the services, for the life of a soldier was regarded as eminently superior to that of a farm worker. Even more important it enabled the peasant to learn how to drive a truck or, with luck, answer a telephone, skills that would make it possible for him to leave the countryside, after service, for what was in his view a much better life in a factory in a city.

There was no insignia for rank in the army but troops were well aware of their commanders at all levels. Commanders (officers) had four pockets in their tunics while the ordinary soldiers possessed only two. This was fine until the border war with Vietnam where strange units met and confusion arose.

Hundreds of thousands of men and women served three years in the PLA and then returned to their jobs in the factories or farms. Many of the older women in the infantry were siphoned off for jobs with the Political Commissar, who represented the interests of the Communist Party, and there were always a number of them who married soldiers; but sexual scandals were as rare as petty theft. Any division committing more than two such misdemeanours in a year was quickly made to feel 'deeply ashamed of itself'.

In those days, the army was always in a state of high alert and it was against a background of fear of a Soviet strike that Edward Heath arrived in Peking in May, 1974, for a welcome usually reserved for heads of state. The leader of the Conservative opposition (he had just lost the spring general election to Harold Wilson) was quite overwhelmed by the reception he received at all levels.

The Chinese honoured Heath for his unyielding support and enthusiasm for the Common Market and 'for taking Britain into Europe'. He was also responsible for the improvement in Sino-British relations while he was prime minister.

The esteem and affection of the Chinese leadership for Heath was never matched by their regard for Mrs Thatcher, though they certainly respect her unbending single-mindedness.

While Mrs Thatcher was leader of the opposition, after having ousted Heath in 1975, she invited me to her office in the House of Commons to discuss China. At that time she was playing with the idea of making a trip to the People's Republic. Naturally, being over-punctual, I arrived early for an appointment at 11 a.m.

As Big Ben struck, I was conducted to her office where after she enquired whether I wanted tea or coffee, she began telling me what she thought of China. Most of this was straightforward stuff, but she kept calling the Chinese 'Chinamen' – a title they abhor. So I tried to tell her not to use the word when in China or when Chinese people were around.

Showing her undoubted character, Mrs Thatcher said, 'We say Frenchmen and Germans. Why not Chinamen?' To which I replied, 'I beg you not to say Chinamen as it is so offensive to them.' I am happy to say that she took my advice when she went to China.

Heath was openly incredulous when he stepped from his airliner on that warm May evening in 1974 to find more than four thousand dancers in brightly coloured costumes performing in his honour.

He was received by Deng Xiaoping, who had taken over many duties from the ailing Zhou. Then he inspected the boy and girl dancers as they sprang about singing songs of welcome under two huge red banners thirty yards long – 'A warm welcome for Mr Edward Heath' 'Long live the friendship between the British and Chinese peoples'.

Suddenly, thousands of Union Jacks, which had been hidden, were waved aloft as he passed by. Heath beamed. Enormous red flags giving the impression of a medieval pageant lined the route from the airport to his guest house in Peking. Hundreds of thousands of Chinese turned out for the occasion. The only difference from a Head of State affair was that this eminent visitor did not inspect units of the forces on parade. British diplomats were quite taken aback by the fulsome courtesies.

They were crowned the next day by an unprecedented interview with Mao himself – in appreciation of the resumption of diplomatic relations with Britain achieved during Heath's prime ministership. The visit was marked, as usual, with official talks, a concert in the Great Hall of the People arranged specially for Heath as a keen musician, a brisk walk along the Great Wall and calls at the Ming tombs and museums.

Before Heath left Peking he received Zhou at his guest house and I was shocked at the change in the Chinese Prime Minister's appearance since the previous year when I had talked to him. I asked about his health and Zhou admitted, 'It is not as good as it was. I shall have to change my ways.' He had less than two years to live.

I flew with Heath to Shanghai where he toured one of the many underground nuclear shelters. We entered by a hidden staircase at Number One Trolley Bus Factory near the city centre and returned to the surface about fifteen yards away by a secret exit. Obviously this was a 'show' shelter embodying an element of comfort not found, I suspected, elsewhere.

Heath enjoyed a great welcome in Shanghai and Canton, the

last city on his itinerary before taking the train to Hong Kong. Both Mao and Zhou told him that it would take thirty to forty years before China became fully industrialised as a great power and during this period her main aim would be internal consolidation rather than development.

Heath obviously made a strong impression on Mao. He visited Peking again over a year later and once more received a surprise summons for talks with the Chinese leader. Mao, who was then eighty-one, had not been seen in public since 1971 but despite his age he still expressed himself with some vigour on the Sino-Soviet problems and constantly underlined his points with illustrations from history. However, his mind was not as good as on the first occasion he had received the former prime minister.

When Heath again visited Peking in the spring of 1987, he conducted its philharmonic orchestra in the Great Hall of the People before an audience of eight thousand. During the concert eighteen blind musicians – some of them additionally handicapped by missing limbs – were led on to the platform and seated beside their instruments. Heath conducted them from the piano using keys instead of a baton. It had taken several rehearsals to achieve this rapport and on the night the blind musicians responded with a brilliant and memorable performance, often smiling broadly as they recognised the maestro's instructions from the piano. A general sitting next to me had tears rolling down his cheeks. At the end, the blind musicians stood to an ovation that went on for several minutes with the entire audience on its feet, clapping their hands above their heads in appreciation of such talent and for the deep sensitivity the conductor displayed in producing such understanding and harmony.

Yet the first article I wrote about Heath was critical. It concerned his announcement in 1963 as one of Macmillan's ministers that Kim Philby had disappeared. He never held this against me and was most friendly and co-operative when he visited Japan as prime minister in 1973. It is sad that his political ability has not been fully utilised since he was at Number Ten.

With the deaths of Zhou and Mao in 1976 and the subsequent trials of the 'Gang of Four' led by Mao's wife, China herself was by 1981 heading for immense changes internally. The political scene was turned upside down with a power struggle of seeming unending proportions. I have discussed these events in my book on Mao (*Mao and the Men Against Him*).

Although I left China in the summer of 1976 to return to London as defence correspondent of the *Daily Telegraph*, I have been back to Peking on many occasions to study the changing military strategy. In some ways I have been able to travel internally more freely than when I was a resident staff correspondent probably because I have been accepted as a reliable commentator with an objective if independent mind of my own. Time means little to the Chinese and advancing years are an advantage rather than an obstacle. Being based in Hong Kong as the Far East correspondent of the *Sunday Telegraph* has enabled me to travel throughout China.

In 1980 I obtained permission to visit Chungdo in the central province of Sichuan and the home of the new premier of China, Zhao Ziyang. He had already introduced a large number of economic reforms designed to increase production and exports. Some years previously he had demonstrated his ability to organise and improve industrial production in his home province, where his free-wheeling economic experiments had been signally successful in a province of one hundred million people.

During 1979, for instance, five major industrial enterprises in Sichuan increased their production by 46 per cent after being granted special autonomy and responsibility for their own profits and losses. As a result similar control was granted to a further one hundred industries in provinces throughout China. Managements were authorised to borrow from foreign banks if state capital was denied to them – an unheard of freedom in communist China and a remarkable departure towards capitalism.

When Zhao took over in Sichuan two thirds of the factories had ceased production while others were half closed. Zhao decided that these disasters were due mainly to too much concentration of power in Peking and too little participation in management by the workers, who thus lacked interest and incentive.

Industrial production improved in 1976 but there were no major innovations until after Mao's death. Zhao then called back all the workers who had been dismissed during the crippling Cultural Revolution.

Revolutionary committees were replaced by experienced managers generally elected by the workers. New rules, more honoured in the breach than the observance, were imposed enabling inefficient managers and workers to be dismissed subject to confirmation by the provincial party. In addition, one hundred large enterprises were allowed to operate freely, retaining a part of the profits on the goods produced after they had fulfilled the target set by the State. The previous year these factories increased their production by 15 per cent and profits by 30 per cent, which more than doubled the average for 1979. Better things were to come. In the four years up to 1980 production increased by an annual average of 29 per cent. And before he left Sichuan for Peking, Zhao increased to six hundred the number of enterprises allowed to 'freewheel' after meeting their industrial targets set by the State.

An 80 per cent tax, however, was levied by the State, leaving 20 per cent for the management to spend; half that figure was devoted to new machinery, about 20 per cent was earmarked for welfare services and 10 per cent to pay increases. All of which represented a tribute to capitalist ideals. British businessmen soon realised another effect of these changes. They were able to deal with managements directly at provincial level – something quite new in China.

Although the foreigner was being welcomed more and more in the principal cities of China there are areas which have remained closed to them since the communist take-over in 1949.

In the summer of 1983 I had the opportunity to visit the ancient city of Kashgar, and Urumchi the capital of the autonomous region of Xinjiang with Pamela, Lady Egremont.

We were certainly objects of considerable curiosity to the women of this remote town. They lifted the corners of their thick brown crochet veils to inspect us – the first foreigners they had seen. Men wearing fur hats and long felt coats 'to keep out the heat' stared at us as they shuffled through the crowds of small children into the mosques, which are open in all the side streets as well as dominating the main square. The thermometer registered well over 90°F.

A massive statue of Mao, badly in need of a coat of paint and repairs, together with a few obvious Chinese offices and department stores, were the only visible signs of communist rule. Indeed, the back streets had hardly changed since the town was the main stopping place for caravans on the silk route between Sian and Samarkand during those centuries before and after Christ when silk in Rome cost its weight in gold. The Chinese were then the only people who held the secret of silk production.

Owing to their 'pale' skins, the Han Chinese from Peking and the west were conspicuous, too, as they walked around the streets. But they maintained an extremely low profile and allowed the indigenous Uighurs to administer themselves within broad guidelines. The Uighurs took full advantage of this and went as far as they could within the basic structure of the state knowing how easily they could be 'clobbered' if things went wrong. Uighur leaders had bridged the gap between Islam and communism and many of them were devout Moslems as well as members of the Communist Party. Only once did I witness a scene between a senior official from Peking and local Uighur officials and that was in the regional capital of Urumchi.

The former British consulate in Kashgar, famous for looking after travellers in the last century, was serving as a lodging house for lorry drivers. Government offices had been built in the once-beautiful grounds.

Along the Karakoram highway, which links China with Pakistan, there was little traffic. But the people who lived in well-built mud huts beside the road were extremely warm and hospitable, offering us tea and dried fruit. They all looked well fed and content. The men gathered in one part of the orchard to play cards while women gossiped in another. One girl was wearing a huge Mao brooch which must have been produced at the height of the personality cult during the Cultural Revolution but she had no idea of its political significance and she thought it was just decorative.

Hundreds of men working on the road, which is plagued by landslides, floods and snow, lived in less glamorous conditions in barrack-like constructions of imported brick. There were plenty of schools but comparatively few of the children appeared to attend them. In one village devoted to rearing horses, a boy of twelve, when questioned about going to school, said no one but a fool would spend the day in a classroom when he could ride around on his own pony.

The large, formerly austere agricultural communes in the extreme west had changed their régime as the former revolutionary committees made way for 'the contract responsibility system', which gave more scope for individual initiative.

The members worked on the commune land to produce rice, fruit and others goods for the State, but once this work was done they rushed to the private plots where they produced goods for the local markets. Although Han Chinese are virtually ordered to keep to one child families this does not apply to the minorities. Large families of six or eight were normal in the communes, although when I was there they had just been requested not to have more than four children. Fancy clothes, television sets and radios provided evidence of the new prosperity that had reached one of the farthest points in China.

The local free markets were packed with excellent meat – but not pork – from the communes, and on the stalls from July to November there were heaps of vegetables and fruit. The people lived as in the Middle East on kebabs and naan, unleavened bread.

There was no fear that these indigenous folk occupying a region that remains strategically important would rise against their rulers in Peking. Lop Nor, the large oasis which houses China's nuclear installations, is only eight hundred miles to the East across the Taklamakan desert from Kashgar.

There were surprisingly few soldiers around considering that the Soviet frontier was only a hundred miles away. The gateway had recently been opened on the border for official government traffic between Russia and China as well as a little local cross-border trade. While relations between the two communist giants had improved, local officials as well as spokesmen in Peking implied that they have far to go. With notices in Arabic and Chinese and free copies of the *Koran* distributed to all Imams, Peking had the Moslem minorities of Central Asia well on its side. But since the rise in Moslem fundamentalism in the early- and mid-1980s, the scene has changed dramatically.

Indeed, over the past decade and a half changes throughout China are striking. During the last days of Chairman Mao and before the earthquake that heralded his death in September 1976, the wide streets of Peking were empty of motor vehicles save for the occasional diplomatic car, bus or taxi. Tens of thousands of workers cycled slowly to work, as they still do, no matter what the weather. Gigantic posters urged 'workers of the world unite' and carried over-sized pictures of 'the beloved' Chairman Mao.

Foreigners sometimes made rude remarks about the Chinese looking like ants because they all – male and female alike – wore dark blue Mao jackets and pants as they went silently about their business. Shops and restaurants were all run by the State. Mercifully, even the bureaucracy could not destroy the quality of Chinese food but the shops were filled with statues, pictures, badges, brooches and embroideries of the Chairman. Few books were on sale other than those *Thoughts of Mao*, while underwear, cooking utensils and furniture were sparse and basic.

I recall the popularity of ball-point pens, which were not on the market, and the delight with which interpreters accepted them as gifts from foreign visitors. Despite their low standard of living the honesty of the people was incredible. I remember a diplomat leaving his suitcase by accident on a crowded railway platform and finding it the next day exactly where he had dumped it with a circle of white chalk around it. His silk shirts and gold cufflinks were all inside as he had packed them.

Dollar bills or yuan notes could be left safely on a desk or dressing-table in the hotels and cities open to foreigners. Radios were rare and only senior cadres could obtain them but every agricultural commune and factory had loudspeakers bleating out the Maoist slogans together with world news with a strong Chinese slant.

The 'broad masses' as Mao dubbed the people, had but little entertainment but important foreign visitors were invited to operas or ballet such as 'The Red Detachment of Women', which was sponsored by Mao's wife. It was also made into a film. Although there were wonderful Chinese conjurers and acrobats there were then few shows in which they could display their unique skills.

In the mid-1980s traffic jams and the pollution they cause

grew to be intolerable due to thousands of new taxis manned by former army drivers, hundreds of foreign businessmen, who have imported cars by paying a large tax, and an increase in the number of diplomatic and official vehicles. Despite over-passes and circular roads, the chronic morning 'rush hour' was and is a nightmare.

Sadly, many beautiful old buildings have been pulled down in the centre of the city to make way for ugly high rise constructions. The municipality has enormous powers and could easily have issued a similar edict to that proclaimed by President de Gaulle that no new buildings might be higher than seven storeys in the centre of Paris. This has preserved the beauty and enhanced the local charm of the French capital, while in Peking the delightful old *hutungs* – compounds of one-storey houses with small, pretty gardens – have been destroyed. Indeed, there are so few old houses left that the authorities are now thinking of preserving, even reconstructing, a few *hutungs* as a sightseeing attraction for tourists. Many of the large and lovely houses, which once belonged to mandarins and, later, warlords, have also been demolished.

One used to drive through the countryside to reach the Summer Palace but the area is now built up with dull blocks of flats. However, day and night 'free' markets abound in all the suburbs of Peking to cater for workers. Not only can one buy bananas from the south but excellent fresh vegetables, crabs and exotic fish together with ducks, chickens, pork and lamb. Until the student demonstrations of May/June 1989 several of the smartest women in Hong Kong took tourist visas to Peking to buy their clothes in the street markets. One needed time and taste but fashionable articles were there to be found. The Friendship Store, that has always catered for foreign residents, still offers large quantities of imported drinks together with wines made in China as a result of joint ventures between the French and the Chinese. In the days of Mao one was extremely fortunate to be served with local beer, then in short supply, but today the selection in most hotels is like London, Paris or New York. The huge bill boards that once carried Maoist slogans are now used to advertise Coca-Cola, soap, a special brand of motor-cycle – and the benefits of the one-child family. Only one picture of Mao remains and that is over the entrance to the Forbidden City. This was temporarily damaged during the 1989 demonstrations, and then repaired.

But the underground operates and is being extended and foreigners are now allowed to use the service, which was denied to them in 1976. By 1986 around five-sixths of the people in the streets of Peking were wearing some form of western clothing. Women frequently had their hair 'permed' and set in a European way rather than the obligatory two short pigtails of the past. Many young women had – I think, misguidedly – taken to high-heeled leather shoes instead of the flat-soled cloth ones favoured by Mao. Indeed, when I tried to replace my black cloth footwear, the salesgirl said, 'Even the peasants wear leather today. Why do you want cloth?' I answered, with truth, 'Because cloth is more comfortable.'

The excellent restaurants we once frequented in the old part of the town grew overcrowded and, without expressing any anti-European views, the line seemed to be that foreigners should eat in one of the many hotels now open for them where Chinese food is good. But I cannot forget the glamorous evenings in a former war-lord's magnificent home where superb Sichuan food was served, or the old Peking Duck eating house. 'The Sick Duck' was also a favourite, so named because the restaurant was near the hospital.

The bookshops (before June 1989) were packed with trans-lations of foreign writers as well as Chinese authors whose works were burned during the Cultural Revolution, but various magazines and some books advocating complete sexual freedom or the introduction of western-type democracy were suppressed. It is interesting that one of the least inhibited and best written daily papers – the *China Daily* – is published in English and, although it generally carries the party line, it omits the jargon foreigners often find off-putting.

In Peking in 1987 the scene was set for Deng to place his successors in key positions in the Communist Party and state hierarchy in the run-up to the vital 13th Party Congress in October. A new Central Committee was elected together with a ruling Politbureau which was to stay in power for the next five to ten years. But this was not to be.

At the meeting of the National People's Congress, China's parliament, in the spring, it was stressed by the then premier,

Zhao, that Deng's policies of opening the door to the West and internal modernisations would continue despite opposition from the extreme conservative hardliners, who had caused the resignation of the party secretary, Hu, the previous January. Zhao, who led the movement to break up the agricultural communes created by Mao in the late 1950s and develop free markets, stressed the urgent need for meaningful internal economic reforms and increased exports to the West.

The two thousand seven hundred deputies cheered the Premier and Hu when they entered the Great Hall of the People in Peking. Hu was making his first public appearance since his resignation in January and so the Congress presented a picture of political unity to China and the world.

We all watched the lively leader Deng march on the platform at the 13th Party Congress and dash around greeting friends, followed by others in the front row who took a long time to walk twenty yards. We were able to see the faces of the delegates as Premier Zhao Ziyang read his report on the 'Advance along the Road to Socialism with Chinese Characteristics'. This took over two and a half hours but few delegates dozed. The main theme is now well known. The door to the West would be open ever wider to technology and experts while, on the domestic front, the industrial and economic reforms would continue. There could be no going back. Zhao proclaimed the 'emancipation' of the minds of the people, battered down by 'many old concepts' that had stifled their thinking, during the Cultural Revolution; but he did mention that corruption 'exists' in 'varying degrees in many sectors'. In addition, Zhao admitted that China's per capita income was 'amongst the lowest in the world' with over seven hundred million people living in rural areas using hand tools to make a living.

Zhao stressed the urgent need to separate the responsibilities of the State and Communist Party which had become confused in the administration.

The agreement with Britain on the future of Hong Kong, and Portugal on the future of Macau was mentioned and Zhao claimed that history will 'prove' that the principle of 'one country, two systems' for national reunification 'is the great innovation showing the political wisdom of the Chinese nation'.

There was an interesting hiccup during the Congress when

the 'elders' who during lengthy discussions at the seaside resort of Beitaiho during the previous summer had agreed to resign, suddenly announced they had no intention of so doing. Acting under pressure from the conservative hardliners they held out for some hours until Deng Xiaoping assured them they could still enjoy the 'perks' of office such as the use of a car and telephone if they kept their word and resigned. It was this group of 'elders' Deng brought back to support him during the student demonstrations in 1989.

But at the Party Congress the new leader Zhao Ziyang, then sixty-eight, impressed me with his self-confident air and firm handshake. It was sensational for him to meet the foreign press at a reception where, between drinks, he stressed his commitment to open the door still further to the West and 'push' forward the ongoing reforms. He was obviously keen to abolish party cells in government offices.

Like his mentor, Deng Xiaoping, Zhao appeared to be extremely fit. He gave up jogging early in 1987 when pressure became too strong for him to take the necessary time away from the premier's desk, but he did devote some of his leisure to learning how to play golf in order to make a good impression when he opened China's second 18-hole golf course in May 1987. Many diplomats said he put up a good show. Zhao's wife, Liang Boqi, who fought beside him as a soldier in the war against Japan, then made one of her rare public appearances with him together with their small grandson. However, like the majority of Chinese leaders, Zhao likes to keep his family life truly private.

Zhao admits enjoying his food and told a group of reporters at the 13th Party Congress, 'I don't diet, I eat what I like and as much as I like.' Together with the late Chairman Mao and his mentor Deng, Zhao is extremely fond of the hot spicy food from the Sichuan area.

After the war against Japan, Zhao served in Canton where he was later persecuted during the Cultural Revolution; members of the Red Guard forced him to wear a dunce's cap as they paraded him through the streets before jeering crowds. After the chaos ended in 1972 Zhao served in Inner Mongolia and again in Canton. But it was in Chengdu in the 1970s that he made his name and became a national figure. The revolutionary committees that ran the agricultural communes of around thirty thousand people slowly disintegrated under directives from Zhao and ordinary village life was slowly resumed.

Zhao gradually became Deng Xiaoping's 'chosen successor', although these words are no longer fashionable. Zhao would have preferred to have remained as premier but Deng was determined to transfer him to the more influential post as party secretary after Hu Yaobang was forced to resign in January 1987.

It was noticeable at the reception shortly after the 13th Party Congress ended that Zhao Ziyang led the other four members of the Standing Committee who smiled but said little. However, Li Peng who replaced Zhao as premier did not lack self-confidence. Well known as the son of a revolutionary martyr he was looked after by Premier Zhou Enlai; thus Zhongnanhai, where the leaders have lived since Liberation, is familiar to him. Basically, Li is a technocrat and a brilliant engineer who specialised in the design and construction of electronic and nuclear power plants. He was trained in Moscow and, perhaps because of this, appears more friendly with Russians than other Chinese leaders. Li was with Hu Yaobang in London and on his European trip when he gave the impression that he was likely to be more cautious than Zhao in moving away from centralised control of the economy. It soon transpired that he is a hardliner.

Hu Qili has charm which he used as head of the Communist Party's propaganda work. He was well known as a staunch supporter of Zhao and all his economic reforms. As the right-hand man of the former party secretary, Hu Yaobang, he believed in giving more authority to banks and commercial enterprises in the provinces. However, Hu Qili was also extremely interested in under-developed agricultural regions as a result of having spent years working in the Ningxia Hui autonomous region where he was sent to till the soil during the Cultural Revolution. Hu Qili is now in disgrace with Zhao Ziyang.

Discussion on changes in the administration and top personnel in many departments of State and Party began within days of the conclusion of the 13th Party Congress.

The bi-monthly magazine the *Red Flag* ceased publication. During the lifetime of Chairman Mao the *Red Flag* dominated all other papers as it updated the leader's thoughts for communist party workers everywhere but, especially, those far away from Peking. It was known as 'the Party's theoretical organ' and I frequently noticed my first interpreter study it, before answering my political questions, in the early 1970s.

While Deng and Zhao stood by their opposition to the western 'one man one vote' type of democracy the average age of the Standing Committee dropped from seventy-seven to sixty-three. But there was no doubt the new 'youngsters', as one elderly Chinese called them, did make a good, perhaps even great, impression not only on the few fortunate foreigners who met them but on the hundreds of millions of Chinese who watched them on television.

Of the seven new members of the ruling Politbureau the most outstanding was Li Ruihuan, mayor of the industrial city of Tientsin who has won high praise from Deng Xiaoping for the dynamism with which his staff have worked to attract foreign capital. As a youthful carpenter he had worked on the construction of the Great Hall of the People and later became one of Mao's 'model workers'. But, unlike most model workers, he was intelligent and is extremely popular with 'the broad masses'.

The other newcomer on the Politbureau, who has been noted by the party on a nationwide basis, is Li Tieying who headed Zhao's economic 'think tank'. Like Zhao he believed, although he does not say so too loudly, that it is far more important for China to improve its productivity than worry about the 'class struggle'. This pragmatic approach is, of course, abhorrent to the conservative hardliners and many hundreds of thousands, maybe millions, of members brought into the Party during the Cultural Revolution.

But Zhao said 'China must terminate the Maoist system of "eating from one big pot" by making individual trading companies responsible for their own profits and losses' and giving more initiative to the provincial leaders. What Zhao called the 'preliminary stages of socialism' really means moves towards pragmatism. He was hampered by out-dated laws which render it difficult to close factories making unwanted or unprofitable goods. The price of food rose sharply and inflation, unknown in the days of Mao, became a serious problem.

The proposed separation of Party and State was generally recognised as an excellent idea but it was difficult to achieve. Again, many untrained and unskilled men and women had senior positions in the communist party cells in the bureaucracy and factories merely watching other people to see their 'attitude' was correct and check that they attended study groups for at least an hour on two or three afternoons each week. 'Study' is a euphemism for classes designed for political indoctrination. The number of party employees in these party cells, who had no other work to do, varied from one section of the administration to another. Ultimately Zhao envisaged the complete separation of the power of Party and State so far as the judiciary, legislature and executive were concerned. Indeed, the Standing Committee was actually working on plans that were first voiced by Deng Xiaoping.

It was interesting that Zhao devoted so little of his two and a half hour address to foreign affairs and defence. Many senior cadres, well known as supporters of Deng – expressed disappointment. Qin Jiwei became defence minister. Qin who served with Deng in the Second Field Army was popular with the PLA who regard him as a really experienced soldier. The only man over eighty who was retained in the Central Military Commission (CMC) was Yang Shangkun who, Deng believed, would be useful in guiding the conservative political commissars in the provinces to give their support to the modernisation programme. Many of them were appointed during the Cultural Revolution when it was 'better to be red than expert' and owe their position and 'perks' to this background.

Although Deng continued to stress that there would be no global war this century, he and China's foreign experts became increasingly concerned by Japan's future military and economic role as the centre of political gravity moves from the Atlantic to the Pacific Ocean. The Chinese defence planners were worried too, by United States' attempts to persuade the Japanese to assume greater responsibility for keeping open – defending – their own shipping lines – especially those to the Gulf. Indeed, they remain apprehensive that the Japanese may take over this role and slowly form a 'blue water' navy in the Pacific. The Japanese military tradition is, they claim, still strong.

Thus guided by Deng, the new younger defence planners bore in mind the possibility that Japan may assume a major military and naval role in the Pacific by the first decade of the next century. Chinese diplomats, even then, confessed their relations with Japan are not always easy although they fully understand the vulnerability of Japanese industry which is dependent on imports – especially of petroleum from the Gulf. The Chinese envisage a sharp decline in Washington's 'clout' in the area as they believe the Americans will ultimately pull out of the Pacific and permit, even encourage, the Japanese 'self defence forces' to increase their strength.

Sino-Soviet relations improved but Chinese defence planners continued to consider possible future border incidents on both Soviet and Vietnamese frontiers, in addition to opposing the Vietnamese military occupation of Cambodia. While China's armed forces were still geared to a defensive role, they reserve the right to re-occupy areas they claim are Chinese such as Taiwan, the Paracel Islands – which they took over at the end of the war in Vietnam – and the Spratly Group in the South China Sea where many Ming dynasty remains and coins have been found and, more important, petroleum deposits are believed to exist.

15 The Power Struggle Emerges in Force . . .

Life in Peking in the early spring of 1989, over a year after the 13th Party Congress, seemed pleasant as the standard of living continued to rise, despite inflation. There was, too, an air of freedom as the Chinese found it easier to travel within the country and invite foreign friends to their homes. In private, however, parents sometimes expressed concern that their children, born during the Cultural Revolution, were showing but little interest in politics. They all wanted to go abroad to study. When this was not possible they enjoyed television, eating out in restaurants while wearing European clothes and reading or pretending to read American newspapers.

What many of my Chinese friends dubbed the easy going life was changed traumatically by the student demonstrations in Tiananmen Square which began in April and the action taken by the PLA to clear the area after Martial Law was imposed on 19 May. People with whom I used to share meals passed me by on the other side too frightened to talk with foreigners – especially foreign correspondents – after the 'hardliners' had taken over and the reformist, Zhao Ziyang, was disgraced.

The death of Hu Yaobang on 15 April provided the catalyst for students to organise demonstrations in favour of greater press freedom, more western-type democracy and an end to corruption in high places. Deng Xiaoping had dismissed Hu in January 1987 and replaced him with Zhao, as general-secretary of the Party, after Hu refused to denounce 'bourgeois liberalism'. But many people now believe this was an excuse and Deng was angered by Hu's 'foot in mouth' jokes which, when made abroad, were embarrassing to him. The students liked Hu because of his reformist views and he talked with them from time to time, without arrogance, as once the late Premier Zhou Enlai had mingled with their fathers. Hu was not disgraced, indeed, he remained a member of the ruling Politbureau and there were reports that he was to be given a new role, just before he died, to act as an intermediary between Party and State: for Zhao Ziyang and Premier Li Peng found it difficult to work together.

Hu had become the cult hero of tens of thousands of students and urban workers throughout China. On the day after he died some six hundred students bicycled from the University in the north of Peking to lay a gigantic wreath in his memory on the Monument of the Martyrs in the midst of Tiananmen Square. The following night some six thousand students and their supporters marched to the Square where they were joined by sympathetic workers. Thousands of students throughout China then ceased to attend lectures as big character posters *dazibao* – the traditional Chinese method of raising political issues – appeared on street corners demanding 'More Democracy', 'An End to Corruption' and 'Press Freedom'. I noted, somewhat to the surprise of the demonstrators, many passersby smiled encouragingly at them and some even made the 'V' for victory sign with their fingers.

Small groups of students then began to doss down in the Square rather than face the long walk back to the University where, in any case, no one was attending lectures or doing any work. The students formed committees as they realized that the many celebrations expected in the immediate future would provide them with global television coverage for their demands. Gorbachev, who was already a student's hero, was expected in Peking on 15 May for a Summit meeting with Deng – the first meeting of Sino-Soviet leaders for thirty years. Further the famous May 4th Movement, which did much to inspire the early communists, including Zhou Enlai and Deng, was about to celebrate its seventieth anniversary and, in addition, the Asian Development Bank was holding a conference in Peking from 4–6 May.

'We felt we had protection from the visitors as well as the prospect of massive publicity,' a student, now in hiding, told me. But after ten days of demonstrations Deng decided it was time to end the disturbances. Thus an editorial, inspired by him, appeared in the *People's Daily* that dubbed the demonstration 'a planned conspiracy', opposed to the Communist Party and the socialist system. It was reportedly read, before publication, to Zhao Ziyang, then on an official visit to North Korea. However, on his return he immediately voiced strong opposition to it. The students and workers – mostly urban workers – were infuriated and, as a result, over a million supporters marched with them to the Square to protest against it.

I saw many slogans being carried on banners by workers as well as students which were anti-Deng in tone 'Thank you Deng: but its now time to say Bye Bye'. However, the banners were far more critical of Premier Li Peng. At first they read, 'Down with Li Peng' then, 'Crush Li Peng' and, finally, 'Hang Li Peng'. About mid-May, as the situation grew more dramatic, hundreds of students went on hunger strike despite the heat and tough camping conditions in the Square where there was but little water and few latrines.

The student committees organised and planned routine marches and demonstrations and they had a squadron of motor cyclists who took orders from the Square to the universities and to communications centres for transmission to other towns. Considerable sums of money were collected in buckets in streets near the Square to provide the students with water and the basic necessities of life. Some days there were more enthusiastic crowds marching to the Square than others, but there was no end to the demonstrations in sight as the date of Gorbachev's visit approached. The students were friendly, and anxious to get their 'democratic' message over to the world. I was constantly invited to 'look at' slogans and announcements in English to see that they made sense.

Deng, for his part, had planned that the Summit meeting with Gorbachev would not only lessen tension between the two Communist superpowers and improve economic relations but would provide a triumphant conclusion to his long and distinguished career. He assumed the Summit would have worldwide publicity and, after basking in the glory of it all for a few weeks, he would finally retire from the vital and key position as Chairman of the Central Military Commission on 1 October when the People's Republic celebrated the Fortieth Anniversary of its proclamation by Chairman Mao Zedong. Further, before the demonstrations, Deng made no secret of the fact that Zhao Ziyang would take over from him, although it was generally assumed Deng would still exert influence in the background.

As all appeals to end the demonstrations fell on deaf ears, the character of the Gorbachev visit changed. The Russian leader was forced to make lengthy detours as he moved around the Square to avoid the demonstrators and he had to enter the Great Hall of the People, for the official banquet, by the back door because the students controlled the two main entrances on the Square and the Avenue of Heavenly Peace. ...

Zhao is reported to have told a small group of friends, after he refused to support the implementation of Martial Law, that he got along extremely well with Gorbachev. Indeed, he implied that they held similar views on the global, economic and financial scene and the policies their respective countries should adopt. Later, he even hinted that Gorbachev's attitude gave him courage and he believed that sooner or later he would be in a position of authority in China.

Deng and the elders in the Politbureau felt they had lost 'face' in a big way. Certainly, what was to be the final act of Deng's career was a failure and the media was far more interested in the students than in the Summit. Indeed, some television crews went off to record demonstrations in Shanghai where newspapers were printing critical reports of the leaders. But many local mayors were clever and when students requested permission to hold demonstrations they were urged to go to Peking and join their comrades there. This provincial influx added to the numbers sleeping in the streets around the Square.

Soon after Gorbachev's departure there were reports of massive troop movements as some foreign diplomats claimed the Army was 'divided from top to bottom on the question of the political reforms the students were demanding'. There were, too, accurate reports that political commissars in the Army were making efforts to re-introduce the daily hour of 'study', compulsory in the days of Chairman Mao, that had been dropped when the modernisation programme was begun. Soldiers had then found it more important to learn how engines worked than to study 'Marx, Lenin and Mao Zedong thought'.

On the night of 19 May, as reports of troop movements

were passed round the Square, Zhao Ziyang visited the students
in an emotional and tearful effort to persuade the hunger strikers
to 'give up'. He told them he should have been there earlier as
he attempted to convey that this was his last chance as well as
theirs. Zhao was closely followed by Premier Li Peng who told
the students he was willing to talk with them and hear their case
in private. When the student leaders demanded that any discussion
they held should be in public and broadcast for the whole nation
to hear, the Premier left them. Many students and their supporters
amongst the urban workers now feel their leaders made a great
mistake in not talking with the Premier on the grounds that they
would certainly have obtained some concessions and dispersed.
Thus the whole tragedy of Tiananmen could have been avoided.
Later that night it was announced that Martial Law would be
enforced the following morning at ten in Peking.

Immediately the students heard the news, which they had
expected a day or two earlier, they established extremely efficient barricades of heavily-loaded buses, lorries and trucks on
all the main routes into the city allowing only private citizens
and vehicles carrying food to pass. When troops arrived from
the 38th Group Army – then generally considered one of China's
best trained and equipped – they were surrounded by students
shouting, 'You are the People's Army: you cannot act against
the People.' The soldiers, who were generally unarmed, turned
their vehicles round and, still surrounded by students frequently
re-enforced by workers, they were lectured on the advantages of
democracy. I drove to three different barricades and saw the
local girls give ice-creams to soldiers, many of whom had the
same accent as they and came from the Peking area. There were
Armoured Personnel Carriers (APCs) at one of the south-western
entrances to the city. The vehicles looked as though they had been
'in store' for a long time as tarpaulins had actually stuck to the
mounted machine guns.

Thousands of supporters from all walks of life rushed to
key points on the outskirts of the city, where the troops were
being held up by students and workers, as well as to Tiananmen
Square where I noticed that the companies of soldiers normally
based in the old Legation quarters nearby and the Great Hall of
the People, did not emerge. Encouraged by the ever increasing
support, student leaders then announced they would remain in

the Square until the meeting of the National People's Congress which was due to assemble on 20 June.

After the initial burst of enthusiasm for the students demonstrating under Martial Law conditions, support from their fellow citizens appeared almost daily to wax and wane as I watched the crowds come and go from a fifth-floor balcony of the Peking Hotel.

The State President, Yang Shangkun, aged eighty-two, took over Zhao Ziyang's post and became acting vice-chairman of the CMC in charge of the day-to-day administration and command of the PLA under Deng Xiaoping's chairmanship. It was Yang, as number three and deputy vice-chairman who had been urging his brother, Yang Baibing, the director of the political commissars in the PLA, to re-activate their role. There were unconfirmed reports that Qin Jiwei, the defence minister, together with the chief-of-staff, Chi Haotian and around thirty senior officials did not appear at their desks for a day or two.

At the time wild rumours were circulated and there was hysterical talk of the possibility of civil war, while some foreigners voiced fears that there would be fighting between units of the defence forces with differing political views. I recall my own amazement and horror, when appearing on Australian television, as the presenter questioned me on when I thought civil war would break out! I replied there was *no* chance of civil war in China.

Deng realised he needed more support, thus he followed the Maoist tradition by re-instating the elders on the Advisory Commission – all in their eighties – who had retired two years earlier at the Party Congress. They were only too pleased to come out of retirement to assist him and Chen Yun, former state president Li Xiannian, Peng Zhen, Wang Zhen and 'Big Sister' Den Yingchao, widow of the late Premier Zhou Enlai, gave Deng their hardline support based on Marxism, Leninism and Mao Zedong thought.

Selected army commanders, whose units were deemed to be loyal, were then called to Peking and a new 'safe' underground headquarters outside Zhongnanhai was established for the implementation of Martial Law. The movement of some troops and all senior officers was through the underground network of roads constructed in the late Sixties when a nuclear attack on the city was feared.

Units were then ordered to move in readiness to encircle Peking from the 27th Group Army in Shijiazhuang, 54th Group Army in Jinan, 39th Group Army in Shenyang, 14th Group Army in Sichuan and 24th Group Army in Chengde (Inner Mongolia) together with the 6th Tank Regiment from Peking and the 1st Tank Regiment from Tientsin. Trains were commandeered to transport the troops to the outskirts of the city while CAAC planes carried senior officers to a little used military airport to the south of the city.

Approximately 130,000 additional troops were deployed around the outskirts of Peking. While all seven commanders of military regions made public statements in support of Deng, there were still one or two Group Armies of 'uncertain loyalty' and, for a time, there was some concern about the Air Force. This was, however, overcome when the defence minister, Qin Jiwei, was shown on television inspecting the troops.

On 3 June the 27th Group Army with token units from all seven military regions supported by APCs and tanks attempted to enter the Square. They were apparently insufficiently armed and this enabled students and some of the more courageous members of the urban work force to surround the tanks, drag out the drivers and set fire to the vehicles. Those who took action against the soldiers were dubbed 'heroes' by many, both in China and abroad by those who watched some of the scenes on television around the world. But they were, and still are, 'hooligans' to the Chinese authorities. After this failure the troops were then issued with AK 47s and tank crews also had machine guns. They then made their way into the Square, driving over tents and killing the students inside.

The authorities told ambassadors and others who later attempted to question them about 'the massacre' in the Square that they were forced to use live ammunition after two attempts to 'clear up' the area had failed. Neither the Police nor the Army possessed hoses that would have enabled them to get rid of the students by dousing them with water, the authorities said. Indeed, had they possessed the necessary hoses, there was insufficient water pressure to render them effective. Few, if any, were convinced.

The world was shocked by a Chinese statement carried on television when an official claimed that 'no one was killed by the

Army in Tiananmen Square.' Undoubtedly students, workers and soldiers were killed in the Square but the majority of deaths took place in nearby streets, and about 4 km to the west at Muxudt. As one German said, 'No one was killed in Auschwitz; Jews, Socialists and Catholics were put into gas chambers and shot in a camp some miles from the town.'

There were, indeed, many unpleasant incidents, some involving foreigners, as the PLA established Martial Law in the centre of the city following the occupation of the Square. One of the soldiers' first tasks was to destroy the impressive statue of Democracy which was, I thought, placed to look straight into the eyes of Chairman Mao's portrait opposite.

The security forces immediately attempted to round up the students and some hundreds were arrested. But despite this, thousands escaped, generally into the countryside to hide with relatives or friends while they grew their hair or changed their appearance when possible. Some managed to leave China and they have established their headquarters in Paris, much to the chagrin of the hardliners now in power in Peking.

To the surprise of many diplomats, the Chinese security forces – the Police and People's Armed Police (PAP) – had placed cameras and special tape-recorders at strategic points in the Square where student leaders were meeting workers. Indeed, they also had cameras in the restaurants of the Peking Hotel where students were sometimes taken to 'wash and brush up' as well as to eat by overseas Chinese. The pictures were used afterwards and given considerable publicity by the PAP in identifying 'hooligans and other anti-Party anti-Government forces'.

While the purge continued foreign embassies evacuated their women and children and reduced their staff to a minimum as businessmen and bankers were advised to close their offices or leave them in the hands of local staff. Serious transportation problems arose as there were no taxis or buses and it was extremely difficult to get to the airport. Few of those foreigners who remained in Peking had any idea of what was happening behind the pre-revolutionary red walls of the Forbidden City where the enlarged Politbureau was said to be in almost constant session. There were many false reports in circulation about the future of Zhao Ziyang and whether or not he would be expelled from the Party and brought to trial for his supportive attitude to the students. There were, too, constant rumours that Deng was ill or even dead. Naturally, officials in the Foreign Ministry could say nothing, but it was eventually released by the official news agency, Xinhau, that the 'open door' policy to the West would continue, while making it clear that no 'flies' or other 'insects' – meaning democracy or western ideas – would be allowed to enter.

The Politbureau was all too obviously attempting to agree on what political actions to take after the purge. They were all aware of the chronic economic situation throughout the State caused by the runaway inflation, a chronic shortage of foreign currency and a dearth of raw materials in the manufacturing industry. The peasants were dispirited because the State had given them IOUs instead of cash for part of their crops. Many of the urban workers, whose factories had closed, were living on the basic wage of 70 yuan a month – around £12.

There was thus some relief that Yang Shangkun had managed to unite the PLA behind him despite the fact that the morale of the troops was low due, again, mainly to low pay – £3 a month, the fact that the modernisation programme was at a standstill and further large scale cuts in the land forces were envisaged. Although the Chinese media was full of praise for the 'heroic' army, that had served the people so well, a senior officer told me, 'Praise doesn't buy pork.'

While foreign diplomats and a handful of rare, outspoken Chinese officials claimed the enlarged Politbureau was 'bogged down' in unending discussions on the succession, the 'broad masses' remained disappointed and dispirited. Cadres, for their part, claimed little could be done in the economic sphere until political decisions were reached.

The hardliners were forced to admit, albeit in private, that China can no longer live in the isolation Chairman Mao achieved after his break with the Soviet Union in the late Sixties. Thus, on the last day of October 1989, Deng Xiaoping begged the former President Richard Nixon, who knows China well, to persuade President Bush to lift the ban on the export of hi-technology to China. And, even more important, he urged that loans from the International Monetary Fund and other financial institutions that were cut off after the 'massacre' of 4 June, be made available again to Peking. At the same time Deng accused the United States of 'gross interference in China's domestic affairs'. Washington, Deng claimed, had encouraged the students in their demands for Western-type democracy. He branded Professor Fang Lizhi, who had taken refuge in the American Embassy in Peking, as a 'traitorous bandit' who was officially accused of 'counter-revolutionary crimes'. Clearly the leadership in Peking fear that the Professor will, one day, be smuggled out of China to emerge as a powerful unifying force of the students and their democratic supporters.

Foreigners, with good Chinese friends, claimed it was extremely difficult to meet them and, when they did, a 'minder' was generally present. The Chinese suggested that there was deep fear and apprehension in the air which was not helped by the lack of news coming from the enlarged Politbureau still reported to be in almost constant session in Zhongnanhai. The fate of the general secretary, Zhao Ziyang, remained uncertain but senior diplomats believed that, although his disgrace was likely to continue, he would not be put on trial as this could, so easily, implicate Deng Xiaoping.

Differences and difficulties between Jiang Zemin and Yang Shangkun became apparent in the autumn of 1989 as Jiang wanted to relax, if not lift, Martial Law, while Yang was keen to maintain it, as it all too obviously increased his power and authority. As a result of economic pressure and the lack of tourists and business men visiting Peking, Deng came down on the side of Jiang. Martial Law was relaxed and in Tiananmen Square, members of the PAP replaced soldiers. Further, a movement to return to their home bases was begun for the many thousands of soldiers who had been deployed in the capital to enforce Martial Law.

There were already serious problems in providing suitable accommodation for the Group Armies as the nights in Peking grew colder. However, Yang still claimed Martial Law was as necessary in Peking as it is in Tibet due to the 'bubbling' discontent. Indeed he advocated that it be retained in its somewhat relaxed state until after the Spring Festival (Chinese New Year).

News of Deng Xiaoping's official resignation and his replacement as Chairman of the Central Military Commission by Jiang Zemin came on 9 November when it made more impact in the Western world than in China, as cadres repeated that 'As long as Deng is fit, all major decisions will be referred to him'. Jiang's appointment came as no surprise to the 'broad masses' as it is in the tradition of the Party and Deng's two previous 'successors', who were also vice-chairman, had been expected to take over in their time. None the less, the announcement was a bitter blow to Yang Shangkun who lost 'face' and power because his new chairman and commander was someone lacking military experience.

On his appointment Jaing immediately called a meeting of the Central Military Commission to discuss not only the streamlining and further cuts that had been in the air for some time, but a major reshuffle. It was disclosed that the general, who had commanded the Group Army which failed to enter the Square on 20 May was, despite his distinguished career, already in prison together with 'scores' of other cadres who had been reported to show sympathy for the reformers. The authority of the seven regional commanders is expected to be reduced in the moves while an increase in the power and authority of the general staff is envisaged. Apparently the future role of the Defence Ministry is still unsettled; so, too, is the date when the new appointments will be announced.

There is now every reason to reduce the numbers of troops deployed on the border with the Soviet Union. Indeed, a year or two ago Deng suggested China's southern frontiers were far more likely to experience sudden limited incidents. This is why Deng formed the Quick Reaction Force so that the border, especially with Vietnam and along the coast, could be protected against intrusions.

But the main military concentration in the reshuffle will be on the Navy and its role, in co-operation with the Air Force, in defending China's claim to the Spratly Islands. This enormous archipelago, once a pirates' paradise, is also claimed by Vietnam, Taiwan, Indonesia, the Philippines and Malaysia and their interest grows with reports that there are considerable deposits of gas and oil amidst the shallow lagoons. Currently, Chinese aircraft based on Hainan Island can only remain a few minutes in the sky over the Spratlys – hence Peking's interest in acquiring in-flight refuelling techniques and equipment. The PLA now have a battalion of Marines deployed on one of the islands.

The defence budget, which now stands at some 7 per cent of the GNP, is most unlikely to be increased. Many units after a short initial training are expected to devote their service to construction work such as road and bridge building. The PLA is always expected to assist the peasants in any crisis in the countryside caused by flooding or landslides and, generally, 'to save the people'.

News of increased democracy in Poland, Hungary, Czechoslovakia and then Rumania caused considerable anguish amongst the hardliners who gave orders that little mention was to be made of it in the Chinese media. But, naturally, the news gradually became known as a result of the BBC and the VOA. But when Bulgaria got rid of its ageing leader, orders were given to 'jam' foreign broadcasts. Thus news of the opening of the Berlin Wall, which appeared in most newspapers on the same day as Deng Xiaoping's resignation, took some time to penetrate amongst the Chinese people.

The students keep themselves well informed, despite jammed frequencies on the BBC, and they and their supporters are excited about events in Eastern Europe which they believe will make an impact on the Chinese political scene. Meanwhile, discontent is increasing, especially in rural areas where over a million local industries have recently closed as a result of lack of raw materials, power or credit, leaving over twenty million people unemployed. This excludes the millions in urban areas. Jiang is supporting Premier Li Peng in his efforts to re-centralise power and the Canton region and coastal belt is beginning to feel the effects of Peking's authority. 'We have turned the clock back and it is not working,' an official said, adding that millions would suffer as a result, unless the reformists were able to resume power in the near future. Few doubt that the pendulum will swing back in their favour within the next year or so. Most people realise that the future of Hong Kong entirely depends on who is in power in Peking when sovereignty is re-assumed in July, 1997. The chances are that reformists will be sitting on the Dragon Throne and the current period when the Chinese nation appears to be economically and ideologically at rock bottom will be little more than a memory.

Epilogue

After visits to China, Vietnam, Japan and Burma each year I return to my *cabanon* in the Alpes Maritimes above Tourrettes-sur-Loup where I make plans for future activities in the places where I have lived and worked. I must go back to India and Pakistan, Sarawak, Kuching in East Malaysia – where I was based during 'confrontation' with Indonesia – Aden, Iraq and, of course, the countries of North Africa. Brussels, too, where I have spent so much time since Nato headquarters left Paris, in my efforts to keep pace with events in the Alliance.

As I plan I look out at a superb view covering the Mediterranean coast from Cap d'Antibes to beyond Nice. Since I bought the wild hillside in the early 1950s the landscape has changed. There was then no road but plenty of good spring water and we hired donkeys or mules to carry our supplies of food and wine up the steep hillside. It was and, indeed, is still a paradise for a keen amateur entomologist as the area abounds in rare and beautiful moths and butterflies. At the end of the Algerian war the local farmers ceased to breed mules, and donkeys seem to have disappeared, so the dung beetles no longer roll their large balls of dung containing their eggs up the hill. Now the road has been extended and there are many modern houses with electricity, mains water and swimming pools. The problem, as always, is the difficulty of finding someone to look after the *cabanon* when I am away and uncontactable in the Far East.

My husband claimed he had never been as happy in his life

as when we were here. We transformed a large old cistern, ten feet deep, into a mini-swimming pool. I have planted flowers and trees and a friend built a splendid round stone table on the terrace, but weeds grow quickly. For days sometimes weeks in summer we wrote or worked in Tourrettes, but the time comes when it is necessary to return to a library in London, Paris or Hong Kong to look at reference books or use press-clipping services. Tokyo has the best Foreign Press Club in the world supported by an excellent library and press cuttings of English language newspapers – it is odd and sad that in other countries the Press Club is a place largely for eating and drinking and not for work.

I must go back to Egypt where I lived for many years to discover how seriously my old friends regard the threat of Muslim fundamentalism outside Iran. I felt echoes of it had reached Muslim tribes in central Asia but I could be mistaken.

During the past few weeks I have developed a strong desire to return to the haunts of my youth in the Balkans. I now want to go to Zagreb, where I studied and made my base for touring the Balkans and central Europe by train, and I must also return to Bucharest where I covered the troubles of 1940 and the civil war in 1941. I feel I should now revisit all my pre-war stamping grounds in Sofia, Belgrade, Athens and even Albania.

My time in future will be divided between modest bases in London, Paris and Hong Kong because I still believe the centre of economic and industrial gravity is moving away from Western Europe to South East Asia. Furthermore, I must study the effects in the Far East of Gorbachev's moves towards global disarmament and the collapse of communism in Eastern Europe. In China, as the elders and 'Long Marchers' die, will the reformers and the young, who have now 'smelled' the Western way of life, follow in the Maoist political tradition? Currently, the changes in China have had a daunting influence on the population of Hong Kong. And what of Japan's future role as an economic superpower? There is still much to do and to write about.

C.H.
December, 1989

Index